Power, Participation, and Protest
in Flint, Michigan

Ashley E. Nickels

Power, Participation, and Protest in Flint, Michigan

Unpacking the Policy Paradox of Municipal Takeovers

TEMPLE UNIVERSITY PRESS
Philadelphia • Rome • Tokyo

TEMPLE UNIVERSITY PRESS
Philadelphia, Pennsylvania 19122
tupress.temple.edu

Copyright © 2019 by Temple University—Of The Commonwealth System
  of Higher Education
All rights reserved
Published 2019

Library of Congress Cataloging-in-Publication Data
Names: Nickels, Ashley E., author.
Title: Power, participation, and protest in Flint, Michigan : unpacking the
  policy paradox of municipal takeovers / Ashley E. Nickels.
Description: Philadelphia : Temple University Press, 2019. | Includes
  bibliographical references and index. |
Identifiers: LCCN 2018057929 (print) | LCCN 2019005059 (ebook) |
  ISBN 9781439915684 (E-book) | ISBN 9781439915660 (cloth : alk. paper) |
  ISBN 9781439915677 (pbk. : alk. paper)
Subjects: LCSH: Municipal finance—Michigan—Flint. | Municipal
  government—Michigan—Flint. | Flint (Mich.)—Economic conditions. |
  Flint (Mich.)—Politics and government.
Classification: LCC HJ9259.F5 (ebook) | LCC HJ9259.F5 N53 2019 (print) |
  DDC 320.9774/37—dc23
LC record available at https://lccn.loc.gov/2018057929

9 8 7 6 5 4 3 2 1

*In solidarity with those who seek
equity and social justice*

Contents

List of Tables and Figures — ix

Acknowledgments — xi

Prologue — 1

Introduction • The Politics of Municipal Takeovers: Power, Participation, and Protest — 7

1 Why Cities Go Broke and Flint's Financial Collapse — 23

2 Saving Cities from Themselves: How States Respond to Urban Fiscal Crises — 30

3 The Policy Paradox of Municipal Takeover: How the Policy Creates Politics — 51

4 Contextualizing the Flint Case: Race, Class, and Contentious Politics — 66

5 The "Development Agenda": Implementing Municipal Takeover in Flint — 89

6 From Development Agenda to Development Regime: Allocating Benefits and Burdens and Interpreting Winners and Losers — 103

7 Defending Democracy: Responding to the
  Municipal Takeover   129

8 From Fiscal Emergency to Public Health Emergency:
  Differing Responses to the Flint Water Crisis
  • Co-authored with Amanda D. Clark   142

  Conclusion • Summary Findings, Implications,
  and Recommendations   159

  Appendix 1 • Research Design and Methodology   167

  Appendix 2   177

  Appendix 3   179

  Notes   209

  References   229

  Index   251

List of Tables and Figures

Tables

Table I.1. Michigan cities under EM, 2013 — 16

Table I.2. Key demographic characteristics of Michigan cities that have experienced municipal takeover under PA 72, PA 4, and PA 436 — 18

Table 2.1. Approaches to state intervention — 35

Table 2.2. Characteristics of state intervention laws by state — 36

Table 4.1. Flint political stakeholders by sector — 77

Table 5.1. Flint mayors, 1975–2017 — 94

Table 5.2. Flint emergency managers, 2002–2015 — 102

Table 6.1. Charter amendment and review ballot questions and results, 2014 — 111

Table A1.1. Interview respondents by race and takeover opinion — 172

Table A2.1. State statutes associated with state intervention — 177

Table A3.1. Key events from Flint's municipal takeovers — 179

Figures

Figure P.1. Claire McClinton at the Water Rate Protest, 2014 — 5

Figure 3.1. Executive order for the elimination of the Office of the Ombudsman, 2011 — 60

Figure 4.1. "Vehicle City": downtown Flint and Genesee County arches, 2011 — 69

Figure 4.2. Flint population by race, 1950–2010 — 71

Figure 4.3. Flint unemployment rate, 1990–2015 — 73

Figure 4.4. Flint poverty rate, 1970–2010 — 74

Figure 4.5. City of Flint ward map, 2012 — 79

Figure 6.1. "EM Law = Dictatorship" sign at "Our Voice Is Silent" demonstration, 2014 — 108

Figure 7.1. Council member Wantwaz Davis at the Water Rate Protest, 2014 — 136

Figure 8.1. Water pickup sign, 2016 — 144

Acknowledgments

My research on municipal takeovers has been met with some resistance. Scholars looking at municipal takeovers, or urban fiscal crises more generally, are not typically amenable to critical perspectives. However, many scholars—including both skeptics and supporters of my epistemological approach—have generously offered critiques and advice at various stages of this research project. Whether reviewing a chapter, offering discussant comments on a conference paper, or providing guidance on a related article, these scholars have imparted wisdom that greatly benefited the research project and, in particular, this book. They include Sawsan Abudabenjeh, Carolyn Adams, Brandi Blessett, Casey Boyd-Swan, Christine Brenner, Marie Isabelle Chevrier, Bev Cigler, Stephen Danley, Lisa Dicke, David Fasenfest, Michael J. Fortner, Shaina Gaines, Christopher Goodman, Patrick Haney, Russell Hanson, Nuri Heckler, Paul Jargowsky, Lorraine Minnite, Adam Okulicz-Kozaryn, Charlene Orchard, Ben Pauli, Monica Schneider, Kathleen Underwood, and Eric Zeemering. I also thank the anonymous reviewers for the manuscript, and for related papers, for their thoughtful comments. Portions of this work were previously published in my article "Approaches to Municipal Takeover: Home Rule Erosion in State Intervention in Michigan and New Jersey," *State and Local Government Review*

48, no. 3 (2016): 194–207, and online in my article with Amanda Clark, "Framing the Flint Water Crisis: Interrogating Local Nonprofit Sector Responses," *Administrative Theory and Praxis* 41 (3), https://doi.org/10.1080/10841806.2019.1621653.

A few acknowledgments deserve special mention. I thank Richard A. Harris, my dissertation chair, for his patience, constructive feedback on the many iterations of this project, and frequent words of encouragement and support. I thank Jan Worth-Nelson and Ted Nelson for sharing their home and their wisdom with me. I loved getting to know them and feel blessed that I was able to share the summer with them while I was in Flint. I thank David Enders for his guidance and support as I revised the manuscript. His excellent editorial suggestions helped make this book more readable and accessible.

This project benefited from a small but diligent team of research assistants, including Katelyn DeBaun-Fee, Suzanne Meade, and Marisa Shepard. To Amanda D. Clark, who began as a research assistant and has become a trusted confidante and collaborator, I extend my sincere appreciation. I continue to be humbled by her generosity and intellectual support. And to the residents, activists, and community leaders of Flint, I express my deepest gratitude for welcoming me into their city. Without them, this project would not have been possible!

This research project, which began in 2012, required significant resources of time and money, and I was fortunate to have institutional and financial support to carry it out. First, the manuscript grew out of my dissertation research, which I conducted as a doctoral candidate at Rutgers University–Camden. A small program, in its infancy when I arrived in 2011, was fertile ground for my intellectual curiosity to grow. I thank the Rutgers University–Camden community, especially the Department of Public Policy and Administration and the Department of Political Science, for providing me with an amazing education and a wealth of support. I also benefited from institutional support from the Department of Political Science at Miami University (Ohio), where I spent a year as the Thomas W. Smith research associate and postdoctoral fellow. I am thankful for the leadership of Kent State University, specifically that of Dean James Blank and department chair Andrew Barnes, for creating a supportive and productive environment in which to finish the research for and writing of this book. I was fortunate to receive additional financial support from various sources, including the Rutgers University TA GA Professional Development Award and the Kent State University Summer Research Grant. I also benefited from institutional support in the form of undergraduate research programs, such as Miami University's First Year Research Experience (FYRE) and Kent State University's Summer Undergraduate Research Experience (SURE).

I offer a special thank-you to a few extraordinary friends. To Prentiss Dantzler, Kirk A. Leach, Jason D. Rivera, and Zachary D. Wood, I owe much gratitude. Without all of them, I may not have made it through my first year of graduate school, let alone the publication of this book. They are an amazing group of scholars, and I count them among my closest friends. To Danielle (Dani) Vilella, my academic cheerleader and dearest friend, I offer special thanks for spending countless hours on Skype discussing my research and reminding me that there is life outside of academia.

And I thank my family: My mom, dad, and brother were my first cheerleaders, pushing me to ask tough questions and encouraging me to find my voice. My daughters, Tessa and Isabella, spent their early childhood moving back and forth across the country. I hope that one day they will look back on those experiences with fond memories. And I hope that studying together at the kitchen table, all of us doing homework together before dinner, reminds them that learning and discovery are team sports. Last, but certainly not least, I thank my partner, Aaron, for being a constant source of support and for giving me the courage to take a leap of faith and pursue my dream.

Power, Participation, and Protest
in Flint, Michigan

Prologue

Let's be clear, there is no daylight between the emergency manager and our right to water.[1]

On December 1, 2011, a state-appointed "emergency manager" (EM) took office in Flint, Michigan, thereby placing the city under state control. The goal was to address the city's fiscal crisis, and Michael Brown, the former Flint official who was appointed EM, began his tenure by cementing his control of Flint's governance. He eliminated the positions of seven political appointees and cut the salaries and benefits of the mayor and city council. Michigan's "emergency manager law"—or municipal takeover, as it is referred to in this book—effectively suspended the governing authority of Flint's local elected officials in favor a series of state-appointed EMs who would run the city for the next three years. Flint also became a test case for a newly strengthened EM law passed just months before. Known as Public Act 4 (PA 4),[2] the policy suspended local representative democracy, purportedly to avoid municipal bankruptcy. Its critics said that it was a political tool that unfairly targeted Michigan's most disenfranchised residents and, in its most recent iterations, was used by a Republican-controlled legislature and governor to reduce the power of political opponents.[3]

Until the fiscal emergency was lifted and the EM removed on April 30, 2015, four men held the EM position in Flint, each implementing draconian austerity measures under the auspices of fiscal responsibility. Reactions to the takeover were mixed. Some decried the municipal takeover in Flint as an affront to democracy. Some supported state intervention. Still others were ambivalent, concerned for the fiscal health of the city, yet uncomfortable with the suspension of local democracy and community control. By early 2016, Flint's takeover experience captured national and international attention as decisions made by the EM led to contamination of the city's water supply, causing the lead poisoning of residents and a legionella outbreak that killed twelve. The fiscal emergency became a public health emergency, now known as "The Flint Water Crisis."[4]

Theoretically, a municipal takeover is intended to be temporary and limited: once a fiscal crisis has abated, the city is supposed to return to its ex ante political status. Yet, as the water crisis and the ongoing political debate over the use of EMs illustrates, Flint has changed: new organizations have developed, new coalitions have emerged and evolved, and people's understanding of municipal takeover has changed. The municipal takeover policy shows a preference for technical rationality, eschewing politics. But a municipal takeover not only fails to avoid politics; it also creates new politics.

With the ostensible purpose of saving money, the EM agreed to move the city's water supply from Lake Huron to the Flint River—a stop-gap measure that was put in place as the city sought to join a new regional water authority and eliminate its contract with the Detroit Water and Sewerage Department (DWSD)—a decision that was projected to save the city $100 million over twenty-five years. A report issued in December 2011 indicated that using the water from the Flint River would require anticorrosion treatment to avoid damage to the city's water pipes; however, in June 2013, a decision was made to not pay for the anticorrosion treatment.[5]

On April 25, 2014, with a bit of pomp and circumstance, the city switched the water source over. Residents immediately noticed a difference in the quality of the water. The water had a funny smell, a different taste, and was discolored. People using Flint city water began to experience rashes, hair loss, and other health problems. High levels of bacteria were found in the water, prompting the city to issue boil water advisories. Despite complaints, the city and EM team continued to vouch for the safety of the water. Mayor Dayne Walling infamously drank a glass of Flint water on live television in July 2015.

As predicted, the untreated water was corroding the city's water pipes, leaching lead into the water.[6] LeeAnne Walters, a local resident who would become a citizen activist, began to suspect something was wrong with her water when her son began to develop a rash each time he came in contact with it. Walters had tests conducted on her water in February and March 2015 that showed lead levels at 104 and 397 parts per billion. That was an exceedingly high number: the federal Environment Protection Agency (EPA) requires action on any water reaching 15 parts per billion; though no action is mandated until at least 10 percent of homes' samples indicate high levels. Nonetheless, state and city officials continued to stonewall residents, providing their own test results showing the water was within regulatory limits. But even the state's Department of Environmental Quality had to admit a problem when more tests found high lead levels and a local pediatrician, Dr. Mona Hanna-Attisha, found a concerning pattern of high blood lead levels in the city's children.[7] In October 2015, the city issued alerts for residents not to use the water and to reconnect to the Detroit supply. But the damage to the health of Flint residents and the physical damage to their homes could not be so easily turned back. Emergency declarations at both the state and federal level occurred in January 2016, but the people of Flint still struggled to have the problem satisfactorily addressed and their voices heard.[8]

It took almost two years and constant pressure from local activists and community organizers for the full extent of the poisoning of the water to be known. Grassroots associations, like the Flint Democracy Defense League (DDL) that had been organizing against the municipal takeover, were early critics of the switch. In July 2014, just months after the switch, Flint City Council member Wantwaz Davis organized a protest of nearly one hundred Flint residents, activists, and community leaders in front of city hall, demanding "national attention" to the issues facing Flint.[9]

Claire McClinton, a DDL cofounder and former labor organizer, attended the Water Rate Protest in July and many other protests, drawing a clear line between the EM and the city's water problems. As noted at the beginning of the chapter, McClinton stated at a protest in August 2014: "Let's be clear, there is no daylight between the emergency manager and our right to water" (see Figure P.1).[10]

In addition to the fact that the Flint water crisis was avoidable, the cover-up of the decisions that brought about the crisis led to residents' total loss of confidence in their government. Outspoken residents, mostly women, were attacked for challenging the official narrative coming from state and local officials. The decision to switch the water supply, as well as the municipal takeover that preceded it, was ostensibly a "color-blind" policy aimed at fiscal stability. Yet the impact of that decision was disproportionately felt by low-income, differently abled, and Black and Latinx residents due to a variety of factors, including the city's demographic makeup and its history of economic and racial segregation.[11]

The water crisis, which continues as of this publishing, and its enduring impact on the city and its residents made Flint the most recognizable contemporary example of municipal takeover in the United States. People around the world began discussing not just the lead in the city's water supply but the culpability of the state-appointed EMs, the governor, and state agency officials. Michigan's EM law became, if only momentarily, the center of attention. "How could this happen?" people wondered. A *Fortune* headline asked: "Did Michigan's Emergency Manager Law Cause the Flint Water Crisis?" Municipal takeover was suddenly politically relevant beyond the boundaries of Flint.[12]

Michigan has one of the most aggressive policies for addressing local fiscal crises in the United States.[13] Though the origins of the policy go back even further, the state's passage of the Local Government Fiscal Responsibility Act, or PA 101, in 1988, marked the first move toward state-directed municipal takeover. The policy has been revised several times, most recently in 2012, with the passing of Public Act 436 (PA 436). Over the past three decades, nine Michigan municipalities have seen the power of local elected

Figure P.1 Claire McClinton, a Flint community activist and co-organizer of the Flint Democracy Defense League (DDL), attending the Water Rate Protest on July 14, 2014, organized by city council member Wantwaz Davis. (Printed with permission from Nayyirah Shariff.)

officials usurped by the state for varying periods of time. At the height of municipal takeover in 2013, six cities, including Allen Park, Benton Harbor, Flint, Detroit, Ecorse, and Pontiac, were governed by state-appointed EMs, placing nearly half (49.5 percent) of the state's Black population under state control.[14] Regardless of intent or disparate impact, the optics, at the very least, suggests systemic racism in state policy and its implementation.

Flint's municipal takeover reshaped local democracy, not only by suspending representative electoral government but also by disrupting the existing order and creating opportunities and incentives that shifted power in the local political system. In Flint, some benefited from the takeover, while others lost. Tasked with correcting the city's budget woes and armed with a newly revised law that gave him sweeping authority, Flint's EM shuttered city offices, laid off employees, restructured collective bargaining agreements, sold city assets, and raised water rates. These decisions reshaped the local political landscape in numerous ways. Tools and strategies designed to "get the local government's fiscal house in order,"[15] when implemented at the local level, have both instrumental and symbolic effects that reshape who may participate politically and how. Municipal takeover determines who wins and who loses, who participates and who protests.

Introduction

*The Politics of Municipal Takeovers:
Power, Participation, and Protest*

> [I] go to various protests, marches, demonstrations, and meetings, and that seems to be, unfortunately, a way of life now. It's like you're always at some meeting, or carrying water bottles around, protesting, or making a video, or hashtagging. You're doing some type of action to voice what's going on in the City of Flint. And it's everything from the water crisis, to the high crime rates, to the no jobs and no living wages. I mean, it's various environmental injustices—it's various issues that we are all tackling at once.
>
> —JIA, community activist, personal interview, 2017

> It's been a constant [state of] chaos, because I think as the community has tried to find a different path forward, it's run up against the various state laws.
>
> —CARL, former elected official, personal interview, 2015

Flint is one of a handful of American cities that has experienced a municipal takeover. Municipal takeover—the state-directed policy of declaring a municipal fiscal emergency, placing the municipality in state receivership, and appointing a manager to implement corrective action, is not common. Historically, except during periods of severe economic downturn like the Great Depression or, more recently, the Great Recession, the number of municipalities placed in state receivership in the United States has never been large. The number of municipal takeovers has been even smaller. This is in part due to that fact that state approaches to local fiscal crises vary considerably, ranging from nonintervention to aggressive interventions such as municipal takeover.[1] Michigan arguably has the *most aggres-*

sive state intervention policy, both in terms of the tools and powers provided under the law and their implementation.[2]

There is little consensus among scholars or the general public about how to refer to these strong state intervention policies: some, like Michelle Wilde-Anderson, have used terms such as "democratic dissolution," while others refer to them simply as "Municipal Fiscal Emergency Laws."[3] Residents of Flint primarily call them "emergency manager laws." In this book, the term "municipal takeover" is adopted to identify state-directed policies for declaring a municipality to be in a state of fiscal emergency and providing mechanisms for intervention that include (1) placing the municipality under state receivership; (2) handing over control of most or all local government decision making to a state-appointed manager, effectively relieving local elected officials of their governing authority; and (3) implementing a combination of tools intended to stabilize the local government's fiscal condition.[4]

Municipal takeovers are a policy of last resort, used when both local government and the local economy are unstable and crisis-prone. A state's concerns regarding credit downgrades, municipal bankruptcy, and fiscal contagion are common motivations for strong intervention.[5] Harold Wolman and colleagues highlighted this: "Cities whose economies are stagnant, whose residents suffer from poverty and unemployment, whose budgets are in chronic fiscal stress, and who require state aid to sustain basic services are a drag on the entire state economy."[6] Municipal takeovers, by design, are intended to be temporary and limited. Yet changes to city governance and the manner in which community members interpret the takeover have long-term political legacies. As such, municipal takeovers present a "policy paradox,"[7] wherein political struggles over conflicting values are often obscured by a discourse of rational decision making, short-term fiscal stability is pitted against local democracy, and neoliberal market solutions are valued over democratic principles of participation and deliberation.

Unpacking the Politics of Municipal Takeover

In public policy, value conflicts are everywhere. As Susan L. Carpenter and W.J.D. Kennedy noted, "Nearly all public controversies entail divergent beliefs about what is right and what is wrong, what is just and what is unjust. Many policy decisions are essentially choices between competing values."[8] There are inherent conflicts in municipal takeover policy: it pits the values of the "market"—rationality, efficiency, and technocratic managerialism—against the values of the "polis"—equality, equity, and participatory democracy.[9] Moreover, the debate over municipal takeover, about both its design and its implementation, illustrates these important value conflicts and the paradoxes that underlie the policy's ostensible rationality.[10]

As such, the policy paradox perspective provides a useful framework for evaluating the current literature on municipal takeovers. As Deborah Stone points out, there are conflicts and trade-offs in public policy.[11] Many scholars within the fields of political science, public administration, policy analysis, and law have declared a "common mission of rescuing public policy from the irrationalities and indignities of politics," otherwise known as the "rationality project."[12] In other words, policy scholars have a tendency to view "policy" as rational, systematic, and scientific, while eschewing "politics" as "an unfortunate obstacle . . . to good policy."[13] Yet, in the case of municipal takeover, *attempts to depoliticize management are inherently political and have important political implications.* When viewed from the perspective of the "rationality project," scholars and practitioners often fail to take into account the role of politics and the values of the polis, including democracy, in the policy process.

Urban Fiscal Crises and Fiscal Stability

The literature of municipal takeovers draws overwhelmingly on economics and public budgeting and finance, focusing on efficiency and stability.[14] From a state's perspective, it is critical to intervene in local fiscal crises.[15] Local fiscal distress can require long-term state aid, becoming a drain on state resources. Failure to address local fiscal crises can lead to municipal bankruptcies and downgraded credit ratings of other localities and the entire state, known as the "spillover effect" or "contagion."

Cities are limited by their legal subordination to state government. While many states have adopted home rule protections to support local autonomy and community control, (which are addressed in more detail below), cities are not free of state intervention under home rule, except in regard to "matters purely local in nature."[16] States have extensive fiscal *oversight* responsibility toward local and municipal governments. In this context, the takeover of a local government by a state is warranted when local fiscal distress threatens the economic or fiscal stability of the region or state.[17]

Anthony Cahill and Anthony James note that state interventions are desirable "in the interest of efficiency," while also recognizing that such policies are at odds with the political value of local control, "which holds that municipalities have significant roles and functions in the political system and that their existence should be supported, not supplanted."[18] These authors conclude, like many of their colleagues, that from a "rational" fiscal and economic perspective, municipal takeovers look like the best alternative, when compared to municipal bankruptcy or doing nothing.[19] Moreover, states have a fiduciary responsibility to guarantee that municipalities meet their obligation to provide services to the public.[20] As a result of the hegemonic "rational-fiscal perspective," little attention is paid to the potential long-term sociopolitical ramifications of municipal takeover policy.

Their ability to skirt the democratic process is not lost on those implementing the takeover policy. In 2011, in Benton Harbor, Michigan, for example, EM Joseph Harris dismissed criticisms that the law suspended local democracy. As one writer put it: "Blissfully free of the checks and balances of democratic government, he [Harris] is living the dream of every frustrated city administrator."[21] Harris said, "Here, I don't have to worry about whether the politicians or union leaders like what I am doing, I have to worry about whether it's the right thing to do. That's the only thing that should matter. I love this job."[22] A true symbol of the "rationality project," Harris seemed to enjoy the freedom to make determinations free from politics and public input.

David Kasdan, an urban studies scholar, notes that it is imperative that these EMs, or "hatchet men," as he calls them, strive for transparency and collaboration.[23] But transparency and collaboration were not on the top of Harris's agenda in Benton Harbor. In the case of Flint, that dynamic, especially the emphasis on collaboration, has had serious implications, not just in the short term, but in the long term as well. More to the point, the nature of the collaboration or partnership matters.

Representative Democracy and Local Control

Municipal takeovers, by definition, suspend local control and representative democracy by removing or superseding the powers of local elected officials. Most criticisms of municipal takeover focus on this element and pay scant attention to the deeper, longer-lasting impact of takeovers on local politics. Whether they are political pundits like MSNBC's Rachel Maddow or protesters in the street, most critics focus on the removal of elected officials, calling it an "affront to democracy." Maddow, for example, posed the following questions regarding Michigan's municipal takeover law:

> Who gets to have a local democracy? Who is considered worthy of being allowed to elect their own local officials? And why is taking democracy away considered to be a prerequisite for fixing a broken place? Should your vote matter, even if the state doesn't like the decisions of the people you elect? Should your vote count?[24]

Here, Maddow focuses on the right to vote for elected officials and the importance of electoral politics and representative democracy. In other words, municipal takeovers are an affront to democracy because local residents are no longer governed by those they elected to represent them.

Under the representative democracy framework, elected officials (and their appointees) must, at a minimum, engage with voters and community stakeholders. State-appointed managers, on the other hand, are freed from the burdens of the democratic process. The primary mechanism for public accountability—voting—is rendered meaningless.

While this criticism is valid, it does not fully capture the reality that unelected officials are making decisions that carry consequences beyond their tenure. Critics overemphasize the issue of representative democracy and electoral politics and do not fully address the broader politics of the policy process. The institutional structure or design of local government, which is modified under municipal takeover, impacts who participates or engages with government and to what extent their involvement influences decision making.[25] Moreover, these changes, including the mobilization of opposition, have effects that outlast the takeover.

In Flint, the EM eliminated citizen's district councils, thereby destroying one of the pathways for residents in low-income areas of the city to "fight blight and rehabilitate urban areas" as a part of the federal government's Community Development Block Grants process.[26] This is an example of how municipal takeovers go beyond the suspension of representative democracy and have the capacity to reshape the ways in which residents engage with local government.

Moreover, the narrow focus on representative democracy and the electoral process opens the "death of democracy" argument up to two important criticisms from takeover proponents. First, municipal takeovers are most commonly implemented in municipalities with already low voter turnout. As such, it could be argued that democracy is already dead, or dying, even before takeover. For example, prior to the municipal takeover in Camden, New Jersey, voter turnout in the 2001 mayoral race was only 26 percent. In 2009, in the midst of the takeover, voter turnout was 24 percent.[27] Second, many supporters of strong state intervention argue that it is not undemocratic because the people who drafted the laws and the governors who appoint the managers are democratically elected, and thus represent their interests.

Legal scholarship on municipal takeovers provides a broader critique, emphasizing the threat to local control. Wilde-Anderson refers to municipal takeover policy as a form of "democratic dissolution," emphasizing, for example, how the Michigan law "empower[s] Emergency Managers to replace all officials elected to govern the city." She states that the law "allows the [state-appointed EM] to literally lock local officials out of city offices, e-mail accounts, and internal information systems, if needed to minimize disruption of 'the Emergency Manager's ability to manage the government.'"[28] Municipal takeovers, from this perspective, are a threat to community control and popular sovereignty, concepts and practices that we hold dear.[29] This is an important critique, but it lacks theoretical specificity as to how this disruption affects local democracy.

A Different Perspective: Power, Participation, and Urban Politics

The suspension of local control, broadly speaking, is a valid concern. However, not all members of the community are equally affected by the political impacts of a takeover. Critics of takeovers rarely delve into the possibility that some members of the community may welcome takeovers, while others may oppose them.[30] Moreover, decades of urban politics and policy research teaches that local politics is more than local elections or local elected officials and that key decisions are made outside of city hall and the ballot box.[31] Municipal takeover, by design, changes the structure and organization of local government and has the capacity to change who is making and implementing decisions.

Recent scholarship suggests that municipal takeovers can be a catalyst for changes in the local governing regime in smaller distressed cities by moving away from a "pro-growth regime" to a "community development regime" comprising high-capacity nonprofits, community development corporations (CDCs), and anchor institutions.[32] The suspension of traditional political processes and the presence of the EM, armed with a range of tools for fixing the city's economic condition, might encourage government departments, particularly the planning department, "to look more creatively at the city's future, creating an opportunity to increase capacity and right size government through public-private partnerships."[33] Municipal takeovers, therefore, create incentives and pathways for nongovernmental organizations to "step in and fill gaps" left by a weak or weakening local government.[34]

Recent scholarship on the subject and the example from Benton Harbor suggest that politics-as-usual is disrupted under municipal takeover. To the extent that takeovers are a shock, they create new opportunities and motivation to mobilize community interests. But, given the differential impact of the policy, community members respond in disparate ways. Much as Naomi

Klein argued in *Shock Doctrine* with regard to entire national economies,[35] this disruption, or shock, creates opportunities for already powerful community interests to gain even more influence in the local political system, further supporting the claim that some entities benefit from the takeover, while others lose.[36]

Municipal takeovers have the capacity to reorder governance and local policy making, and create new constituencies, by changing the "rules of the game."[37] Municipal takeover policies, like all policies, are "political forces that [have the capacity to] reconfigure the underlying terms of power, reposition actors in political relations, and reshape political actors' identities, understandings, interests, and preferences."[38] Insomuch as community interests are aligned with the policy's market-focused design and its development-focused agenda, they will reap the benefits of the policy (e.g., the sale of city assets and the privatization of services).

On the flipside, the policy may also have "self-undermining effects," wherein the "social consequences" of the policy, such as the disproportionate burden placed on already marginalized groups (e.g., low-income residents, the elderly—including retirees and pensioners—and Black and Latinx residents), can "reshape actors' preferences and capacities . . . in ways that diminish political support and expand opposition coalitions."[39] In other words, municipal takeover, with its lack of democratic process and disparate allocation of resources and incentives,[40] can shape peoples' understanding of their place within the local political order and how they should conduct themselves. Municipal takeover, therefore, does not avoid politics—it creates new politics.[41]

Policy implementation is like a "coordination game," in which distributive issues, such as who gets what and how, depends on the "relative power of the actors."[42] How political actors respond to these changes depends, in part, on whether or not they are included in the new—even if temporary—power structure. On the one hand, high-capacity nonprofit organizations, such as universities, hospitals, community development corporations, and foundations that have a development-focused agenda, are well placed to benefit. On the other hand, given the burdens placed on residents, coupled with the perception that the takeover is a threat to local democracy, the shock of the policy has the capacity to mobilize grassroots groups and community residents that were dissatisfied with the previous arrangement and motivated to question or interrogate the emergent governing structure.[43]

Moreover, grassroots organizations not only organize protests, bringing visibility to their specific policy concerns, but also help frame the issue more broadly by identifying the underlying problem and its causes. Framing is used to inform people's interpretation of the issue,[44] using symbols, stories, and metaphors to mobilize and organize an opposition movement.[45] As such, community-based nonprofit advocacy groups and residents may coalesce around a narrative that further undermines the new policy. For example, Flint's leading opposition group, the DDL, was instrumental in drawing a clear link between the choices made by EMs and the Flint water crisis, providing a platform for whistle-blowers to come forward.

Race is another important dimension of municipal takeovers that is overlooked by the "rationality project," though evident in much of the criticism of municipal takeover policies highlighted above. An important social construct that organizes people's realities, race plays a significant role in how takeovers are perceived. In Michigan and New Jersey, municipal takeovers have primarily been applied to majority-Black cities, making discussions about race significant.[46] Claire McClinton, the leader of the DDL, noted:

> [The] Emergency Manager Law, signed by Governor Snyder, was driven by the perception that Black elected officials are dysfunctional, incompetent, and corrupt, and cannot be trusted to manage the affairs of the city.[47]

After the takeover of Detroit in March 2013, nearly half of Michigan's Black population lived in a city with a state-appointed manager and for all intents and purposes without an elected local government.[48] Table I.1 shows demographic information for cities that were under EM at its height of use in 2013.

Recent legal battles highlight the important and historically overlooked issue of race in municipal takeovers. On November 19, 2014, the U.S. District Court for the Eastern District of Michigan ruled that a lawsuit brought by plaintiffs throughout Michi-

TABLE I.1 MICHIGAN CITIES UNDER EM, 2013

Locality	Population	Black/ African American	% Black	% of State's Black population
Michigan (state)	9,883,640	1,400,362	14.17%	
Allen Park	28,210	604	2.14%	0.04%
Benton Harbor	10,038	8,952	89.18%	0.64%
Detroit	713,777	590,226	82.69%	42.15%
Ecorse	9,512	4,415	46.42%	0.32%
Flint	102,434	57,939	56.56%	4.14%
Hamtramck	22,423	4,317	19.25%	0.31%
Pontiac	59,515	30,988	52.07%	2.21%
Total Black population under EM, March–April 2013		693,124		49.50%
Sources: U.S. Census Bureau 2010b–i.				

gan against the state's takeover law could move forward on the claim that takeovers disproportionately affect Black and African American residents and could be considered unconstitutional for violating the Equal Protection Clause in the Fourteenth Amendment, which prohibits discrimination on the basis of race.[49] However, the U.S. 6th Circuit Court of Appeals declared that while the law "might not be a 'perfect remedy,' it is 'rationally related' to turning around local governments."[50]

Flint: A Case Study of Policy-Making Politics

Over the past three decades, ten Michigan municipalities have seen the power of local elected officials reduced or usurped by the state for varying periods of time under the auspices of helping fiscally distressed municipalities.[51] Theoretically, these municipal takeovers are intended to be temporary and limited: once the fiscal crisis is abated, the city is supposed to return to its ex ante political status. Yet, the response to municipal takeovers has been mixed, and little is known about the political impact of these state interventions.[52]

To examine how municipal takeover policy has created a new politics, I have adopted a policy-centered single-case research design.[53] As Jacob Hacker, Suzanne Mettler, and Joe Soss have pointed out, in a policy-centered analysis, "policy serves as the focal point for a broader analysis of how political forces shape governance and how government actions reshape the society and polity."[54] In other words, this research project centers the concept of policy design and policy implementation. Thus, we can unpack the policy paradox of municipal takeovers by using the policy as an analytic lens and using Flint as the site of investigation.

This book uses the Flint case to examine how a takeover unfolded, what choices were made, and how community residents and community leaders made meaning out of and reacted to the experience. Flint, Michigan, was selected for its analytic and practical utility. After decades of White flight, economic disinvestment, and neoliberal policies, Flint, like many other deindustrialized cities, faced a staggering structural deficit,[55] and under the auspices of fixing Flint's fiscal emergency, Michigan placed the city under emergency financial management.

Like most cities that have experienced municipal takeover, Flint is a small city.[56] With a population hovering around 102,000, according to the 2010 Census, the city is substantially smaller than the largest takeover city, Detroit, which had a population of more than 711,000 at the time of the takeover.[57] It is, however, quite a bit larger than other cities that have experienced municipal takeovers. The population of Camden, New Jersey, for example, was approximately 77,000 in 2010, and Pontiac, Michigan, has a population of almost 60,000. Most cites in Michigan that have been placed under a state-appointed EM are even smaller, as indicated in Table I.2.[58]

Regardless of size, Flint is in other ways typical of the small cohort of cities that have experienced municipal takeover, making it a useful case to "probe causal mechanisms" and develop an explanation of how the takeover changed local politics that is applicable and testable in other takeover cities.[59] In other words, because Flint is similar to other cities placed under a state-appointed EM, it is, with regard to local economic and sociopolitical conditions (e.g., shifting demographics, decreasing revenue with increasing demands, and internally contentious

TABLE I.2 KEY DEMOGRAPHIC CHARACTERISTICS OF MICHIGAN CITIES THAT HAVE EXPERIENCED MUNICIPAL TAKEOVER UNDER PA 72, PA 4, AND PA 436

Locality	Years of intervention(s)	Population (2010)	Population change (2000–2010)	Housing: % vacant lots	% Black (2010)	% Population below poverty*
Allen Park	2012–2014	28,210	−4.01%	5.13%	2.14%	8.4%
Benton Harbor	2010–2014	10,038	−10.54%	18.04%	89.18%	n/a
Detroit	2013–2014	713,777	−24.97%	22.83%	82.69%	36.0%
Ecorse	2009–2013	9,512	−13.79%	19.76%	46.42%	n/a
Flint	2002–2004 2011–2015	102,434	−18.04%	21.14%	56.56%	38.5%
Hamtramck	2000–2007 2013–2014	22,423	−1.84%	18.75%	19.25%	46.0%
Highland Park	2000–2009	11,776	−29.52%	23.73%	93.51%	n/a
Lincoln Park	2014–2015	38,144	−5.12%	9.72%	5.92%	16.5%
Pontiac	2010–2013	59,515	−10.29%	17.96%	52.07%	33.5%
Three Oaks	2008–2009	1,622	−11.03%	14.93%	1.11%	n/a
Michigan (State)	n/a	9,883,640	−0.55%	14.56%	14.17%	15.7%
Average†		99,745	−12.91%	17.20%	44.89%	29.82%‡

Sources: U.S. Census Bureau 2000, 2010a–i; 2008–2010 American Community Survey.

*Estimate, 2008–2010 American Community Survey.
†Average does not include state figures.
‡Average for available estimates.

politics), a useful case through which to examine *how* the policy reshapes governance and local democracy.

A Note on Research Methods

Research that examines how policies are "reshaping governance in enduring ways," is particularly amenable to a qualitative research design, as it requires in-depth, process-oriented, and context-specific investigation.[60] As such, the research for this book was carried out over a period of five years, but the bulk of the heavy lifting was done between March 2015 and September 2017. During that period, I spent a significant amount of time in Flint: sitting in coffee shops, attending community meetings, conducting interviews, and reading archival reports in the local public library.

This book draws heavily on interviews conducted during my fieldwork. In total, forty-eight interviews with community leaders and actively engaged Flint residents were transcribed, coded, and used in the analysis. Of these semi-structured interview participants, seventeen were Black (35.4 percent), twenty-nine were White (60.4 percent), and two were Latinx (4.2 percent).[61] While this does not reflect the population of Flint, where 56.6 percent of the population identifies as Black or African American,[62] the larger proportion of White participants is due in part to the nature of Flint's business and nonprofit elite, who are disproportionately White. Additionally, due to the nature of snowball sampling, White community leaders often referred other White community leaders and residents.[63]

The findings outlined in this book are based not only on these interviews but on an extensive review of city documents and city-affiliated websites, local and regional newspaper articles, and social media as well as attendance at city council meetings, charter review meetings, and community programs.[64] (My research design and methods are described in detail in Appendix 1.)

Organization of the Book

The organization of the book addresses this question: How does the implementation of municipal takeover reshape local democracy?

The next two chapters explore the fiscal and legal dimensions of municipal takeovers. First, Chapter 1 examines why cities go broke, exploring both internal and external factors that impact local fiscal health. This chapter explores the explanations for why Flint has repeatedly found itself facing fiscal distress—and two municipal takeovers. Chapter 2 then explores the variation in state responses to local fiscal crises, highlighting how Michigan compares to other states.

Chapter 3 lays out the project's theoretical framework. Building on Deborah Stone's policy paradox perspective, this chapter outlines how these ostensibly "apolitical" policies create new politics.[65] I argue that a municipal takeover represents a shock to a municipality, because it disrupts the political status quo by appointing an EM and placing the local government under state oversight. Though the policy is technically temporary, a shock of this nature has a long-term impact on local political institutions and processes. Actions undertaken by the state have broad implications for local governments and for urban democracy.

Chapter 4 begins my analysis of Flint's municipal takeover by contextualizing the Flint case. In order to fully understand the impact of the policy—particularly how contextual factors mediated policy impact—this chapter provides the necessary demographic, economic, and political background. I focus on Flint's history as the "Vehicle City," and highlight the city's evolution from a factory town to a distressed city. This chapter also provides a review of the city's political stakeholders. I pay particular attention to how the rise of the General Motors Corporation led to the growth of major political players such as the Charles Stewart (C. S.) Mott Foundation, labor unions, and a host of community and labor organizers.

Since 2002, Flint has experienced two municipal takeovers, four EMs, and thousands of executive orders, resolutions, and directives. Under the authority of EMs, the city of Flint went through significant changes. Chapter 5 traces the implementation of the municipal takeover in Flint, illustrating how the EMs relied on the "development regime," giving organizations such as the C. S. Mott Foundation and the Flint and Genesee Chamber of Commerce a prime seat at the decision-making table.

Chapter 6 then highlights key events and decisions that were made under EMs, identifying the policies' instrumental and symbolic feedback effects.[66] While the development regime gained access, a disproportionate resource burden was placed on low-income and Black residents. These disparate policy burdens had both instrumental (e.g., resource) and symbolic (e.g., interpretive) effects. The chapter first examines the policy's instrumental effects, identifying the disparate allocation of resource benefits, resource burdens, and participatory access. The chapter then outlines, broadly, how different constituent groups made meaning out of the policy, focusing primarily on their interpretation of winners and losers.

Chapter 7 shifts the focus away from the top-down analysis of Chapters 5 and 6 by focusing on how grassroots groups translated the symbols, stories, and metaphors of policy resistance into action. The chapter focuses on grassroots and participatory responses to the takeover in two areas: protest and charter review. The chapter begins with a review of how the Flint DDL framed the takeover and mobilized opposition through contentious politics—particularly protest. The chapter then outlines how the charter review process also served as a platform for dissent. Though formal in nature, this forum for participatory engagement provided an important venue for the grassroots community, including opposition leaders, to inform local decision making and address changes made under the takeover. This chapter highlights how progressive activists, Black community leaders, and community organizers mobilized against the takeover and the development agenda, illustrating how the ostensibly apolitical takeover policy created new politics.

Chapter 8 further illustrates how Flint's takeover created new politics by investigating the divergent responses of two important political stakeholder groups: the high-capacity nonprofits that drove the city's development agenda and the grassroots associations that mobilized in opposition. Paying particular attention to whether and how these groups addressed the topics of race, class, and power in their framing of the Flint water crisis, the chapter illustrates how the grassroots groups, often working with little to no institutional support, framed their concerns around broader issues affecting the city: power and inequality, justice and rights, and democratic accountability—frames clearly linked to their earlier efforts to challenge the takeover policy. This is in stark contrast to the high-capacity nonprofits, which were more embedded in the city's power structure and thus slower to express concerns, eventually framing their concerns around immediate individual and community needs.

The Conclusion presents policy recommendations. This chapter presupposes that policies should be designed to foster democracy, not undermine it. Community representatives should have an active role in addressing the fiscal concerns of the city. The preceding chapters provide empirical evidence of how municipal takeovers, which restrict democratic participation in order to expedite decision making, have political consequences. This chapter presents possible alternative models, including those adopted in other cities. Programs such as participatory budgeting give citizens the power to identify community needs and allocate government funds accordingly. Though in their infancy in the United States, such programs provide a model for fiscal decision making that seeks to increase trust in local government and foster a "renewed political culture in which citizens . . . serve as democratic agents."[67] While it can be challenging to fully incorporate all voices during a fiscal crisis—such programs provide evidence that there are ways in which local budgeting could be improved.

1

Why Cities Go Broke and Flint's Financial Collapse

Flint, Michigan: A Hollow Frame of a Once Affluent City
—PATRICK GILLESPIE,
CNN Money, March 2016

Local governments provide many of the services residents take for granted, from garbage collection to education. Municipalities maintain local infrastructure, pave roads, distribute potable water, manage sewage systems, and provide police and firefighters. In order to provide these services, local governments levy taxes and issue bonds. The fiscal health of a city is dependent on making sure revenues cover expenditures.

This chapter explores issues of local fiscal health and broadly examines the explanations of how Flint has become, according to the title of a 2016 news story, a "hollow frame of a once affluent city."[1]

Why Cities Go Broke

The fiscal health of local governments falls on a continuum. Some municipalities do well, while others struggle. As Benoy Jacob and Rebecca Hendrick point out, there are a host of factors that impact local government finances, "and no single metric is able to fully account for the various components of financial condition."[2] There are internal decisions, external environmental factors,[3] and historical contingencies that influence local fiscal conditions.[4] City finance, Eric Monkkonen argues, is an element of the political economy, "for the shaping and operating of cities has required internal political adroitness in addition to a healthy economic system."[5] Fiscal crises are therefore neither exclusively internally created, nor externally caused; both are relevant.

Cities that experience long-term deficits are considered "structurally distressed."[6] Structurally distressed cities must balance competing demands: reducing costs and increasing revenues. Why some cities avoid crises while others do not may be explained in part by how local city officials balance these competing demands. Carl, a former elected official in Flint, noted that a strong local government is necessary to provide adequate services.[7]

Local decision-making practices, including institutionalized budgetary processes for balancing competing demands, can undermine the strength and stability of local government finances. Ester Fuchs, for example, argues that the nature of local governing regimes has a significant impact on mitigating municipal financial crises. In her book *Mayors and Money: Fiscal Policy in New York and Chicago*, Fuchs focuses on the municipal fiscal conditions of both cities in the 1970s.[8] Fuchs argues that while New York went broke, Chicago avoided a crisis "because its leaders were able to deflect interest group demands for increased spending."[9]

Interestingly, and to some extent telling of current debates regarding fiscal stability versus racial and social equity, Fuchs reflects on the attitudes many have about two notable mayors, Richard J. Daley of Chicago and John Lindsay of New York:

> Vilified in the 1960s for his callous approach to Chicago's ghetto violence, Daley became a hero in the 1970s for shrewdly managing the city's finances. In New York, John Lindsay was synonymous with 1960s politics, and his legacy has been the antithesis of Richard Daley's. Lindsay was both the white knight who saved New York's ghettos from burning and the profligate mayor whose spending gave rise to New York City's 1975 fiscal crisis. While Daley's reputation over time has risen, Lindsay's has declined: *fiscal prudence is now more valued than racial harmony.*[10]

Local governments not only must balance competing demands for resources; they also must do so in a complex political environment that often pits financial stability and governmental efficiency against social equity or political equality. As Fuchs pointed out, "While interest group pluralism is highly valued in a political democracy, it is often disruptive and detrimental to policies which promote local fiscal stability."[11] Furthermore, interests shift during times of fiscal crisis. While demands typically center on efforts to "improve or expand government," during times of austerity, "development interests acquire a newfound legitimacy and groups which contribute least to the tax base are most likely to be ignored."[12] In Chicago, the city avoided the financial crises that plagued many large cities by consolidating fiscal power, but it did so at a cost: keeping special interests, including the city's growing Black political interests, out of the [fiscal] decision-making process.

Moreover, local budgetary policies must be contextualized historically to understand how mayors and their administrations are "constrained by [local] fiscal policy-making structures that had developed decades before they took office."[13] In other words, budgetary decision-making processes, including the management of competing interests, can become institutionalized, constraining later options.[14] Take, for example, the significant role of public employee unions. Political discussions of municipal finance cannot be fully understood without considering the cost of public employee salaries, benefits, and pensions and, relatedly, the role of public employee unions as a key interest group.[15] First, public employee wages and benefits make up the lion's share of local government expenditures, accounting for 41 percent of local government general spending.[16] And, as Sarah Anzia and Terry Moe report, public-sector unions and collective bargaining are a powerful factor in increasing the costs incurred by local government, particularly when it comes to employee benefits.[17] Early collective bargaining agreements both shape and constrain future budget choices.

There are also numerous other factors, including internal factors, such as community needs, resources, and political culture, and external environmental factors, such as intergovernmental constraints, disaster risk, and external economic conditions.[18] Thus, local budget and finance scholar Hendrick's assessment: "Although government officials determine the actual levels of services provided or taxes collected, the environment limit their options."[19]

The finances of a city, like an individual, are affected by shifting patterns in employment and housing. Detroit is a prime example of a city where changes in the economy were manifested in the city's financial condition. While some have argued that Detroit's recent bankruptcy and state takeover in 2013 can be attributed to the housing bubble fueled by subprime mortgages and the subsequent foreclosure crisis,[20] others posit that a deeper historical account is necessary. George Galster, for example, suggests that Detroit's current fiscal distress is not just due to contemporary political economic forces but is also built on decades of urban decline.[21] He further argues that three other structural and historical factors are necessary to understanding Detroit's financial crisis: mass suburbanization of the city's industrial, retail, and commercial tax base fueled by the auto industry's departure from the city and subsequent "White flight"; expansion of the suburban housing market, which further exacerbated city-suburb racial and economic inequality; and reductions in federal and state revenue sharing.[22] Each of these factors illustrates how economic, social, and political situations combine to reduce local revenue. Less explicit, however, is that these historical patterns have also placed new internal demands on city officials for services and expenditures.

Flint's Financial Crisis

Flint's fiscal crisis differs in important ways from those of Chicago, New York, Detroit, and other large urban areas. Deindustrialization came later to Flint than other Rust Belt cities.[23] In the late 1970s and early 1980s, while other cities faced fiscal crises brought on in part by deindustrialization and suburbanization, Flint was just beginning to experience job losses. At the end of World War II, Flint's per capita income was 30 percent higher than the national average.[24] With a peak population of nearly 200,000 in the 1960s, it was once the second-largest city in the state of Michigan, smaller than only Detroit. But by 2010, the U.S. Census Bureau reported a fourth straight decade of double-digit population decline. Flint is the quintessential "shrinking city."

Flint's prosperity, in many ways, has been tied to General Motors (GM). As the auto industry modernized, outsourced jobs, and shut down plants, Flint suffered. In 1978 more than 80,000 Flint-area residents were employed by GM. By 2005 only 8,000 Flint-area residents were employed by GM, and by 2008 approximately 7,100 hourly and salaried employees remained.[25]

After decades of economic boom, the bust was painful. From 2000 to 2010 the city saw an 18 percent decline in population, and the U.S. Census estimated that in 2013 the city had dropped below 100,000 residents. As GM closed plants and people were laid off, many residents left and the city's tax base deteriorated. Overall, property values decreased by 20.7 percent from 2001 to 2010.[26] With declining revenues, city streets went unpaved and public lawns unmowed. The city is pocked with abandoned homes and boarded-up buildings. As the water crisis unfolded, news media flocked to the city, eager to take photos of the city's decline—often referred to by locals as "ruin porn." There is plenty of it.

Limited resources also meant more contentious politics. The back-and-forth, highly antagonistic nature of politics in Flint is discussed in more detail in Chapter 4, but it is worth noting here that Flint's financial condition was the result of a perfect storm: economic change increased demand for services as revenues decreased, escalating internal political tensions that sometimes led to poor budgetary decisions and further policy constraints on the city's ability to increase revenue.

As a result, the city faced chronic budget shortfalls. Eric Scorsone, a senior economist at the Michigan Senate Fiscal Agency in 2010 and current senior deputy state treasurer, noted, "The inability to sustain a positive fund balance is symptomatic of structural budgetary constraints. The City of Flint's fund balance/accumulated deficit history is an example of a city that has recurring deficits."[27] In 2001 the city had a $26.6 million general fund deficit.[28] The city's financial condition stabilized after the state intervened and put in place the city's first emergency financial manager (EFM).[29] The EFM, Ed Kurtz, helped shift the general fund deficit to a $6.1 million surplus by June 30, 2005.

The progress was short-lived. By 2010 the city's net assets were $48.1 million in the red and the general fund deficit was $14.6 million.[30] Mike Brown, who later became EM, reflected on the causes of the city's financial condition in 2012: "It's hard to tie it to one thing," but he suggested that 80 percent of the city's costs were related to employee costs.[31] The conservative news outlet Michigan Capital Confidential placed the blame for the city's return to financial distress on labor settlements and litigation. "At a time when the city's revenue was evaporating, its expenses were rapidly escalating," the news outlet reported.[32] Expenditures on labor, Eric Scorsone and Nicolette Bateson argued, were "at alarming levels."[33] While employment numbers decreased, expenses increased:

> The number of full time equivalent employees (FTEs) decreased from 1,227 (at the *beginning* of fiscal year 2003) to 767 (at the end of fiscal year 2010). This was a decrease of 460 employees or 37.5 %. During that same time period, total wages and benefits went from $79.6 million to $93.2 million for an increase of $13.6 million or 17.1 percent. If retiree healthcare were excluded, the increase based on what is considered active employee wages and benefits would be 10.2 %. A significant portion of active employee expenditures is related to pension and healthcare costs.[34]

Labor union demands and so-called legacy costs of pensions and health care are important factors in Flint's fiscal health. However, reducing these costs comes with trade-offs. For example, public-sector employee layoffs have a disparate impact with regard to race. According to the U.S. Census's Center for Economic Studies, Black employees made up approximately 24 percent of the public-sector workforce living in Flint from 2000 to 2016.[35] Importantly, the proportion of public-sector employees that are Black decreased from 28.3 percent in 2001 to 22.5 percent in 2015; this is in contrast to the proportion of public-sector workers who are White (non-Hispanic), which increased from 67.2 percent in 2001 to 72.6 percent in 2015.[36] In other words, as the total number of public-sector employees in Flint has decreased—due in part to reduction in the number of city employees—the *proportion* of jobs held by Black employees has decreased as well.[37]

An additional consequence of reducing the city's workforce is that the city is less able to respond to increasing demands. For example, as the city continued to face population loss, and homes were abandoned, crime increased. In 2010 the city experienced 761 arsons, with the highest rate taking place from March to May, after the city laid off 23 firefighters.[38]

In reality, there were multiple factors that placed the city back in the red. Labor settlements with city police and fire unions, litigation, and further declining revenues converged to cause the city's financial condition to decline.[39] In addition to continued population loss and increased demands for services, Flint, along with other cities throughout the state, also experienced a decrease in revenue sharing from the state. According to the Michigan Municipal League, between 2003 and 2013, Flint lost nearly $60 million in revenue sharing. This loss of revenue, as sociology professor Jacob Lederman points out, is larger than Flint's entire 2015 general fund budget.[40]

Long-term structural deficits can have devastating consequences. Local fiscal distress can be a drain on state resources (i.e., through long-term state aid), and failure to address local fiscal emergencies can lead to municipal bankruptcies or downgraded credit ratings of other localities and the state (i.e., "the spillover effect"). As a result, states have developed a range of policy tools to monitor and intervene in local financial affairs.

2

Saving Cities from Themselves

How States Respond to Urban Fiscal Crises

> We want more of an active local government that's actually strong enough to deal with violence [and] strong enough to provide a quality education [and] stable neighborhoods under some really difficult circumstances. We'd like to see government as part of the solution, [but] ... the agenda out of Lansing was that government, in general, was part of the problem.
>
> —CARL, former elected official, personal interview, June 2015

Municipal takeovers, and state interventions more generally, provide mechanisms to monitor urban fiscal health and, if necessary, address local financial crises. Municipal takeover policy history in Michigan highlights three important themes: (1) City fiscal crises are not a new phenomenon, and policy interventions have evolved over time. (2) The evolution of the policy is, in part, related to political tensions over who has the authority to address local fiscal crises. (3) State interventions have often been insufficient for addressing long-term fiscal stability.

In this chapter I examine the history of state intervention and the development of municipal takeover. I highlight the increasing power of state government to intervene in local affairs, using Michigan's evolving state intervention strategy as an illustrative case study.

The Roots of Municipal Takeover

The roots of municipal takeover date to the late nineteenth century. Beginning in the 1850s, local governments took on significant public debt to build railroads and develop real estate, resulting in a flood of local government defaults that were instrumental in creating the economic depression of 1873. According to Eric Monkkonen, there were 941 municipal bond defaults between 1854 and 1929. During the Great Depression that number increased almost 400 percent; by 1935, 3,251 municipalities had defaulted.[1]

Missouri was the first state to create a process for state-imposed receivership in the mid-1870s in an attempt to deal with the municipal default crisis.[2] But the first state-imposed takeover took place in Memphis, Tennessee, in 1880. The intervention was "so controversial that it resulted in a challenge to the state receivership law" that was eventually taken up by the U.S. Supreme Court.[3] In *Meriwether v. Garrett*, the Court ruled that the state, via the court, had a right to force the city into receivership, adding, "The receiver appointed by the court was invested with larger powers than probably any officer of a court was ever before intrusted [sic] with."[4] Of particular relevance here is the Court's statement on municipal governments and the right of a state to repeal a city's charter:

> The right of the State to repeal the charter of Memphis cannot be questioned. Municipal corporations are mere instrumentalities of the State for the more convenient administration of local government. Their powers are such as the legislature may confer, and these may be enlarged, abridged, or entirely withdrawn at its pleasure. This is common learning, found in all adjudications on the subject of municipal bodies and repeated by text-writers. *There is no contract between the State and the public that the charter of a city shall not be at all times subject to legislative control.*[5]

Eight years prior, in 1872, the oft-cited Iowa State judge John Dillon wrote what is now a famous opinion on municipal power and its subordination to the state:

> Municipal corporations owe their origin to, and derive their powers and rights wholly from, the legislature. It breathes into them the breath of life, without which they cannot exist. As it creates, so it may destroy.[6]

Dillon's Rule, as it is now known, became the "bible on municipal law."[7] Dillon's views were highly influential in the *Meriwether* case. The judge's comments were derived from the public perception that local governments were irresponsible and wasteful, as evidenced by the large upsurge of municipal defaults on loans in late nineteenth-century America.[8] Under Dillon's Rule, Lyle Kossis argues, "City policymaking was legal *only* if it was expressly authorized by local charter, incidental to express powers in the local charter, or essential to accomplishing the declared objectives of the city."[9]

The subordinate role of municipal government was affirmed under federal constitutional law in *Hunter v. Pittsburgh* in 1907. Addressing the [Federal] constitutionality of merging smaller suburbs with the city of Pittsburgh, Justice William Henry Moody wrote:

> Municipal corporations are political subdivisions of the State, created as convenient agencies for exercising such of the governmental powers of the State as may be entrusted to them.... The number, nature and duration of the powers conferred upon these corporations and the territory over which they shall be exercised rests in the *absolute discretion of the State*.... The State, therefore, at its pleasure may modify or withdraw all such powers, may take without compensation such property, hold it itself, or vest it in other agencies, expand or contract the territorial area, unite the whole or a part of it with another municipality, repeal the charter and destroy the corporation. All this *may be done, conditionally or unconditionally, with or without the consent of the citizens, or even against their protest.*[10]

The opinion continues: "In all these respects the State is supreme, and its legislative body, conforming its action to the state constitution, may do as it will, unrestrained by any provision of the Constitution of the United States."[11]

As Kossis notes, "In light of the almost unanimous acceptance of the substantive principles underlying Dillon's Rule, the tenor of this holding is not surprising."[12] In fact, when state-imposed receivership escalated again during the Great Depression, objections "were non-existent, as states fell into a pattern of imposing receivership on fiscally distressed cities."[13] Mechanisms for intervention were established, with the first state financial control board being implemented in Manchester, New Hampshire, in 1921.[14]

By the mid-1930s municipal defaults had become a national problem, and as a result the federal government passed the Municipal Bankruptcy Acts of 1934 and 1937 to provide mechanisms for orderly debt adjustment for municipal governments.[15] While the new legislation offered support to local governments, states continued to intervene. According to David Berman, some states took complete control of local governments that were in fiscal distress, continuing to place them under receivership.[16] In Oregon, for example, the state legislature responded to local fiscal crises brought on by the Great Depression by passing legislation that allowed state courts to place municipalities that defaulted on their bond payments under receivership.[17]

World War II and the affluence of the postwar period reduced concerns about municipal defaults; however, the 1970s brought another cycle of urban fiscal crises. Large cities such as New York City, Chicago, and Philadelphia faced such crises and were placed under financial oversight by the state, renewing discussions about the benefits of strong state interventions via fiscal emergency laws. Many states developed such laws in a proactive attempt to cope with the consequences of local financial emergencies.[18] Today there remain significant differences in how states deal with local financial emergencies. Some states do little, some states deal with it on a case-by-case basis, while others have adopted general legislation.[19] Eric Scorsone has identified some of the characteristics that municipal fiscal emergency laws share. In addition to "defin[ing] the conditions that would trigger a crisis," such laws outline what governing bodies should do "once the crisis is established" and many define "exit" strategies. Enforcement of the laws varies from state to state.[20]

There are numerous ways to categorize state fiscal emergency laws. In this analysis, I draw on the typologies developed by the Pew Charitable Trusts in its 2013 report "State Role in Local Government Fiscal Distress" and Scorsone's 2014 white paper, "Municipal Fiscal Emergency Laws."

Nineteen states have some form of intervention laws on the books.[21] Of these, three states, Connecticut, New York, and Massachusetts, are special legislation states that address local fiscal concerns on a case-by-case basis. The remaining sixteen, including Michigan, have general legislation in place to monitor and address local fiscal conditions.[22] Moreover, some states are more aggressive than others in how they intervene: some simply monitor fiscal conditions, while others allow for stronger forms of state intervention. Anthony Cahill and Anthony James note that "the most extensive form" gives state officials the power to "supplant local decision-making authority."[23]

Table 2.1 shows that policies vary in terms of both who is given authority to carry out local reforms and the tools available to them. Pew has created a typology of state interventions, identifying three groups that carry out the policy and six "intervention practices" utilized by states. Some states, including Michigan, allow for a single individual—whether they are called a receiver, a chief operating officer, or an emergency manager—to hold sole authority in "tak[ing] charge" of the local government's budget and operations. Other states, like Pennsylvania, designate an agency to oversee a city's fiscal reforms. Yet others, such as Illinois, provide for a financial control board.[24]

Table 2.2 demonstrates that, as far as tools available for intervention, "no two states are alike,"[25] and highlights that state approaches to takeovers vary by legislative type (general or special), to whom authority is given (a state agency, a board, or a single person), and by the tools and strategies allowed under state law.[26] (A list of relevant state statutes is included in Appendix 2.)

Many states that adopted state intervention laws in the wake of New York City's 1970s fiscal crisis have continued to revise their laws. Ohio, for example, first adopted its emergency financial law in 1978 to address the fiscal crisis in Cleveland and updated its law in 1996 to include townships and counties.[27] New Jersey has one of the oldest state intervention laws, dating back to the Great Depression, but legislators significantly revised it by passing the Municipal Rehabilitation and Economic Recovery Act (MRERA) in 2002 to address the ongoing fiscal crisis in the city of Camden. New Jersey again intervened in municipal

TABLE 2.1 APPROACHES TO STATE INTERVENTION

Group responsible	Receiver, financial manager, overseer, or coordinator	A single individual, who may go by different titles, is given the authority to control some level of municipal fiscal affairs and/or general management.
	State agency or department	Role of state agencies varies; may play significant role on a financial control board
	Financial control board—local or state	A state-appointed body, composed of any number of people, with a mix of public managers and private citizens who have expertise in finance and accounting, put in place to oversee local fiscal and managerial affairs
Intervention tool	Debt	Approving bond sales or renegotiating terms of existing bonds
	Labor	Reducing labor costs by renegotiating existing labor contracts or shared service agreements
	Taxes, fees, and credits	Increasing existing taxes and fees or implementing new ones
	Emergency financing	Providing state loans (often no- or low-interest loans), grants, or credit guarantees (This can include economic development financing.)
	Technical assistance and budget approval	Auditing records, creating a financial plan or balanced budget, negotiating and approving labor and other contracts, and approving spending
	Dissolving or consolidating local government involuntarily	Allowing for the disincorporation or dissolution of a city and consolidating it with other nearby jurisdictions

Sources: Pew Charitable Trusts 2013; Weikart 2013; Scorsone 2014. From Nickels 2016. Reprinted with permission from *State and Local Government Review.*

TABLE 2.2 CHARACTERISTICS OF STATE INTERVENTION LAWS BY STATE

	Group responsible	Debt	Labor	Taxes/fees	Finance	Budget	Dissolve
General legislation							
FL	Board				X	X	
IL	Board	X	X	X	X	X	
IN	Receiver		X		X	X	
ME	Board	X		X	X	X	
MI	Receiver	X	X	X*	X	X	X
NC	Board	X		X		X	
NH	Agency				X		
NJ	Receiver or board	X		X	X	X	
NM	Board				X	X	
NV	Agency	X	X	X	X	X	X
OH	Board	X				X	
OR	Agency	X				X	
PA	Receiver or board	X	X	X	X	X	
RI	Receiver or board	X		X		X	
TN	Board	X		X	X	X	X
TX	Judiciary receiver					X	
Special legislation							
CT	Board	X	X	X		X	
MA	Board	X		X	X	X	
NY	Board	X	X		X	X	

Sources: Pew Charitable Trusts 2013; Weikart 2013; Scorsone 2014;† review of state legislative websites (see Appendix 2).

* Under Michigan law, the emergency manager can increase fees. Tax increases can be proposed but must go before the voters for approval.

† Scorsone did not include New Hampshire, New Mexico, and Oregon in his analysis, as they do not require a receiver or board, only monitoring by a state agency.

affairs, taking over Atlantic City, naming one of Michigan's well-known EMs, Kevin Orr, as an advisor to the EM team.[28]

Michigan's law, much like the others, has also evolved over time.

Michigan's Evolving Approach to Local-State Relations and Urban Fiscal Crises

Michigan's legislation is among the most aggressive municipal takeover laws in the country. Paradoxically, Michigan is also a so-called strong home rule state, and, in the late nineteenth century, one of the most prominent supporters of municipal autonomy and home rule in the United States was Michigan Supreme Court judge Thomas Cooley.[29] In an 1871 opinion regarding the constitutionality of a state-imposed local board of public works in the City of Detroit, Cooley wrote, "Local government is a matter of absolute right; and the state cannot take it away."[30] Cooley sought to "shelter local governments from powerful private interests that were often protected by state politicians as they perverted public interests of communities for private gain."[31] Cooley's philosophy, which became known as the Cooley Doctrine, stood in opposition to Dillon's Rule. Moreover, Cooley believed that local governments were central to the development of democratic equality and the enhancement of local self-government.[32] Despite this historical legacy, Michigan has become "a state of [constitutional] home rule, local autonomy, *and Emergency Managers,*"[33] the latter a result of decades of home rule erosion perpetuated not just by the legislature and the courts but also by cities and voters themselves.[34]

Michigan's home rule laws are both constitutional and statutory. The primary provisions in the constitution regarding municipal home rule are Article VII, § 2 and 22, which both emphasize broad local control. Section 2 references county charters: "No county charter shall be adopted, amended or repealed until approved by a majority of electors voting on the question." Section 22 refers to cities and villages, noting that

> city and village [sic] shall have power to adopt resolutions and ordinances relating to its municipal concerns, prop-

erty and government, subject to the constitution and law. No enumeration of powers granted to cities and villages in this constitution shall limit or restrict the general grant of authority conferred by this section.[35]

The second provision, Section 22, is the foundation of home rule in Michigan and is the most pertinent to the discussion on municipal takeover.[36] These constitutional provisions both provide a framework for municipalities to craft their own city charters and choose how they wish to be governed (e.g., a strong mayor or council-manager) and restrict the legislature from passing local or special laws that affect local government authority without prior approval of the voters in that particular district. Michigan thus is restricted from adopting a special legislation or case-by-case model to address municipal fiscal crises.[37]

Michigan's constitutional home rule protection, however, is not self-executing. Instead, the Home Rule City Act of 1909 serves as the primary executing statute. The statute allows local governments to incorporate and adopt their own charters and enumerates allowable charter provisions. The Home Rule City Act also describes limitations on municipal powers. Since its first adoption in 1909, the Home Rule City Act has been amended numerous times to further restrict municipal autonomy. The Citizen's Research Council (CRC) of Michigan noted that "the current implementing legislation [the Home Rule Act] for municipal home rule is . . . subject to legislative interference and the legislature often shows little self-restraint in interfering in local affairs."[38] As the CRC implies, the state legislature often oversteps its bounds in interfering with home rule protections. The Home Rule City Act, for example, was amended in 1988 by the passage of PA 101, allowing that an "Emergency Financial Manager may exercise the authority and responsibility provided in this act to the extent authorized by Act No. 101 of the Public Acts of 1988."[39]

Writing on behalf of the CRC, the Michigan Municipal League, and the Michigan Association of Municipal Attorneys, David Morris argued that Michigan's home rule principle was being eroded not just by revisions to PA 279 but by other legislative actions. He noted, "Every year . . . bills are introduced which would diminish home rule discretion" either by "prohibiting what a city might otherwise opt to permit, or by permitting what a city might otherwise wish to prohibit." He cited several examples, among them "local regulation of firearms . . . location of day care facilities . . . and the regulation of mobile home parks and mobile homes."[40] The result is that the Michigan legislature, regardless of being in a strong home rule state, nevertheless plays a strong role in determining municipal autonomy by limiting or restricting both how municipalities govern themselves and how they raise revenue.

But legislators are not the only ones interfering in municipal autonomy. Voters and cities undermine the strength of home rule and local autonomy in Michigan as well.[41] Two such examples are the Headlee Amendment of 1978 and Proposal A of 1994. The Headlee Amendment was a voter-approved constitutional amendment that aimed to reduce the tax burden on residents by reformulating state-local relations.[42] Headlee, named for its author, Richard H. Headlee, restricts property-tax revenue growth to the rate of inflation; therefore, any jurisdiction with potential revenue that exceeds the limit is required to reduce their tax rate. As such, the amendment effectively placed a limit on local government taxing power but required that "the proportion of total state spending paid to all units of local government, taken together as a group, shall not be reduced below the proportion in effect in fiscal year 1978–79."[43] In other words, the state reduced the amount of spending paid to local governments but could not go lower than 41.6 percent of total state spending.[44] The Headlee Amendment "tied local and state revenues together and in the end may have degraded local autonomy to such an extent that state control over local government became imperative."[45]

In 1993 the Michigan legislature passed a bill abolishing all use of local property taxes for schools, with no alternative revenue source proposed. Ultimately, this forced the voters to approve a major tax overhaul, which they did the following year in Proposal A. That proposal further bound state and local finances by prohibiting local governments from using property taxes to fund schools and required that they hand over control of K–12 education funding to the state. In effect, Proposal A imposed a taxable value cap on local governments, limiting the growth of property values for tax purposes to less than the rate of inflation.

The electorate, however, has shown interest in strengthening home rule protections, or at least a discomfort with state intervention in local affairs, as evidenced by the 2012 referendum on Michigan's municipal takeover law, PA 4 of 2011, which repealed the law by popular vote.

Michigan's Municipal Takeover Law

In Michigan, the foundation for later municipal takeover legislation came with the adoption of the Emergency Municipal Loan Act, PA 243, in 1980. The act addressed the financial issues that plagued Wayne County, which includes the city of Detroit. Wayne County is unique in that the county pre-dates the establishment of Michigan as a state, and in the 1980s was one of the most populous and urbanized counties in the nation.[46] According to the CRC, by 1970 Wayne County's financial problems were "staggering."[47] The research organization notes:

> There were too many elected officials, too much cronyism, too many semiautonomous departments. Wayne County was facing ever more critical problems, but no one was in charge. The role of the county commission was too broad, encompassing both legislative and executive functions, and at the same time too narrow, rendering it powerless to prevent excesses in operations headed by elected, or even appointed, officials. The commission structure was recognized as causing some, and inhibiting resolution of other, fiscal and operating problems.[48]

In 1976 the state of Michigan, via the Michigan Municipal Finance Commission, ordered Wayne County to balance its budget. Instead, the city's budget deficit grew. The CRC argues that the county's problems stemmed, in part, from the political divisions between Detroit and the suburbs and between Black and White residents, as well as a shrinking tax base that could not keep up with costs.[49]

In 1979 Wayne County became the first county in the United States to go into default since the Great Depression.[50] Unable to meet payroll, the county was struggling to deliver necessary services. In response, the state adopted PA 243 of 1980, which created a state-level board with the ability to allocate emergency funds in the form of loans to distressed locales. The bill also stipulated that, in accepting the loan money, the local government was required to adopt a long-range plan to balance its budget and "employ a full-time professional administrator or contract with a person with expertise in municipal finance and administration to direct or participate directly in the management of the municipality's operations until otherwise ordered by the board" (Emergency Municipal Loan Act, PA 243 of 1980). Michigan also took the step of giving the state loan board the power to not only investigate local financial records and obtain sworn testimony from local officials but also issue orders to the municipality receiving loan money.

Throughout the 1980s, many local governments in Michigan, as elsewhere, continued to face fiscal instability. During the early 1980s the city of Ecorse experienced a series of economic challenges, including business disinvestment and population loss, which translated to reduced property tax revenues. By 1986 the city's population had dropped from a peak of twenty thousand to approximately twelve thousand.[51] According to Robert Kleiman and Anandi Sahu, "more than half of the residents were senior citizens living on fixed incomes in tract houses built after World War II for the returning GIs and factory workers. In 1984 the city failed to pay its Police and Fire pension plan contributions and other utilities."[52] By 1986 the city was facing a general fund deficit of $4.5 million and stopped paying creditors, including the Detroit Water and Sewerage Department. When the city failed to adopt its 1986–1987 budget, Judge Dunn ruled the city out of compliance with the Uniform Budgeting and Accounting Act (PA 621 of 1978) and appointed a receiver.[53]

The court-appointed receiver, Louis Schimmel, had an unprecedented level of control over Ecorse's government functions. During his tenure, Schimmel eradicated the city's debt by eliminating nonessential services, contracting out services such as public works and animal control, and selling off city assets.[54]

The receiver was viewed by many as "vitally needed to bring the city's bureaucracy and financial management under control."⁵⁵

PA 101 of 1988 and PA 72 of 1990

Seeking to bring the power of the receiver back under state legislative, rather than court, control, the Michigan legislature enacted the Local Government Fiscal Responsibility Act, PA 101, in 1988. Written by Republican Michigan senator (and later governor) John Engler, the legislation provided the state with a mechanism to determine fiscal distress and a process for state intervention, including appointing an emergency financial manager, modeled after Ecorse. PA 101 was replaced in 1990 with the adoption of the Local Government Fiscal Responsibility Act, PA 72. PA 72 was passed under Democratic governor James Blanchard but was not utilized for a decade. Hamtramck was the first city to be placed under an EFM in 2000, under then-governor Engler. Two other cities followed shortly: Highland Park in 2001 and Flint in 2002. As the Great Recession began to impact the state, more cities were placed under state control and appointed EFMs. From 2008 to 2010, under Democratic governor Jennifer Granholm's administration, the list included Three Oaks, Ecorse, Pontiac, and Benton Harbor.

PA 72 identifies several mechanisms through which the Michigan Department of the Treasury (Treasury) is made aware of a local government's financial distress. These mechanisms include notification by a creditor, the mayor, city council, or chief administrative officer of the local government unit; a petition from registered voters, pensioners, employees, or bondholders; or a resolution put forward in the state Senate or House. The latter was the mechanism used in Flint's 2002 takeover, when State Senator Bob Emerson submitted a resolution for the Treasury to conduct a review of Flint's financial condition.⁵⁶

Under PA 72, if the Treasury is notified, the department then conducts a preliminary review to evaluate whether there is a financial emergency. There are nine conditions, of which the local government must meet only one, that will lead to an appointment of a formal Financial Review Team by the governor. The conditions include default on payment of principal or interest of a bonded obligation; failure to transfer employee taxes, taxes collected for another government, or pension contribution to the appropriate entity; failure to pay wages or compensation for thirty days or more; indication that the city's accounts payable exceeds 10 percent of total expenditures; failure to eliminate any fund deficit within two years; or 10 percent or greater operating general fund deficit.[57]

Members of the Financial Review Team have sixty days to conduct their investigation and report their findings to the governor. PA 72 stipulates that the review team members can categorize their findings as follows:

(a) serious financial problem does not exist in the local government;
(b) A serious financial problem exists in the local government, but a consent agreement containing a plan to resolve the problem has been adopted pursuant to 14(1)(c);
(c) A local government financial emergency exists because no satisfactory plan to resolve a serious financial problem exists.[58]

If the governor, upon examination of the review team's findings, determines that a financial emergency exists, the governor can then assign the "responsibility for managing the local government financial emergency to the local emergency financial assistance loan board. . . . The local emergency financial assistance loan board shall appoint an Emergency Financial Manager."[59]

The law also identifies the qualifications and conditions of service for an emergency financial manager. Besides being competent, the EFM cannot have been elected to, appointed to, or working for the community they are to be managing in the last five years. Where the EFM resides is not a criterion: the manager serves "at the pleasure of the Local Emergency Financial Assistance loan board" and can expect "compensation and reimbursement for actual and necessary expenses from the local government." Finally, the manager has the authority to "appoint additional staff and secure professional assistance" when necessary.[60]

Under the law, the EFM can engage in a range of activities to address the local government's financial emergency. Scorsone identifies fifteen activities that "among other things, the EFM may do," including "implement a written financial plan"; amend, revise and approve or disapprove the budget of the local entity; and "exercise all appropriate authority regarding union contract negotiations."[61] The list also includes "within charter limits, sell assets to meet current or past obligations."[62]

Of particular importance to this book is the section on "orders," because that section makes evident that all orders that the manager "considers necessary to accomplish the purposes of this act, including, but not limited to, orders for the timely and satisfactory implementation of a financial plan developed pursuant to section 20," are "binding on the local officials or employees to whom it is issued."[63] In other words, *these orders are lasting, legally binding decisions.*

While in some instances a local government may opt to overturn such orders, doing so requires following the rules set out in the city's charter (i.e., following the traditional policy process for passing a local ordinance or order). Under PA 72, "The statutory process is focused on financial challenges such as internal control problems, cash flow shortage, or fund deficits."[64] What it does not do, Scorsone argues, is address any "long run economic problems that may be present in these communities" because such problems "are not easily or readily addressed through a consent agreement or EMF [sic] process."[65] As such, the Financial Review Team must ignore "the long-term economic and fiscal health of the community" and stay "focused on the issue of addressing short- and medium-term adverse financial problems."[66]

PA 4 of 2011

By 2011, many local governments across Michigan were feeling the financial pressure of the economic downturn, increasing post-retirement costs, and cuts to state revenue sharing. In response, the newly elected Governor Snyder sought to update PA 72 by giving the state, and its designee, more authority.[67] PA 4 took effect in March 2011, asserting:

The legislature hereby determines that the health, safety, and welfare of the citizens of this state would be materially and adversely affected by the insolvency of local governments and that the fiscal accountability of local governments is vitally necessary to the interests of the citizens of this state to assure the provision of necessary governmental services essential to public health, safety and welfare. The legislature further determines that is it is vitally necessary to protect the credit of the state and its political subdivisions and that it is necessary for the public good and it is a valid public purpose for this state to take action and to assist a local government in condition of fiscal distress.[68]

PA 4 revised the process for intervention and gave greater powers to the state-appointed manager. It also dropped the term "financial," opting for just "Emergency Manager."[69] This was both substantively and symbolically important, as it indicated that the manager had broader authority under the new law—authority, proponents hoped, that would help address structural deficits, not just balance the budget. Under PA 4, the number of "triggering events" that would set in motion the path to municipal takeover was expanded to include failure to file timely annual financial reports or audits, breaches of deficit elimination plans, receiving downgraded assignments on long-term debt ratings, or "the existence of other facts or circumstances that in the state treasurer's sole discretion for a municipal government are indicative of municipal financial stress."[70]

A triggering event would then lead to a preliminary financial review by the Michigan Department of Treasury. If there was "probable financial stress," the treasurer's office would recommend to the governor that a formal Financial Review Team be appointed. Much like under PA 72, the eight-person review team would determine whether the local government faced mild financial stress, severe financial stress, or a financial emergency. The review team had authority to review the accounts and records of the local government unit, draw on the expertise and services of other state agencies and employees, and if necessary negotiate and sign a consent agreement with the chief administrative officer of the municipality.[71] If it was determined that the local government was in a financial emergency, and it did not have a viable plan, the review team would recommend the appointment of an EM.

Unlike PA 72, however, if the review team found a financial emergency, the governor, not the loan board, would directly appoint an EM. And, as the law noted, the "emergency manager shall serve at the pleasure of the governor" but may delegate oversight to the state treasurer.[72] This addition helped streamline the process by eliminating the loan board, and further consolidated the oversight of the EM under the governor.

Other changes were made under PA 4. First, the law no longer restricted the selection of an EM based on their past involvement in local government; a mayor or former city employee could now be appointed to serve as EM. This turned out to be important in Flint, where two of the four EMs, Michael Brown and Darnell Earley, were previously employed by the city of Flint and had served as interim mayors. The method for compensating the EM was also spelled out, noting that the expenses of the EM would be paid by the local government.

Most importantly, the 2011 law gave the EM *enhanced* powers, including the authority to terminate collective bargaining agreements, reduce or eliminate the pay and benefits for local elected officials, and recommend consolidation or dissolution of municipal governments.[73] PA 4 explicitly outlined more than thirty actions that could be undertaken by the EM. For Flint, the most important provisions were the authority to change staffing levels, remove or replace "administrators, other than elected officials, from office" as well as "any office, board, commission, authority" under the local government unit. Also of importance in Flint was the EM's ability to merge or eliminate local government departments, sell or lease local assets, and "enter into agreements with other units of municipal government to transfer property of the municipal government." Also significant for Flint was that the EM was placed in charge of the local pension board. Paired with the ability to replace board members, this meant that the EM had significant control over pension board decisions.[74]

Though not directly influential to the Flint case, the state's authorization for the EM to "recommend to the state boundary commission that the municipal government consolidate with 1 or more other municipal governments" and "disincorporate or dissolve the municipal government and assign its assets, debts, and liabilities as provided by law" was also important for symbolic reasons.[75]

Moreover, the law stipulated that the EM had sweeping jurisdiction to

> take any other action or exercise any power or authority of any officer, employee, department, board, commission, or other similar entity of the local government, whether elected or appointed, relating to the operation of the local government. The power of the Emergency Manager shall be superior to and supersede the power of any of the foregoing officers or entities.[76]

PA 4 was the "centerpiece of the fiscal program" developed by Michigan's majority Republican legislature in 2011.[77] Supporters of the law argued that it was an "efficient and nimble response to the budget crisis confronting local governments in the wake of the housing crash and near collapse of the auto industry."[78] But not everyone agreed, and some suggested ulterior motives behind the legislation.

While there was little public outcry regarding earlier state interventions, which focused primarily on balancing local budgets, in 2011 many Michigan residents were growing concerned over the increased powers and utilization of Michigan's municipal takeover law. Only fifty-three days after taking office, Governor Snyder proposed PA 4 and was defending it to the press. Snyder was criticized by various constituencies for proposing PA 4 because it would "authorize state-appointed Emergency Financial Managers of municipalities and school districts to unilaterally amend or eliminate local union contracts."[79] Among the most vocal critics were labor leaders, who called the legislation "an assault on collective bargaining."[80] In defending the bill, the governor said "the language of the bill may not reflect how those new powers are implemented in practice," and he "pledged to have 'a good dialogue with organized labor about what's going on and how we can do this constructively.'"[81]

Concern about the passage of PA 4 and the increased powers of the state-appointed EM led to the formation of Stand Up for Democracy, a coalition of community organizations and activists, faith leaders, and unions that sought to overturn PA 4 through a referendum. When the campaign had successfully secured 200,000 signatures to put the issue on the ballot in 2012, the state legislature began discussing replacement legislation.[82] That year, 53 percent of Michigan voters supported Stand Up's measure, overturning PA 4.

PA 436 of 2012

Undeterred, the Michigan legislature passed a new version of the law a month after the election. The Emergency Financial Manager Law, Local Financial Stability and Choice Act, or Public Act 436, went into effect in March 2013. PA 436 made some changes to the state's municipal takeover policy, which included requiring the salary of the EM to be paid by the state, and gave local government the ability to vote out an EM after eighteen months. In addition, the new legislation outlined the process for addressing municipal fiscal distress, which included the option for one of the following:

1. Consent Agreement option
2. Emergency Manager option
3. Neutral Evaluation Process option
4. Chapter 9 Bankruptcy option

Not everyone was impressed. One of the more controversial elements of the new policy was the stipulation that PA 436 could not be repealed by public referendum, as PA 4 had been. As Scorsone notes:

> If you really carefully read PA 436, what you actually find is that a local government can choose consent agreement, for example, but actually the state treasurer has to agree

that that is the right approach. If they don't agree, [the state treasurer] can force [the local government] to go back to one of the other options. So, it is a choice, but perhaps a bit of a constrained choice.[83]

A "New Normal"

Understanding the causes of and response to local fiscal distress is vital. Local fiscal conditions are contingent on a range of internal and external factors. In order to provide adequate services to meet the needs and demands of residents, businesses, and other interests, city officials must make tough decisions, often balancing competing demands. But ultimately, local governments are creatures of the state. So, when cities go broke, states intervene.

Municipal takeover policy, its development, and its application have evolved over time. The design of the policy varies across states, in terms of the powers provided to the party responsible as well as the tools and strategies provided for under law. Moreover, the tensions between fiscal stability and community control have long framed the debate about whether states should intervene in local affairs and, if so, the extent to which the state should wield its power.

While state intervention is not a new response to cities in financial trouble, state governments are becoming increasingly aggressive in how they address local fiscal crises. For example, Joshua Sapotichne and colleagues refer to Michigan's takeover law as "a brave new world for state intervention."[84] Lawrence Martin, Richard Levey, and Jenna Cawley suggest that the great recession of 2008 created a "new normal" for local government through the implementation of "long overdue reform" of financial, service, and employment policies across states.[85] While the authors look at a broad range of strategies, the use of strong state interventions such as municipal takeover is but one (albeit extreme) way that state and local governments have implemented financial, employment, and service reforms, thereby altering the post-recession political landscape.[86]

What are the implications for local governments, and for urban democracy more generally? Michelle Wilde-Anderson suggests that municipal takeovers "go too far in suspending local democracy . . . and do much too little . . . at addressing the underlying causes of persistent decline."[87] The "popularity," or increased utilization, especially in Michigan, of the takeover strategy has led to the development of training centers for EFMs. One such training, hosted by the investment-banking firm Stout Risius Ross in collaboration with Turnaround Management Association, brought in 350 participants from across the country, including representatives from California, Michigan, New York, and Ohio.[88] Topics of the training included, among other things, dealing with a unionized workforce.

While the threat of municipal bankruptcy or credit downgrades may be motivations to seek intervention, such action implies, as several scholars have pointed out, that the state government has the expertise and the means to "do it better."

But does it? And what happens to local political participation when democracy is suspended?

3

The Policy Paradox of Municipal Takeover

How the Policy Creates Politics

It's not good. The end result, today, is that Flint's finances are stable and the level of service is incredibly low, and it does not bode well for fostering future growth.... If the house is on fire, you might not be able to rebuild the house, but you have to put the fire out.[1]

Michigan's takeover laws have certainly faced controversy. Prior to a 2012 statewide referendum on PA 4, the municipal takeover law, Michigan governor Rick Snyder attempted to justify the state's aggressive approach to state intervention in an editorial in the *Detroit Free Press*.

Snyder argued that takeovers are good for communities in distress: "It's not about takeovers or control. It's about helping communities and schools get back on solid financial footing and adapt to changing circumstances and fiscal realities." Pivoting to address the concerns of public workers who saw such aggressive state interventions as a threat to unions, Snyder wrote, "It's not about voiding contracts or circumventing collective bargaining, but about ensuring fair contracts and benefits while recognizing that the past status quo simply isn't sustainable anymore." To answer citizens deeply worried about political disenfranchisement and whether their votes count, he offered this justification:

"It's not about voting rights. This updated measure was passed after a thorough legislative process and robust public discussion. Emergency Managers are accountable to me and the Legislature, all of whom are elected."[2]

At the time, numerous cities across the state, including Benton Harbor, Ecorse, Flint, and Pontiac, were under the management of state-appointed EMs. Protests were being staged throughout the state, and lawsuits claiming that PA 4 violated the state constitution had been filed.

Snyder's editorial provides an excellent frame for understanding some of the most important value conflicts that surround municipal takeovers and the complexity of resident responses, particularly as they relate to politics, democracy, and local control. These conflicts have received little attention from scholars and policy makers, who are often more interested in the fiscal and economic dimensions of takeovers. Even among those who have criticized municipal takeover policy, lamenting the "death of democracy" and the suspension of elected local officials, little notice has been paid to municipal takeover's impact on local politics over time.[3]

While proponents of municipal takeover policy aim to depoliticize local decision making through technocratic, expert-led implementation, the policy is rife with political value conflicts: as one side pursues limited government and fiscal stability, the other perceives a loss of local control and a threat to social equity. In some instances—the Flint water crisis, for example—balancing the budget with little regard for traditional checks and balances on power can have significant political, social, public health, and financial consequences.

Municipal takeovers are aimed at removing politics from the equation but are inherently political in nature and have lasting political impacts. These policies not only are guided by a political ideology of smaller, reform-style government; they also quite literally shape who gets what, when, and how. While the takeover is temporary, those who implement state intervention policies "assume that states can help bring both immediate and long-term improvements that survive long after the state-appointed interveners have departed."[4]

In other words, state intervention is intended to be temporary on the one hand but durable and lasting on the other. The suspension of local governing authority is temporary, but changing union contracts, selling assets, eliminating and restructuring government offices, and shrinking local government are not. Municipal takeovers are a "policy paradox."[5]

Deborah Stone's policy paradox perspective provides a useful conceptual framework for understanding the politics of municipal takeovers. As Stone points out, there are conflicts and trade-offs in public policy, especially between the values of the "market" and the "polis."[6] As neoliberal ideals about privatization, market solutions, and technocratic rationality are put forth as solutions to urban fiscal crises, or as models for governance more broadly, democratic principles of popular sovereignty, community control, and participatory governance are marginalized.[7] David Fasenfest argues, for example, that municipal takeover of Flint was a prime example of a neoliberal approach to urban decline, wherein austerity politics, such as privatization, "privilege [a] financial rather than a social solution to a community's ills."[8] Municipal takeover, in which an EM is freed from the messiness of politics, is a rational and systematic approach to addressing urban fiscal crises. After all, politics, from the perspective of the "rationality project" is "an unfortunate obstacle . . . to good policy."[9]

Building on Stone's work, I argue in this chapter that politics must be "brought back in" to our analysis of municipal takeovers by focusing first on how power is manifested in the EM's policy agenda and how implementation of the policy at the local level has important instrumental and symbolic effects, creating winners and losers and forcing some actors to find new modes of participation. I first explore how municipal takeovers are a shock to the political status quo, creating opportunities for elite interests whose values align with the objectives of the policy to take a seat at the proverbial decision-making table. I then outline how, through policy implementation, municipal takeover creates political winners and losers. Carried out with the ostensible purpose of stabilizing the budget, a takeover reduces the local government footprint, which has important instrumental and symbolic effects.

Bringing Politics Back In: Power and Conflict under Municipal Takeover

Bringing politics back in to an analysis of public policies, particularly municipal takeover, is about more than elections or political parties; it is about who has power and how they use it. While some literature focuses solely on the power of local elites,[10] governing regimes,[11] or who is setting the governing agenda,[12] my analysis examines power from the top down *and* the bottom up.[13] In this analysis, power is not the sole purview of the political elite, nor is it dispersed equally among competing interests.[14] Instead, power is manifest in different ways by different constituencies, depending on their place and perceived value in the local political system. In other words, power is not located solely *within* government, or the governing regime; the nature and use of power is *contingent* on government action and mediated by historical, political, and economic contexts.[15]

Top Down: Governing Regime Power

Our understanding of the nature of local government has evolved. Given the challenges that local governments face, including low voter turnout, declining revenues, and increasing demands for service—not to mention federal retrenchment and neoliberal politics of austerity and privatization—we have shifted from talking about urban *government* (e.g., the formal institutions of the "local state") to talking about urban *governance*, wherein the power to carry out locally relevant decisions is dispersed among a network of actors, as illustrated by the rise in public-private partnerships.

This network of actors, sometimes referred to as the "urban governing regime," is composed of public, private (e.g., business), and nonprofit organizations with overlapping political interests. The power of the urban governing regime may be changed, however, if the regime's capacity to carry out their agenda or political interests shift.

Recent literature on regime change examines how a scandal or other shock to the political status quo may set off a transformational process whereby one regime is replaced with another.[16] Richard Harris, in his assessment of municipal takeover in

Camden, New Jersey, found that the convergence of a weakening "pro-growth regime" with the disruption of the political status quo vis à vis that city's takeover created favorable conditions for the emergence of a new "community development regime."[17]

Thus, a municipal takeover, which represents both an economic shock (e.g., the financial emergency) and a political shock (e.g., the suspension of local democracy), opens a window of opportunity for interests to be realigned and a new governing regime to emerge.[18] In a distressed city, where ongoing economic disinvestment has weakened the local business community, high-capacity nonprofit organizations have filled this governing void.[19] Therefore, the development-focused agenda of the EM mobilizes similarly focused nonprofits. This phenomenon was not evident in only Camden but in Benton Harbor. For example, under Joe Harris's term as EM, he steered a major contract for a golf course development to a local nonprofit economic development corporation backed by Whirlpool, the world's largest home-appliance manufacturer, which has its headquarters in Benton Harbor and has long dominated economic life there much the same way GM did in Flint. Meanwhile, critics of the takeover were refused access to city hall.[20]

The EM and his cadre of advisors are freed from internal checks on power—such as voting or public deliberation—to set and carry out their agenda. The state, driven by the presupposition that local fiscal crises are the result of local mismanagement and waste, thus expands the powers of the state-appointed "expert," who relies on technocratic rationality, to "fix" the city's problems.[21]

Bottom Up: Grassroots Power

It is insufficient, however, to focus solely on the governing regime. Such a perspective blinds us from considering the ways in which municipal takeovers mobilize opposition. A takeover disrupts the political status quo by appointing an EM and placing the local government under state oversight, thus changing the rules of the game. Traditional pathways to influence the governing agenda are suspended or eliminated.

The takeover also reshapes local institutions that had once

served as pathways for community interests to voice their concerns. Though the policy is technically temporary, a shock of this nature has long-term impacts on local political institutions and processes, especially if the changes are maintained post-takeover. Additionally, the takeover may serve another function: creating a shared sense of identity for those excluded and presenting opportunities for "coalescence and mobilization of an opposition [movement]" that would not have occurred otherwise.[22] The shock of a takeover, therefore, also creates the conditions under which opposition is organized and resistance voices are mobilized.

Changing the Rules of the Game: The Instrumental and Symbolic Effects of Municipal Takeover

A policy-centered analysis, which captures both the top-down processes (e.g., how changes to government structures reorganize decision making) and bottom-up processes (e.g., how policy design and implementation shape people's perceptions of power and create new constituencies) is necessary to understand how municipal takeovers create new politics.[23]

The premise that policies create politics is well supported by decades of research.[24] Policy decisions create constituencies and interests, thereby affecting future policies and politics.[25] Moreover, policies shape democracy by highlighting the ways in which vested interests "reconfigure arrangements of power in society."[26] Public policies thus have the capacity to "reorganize power relations" and "mobilize or pacify constituencies."[27] Municipal takeover therefore has the capacity to restructure local politics by "defining who belongs in the political community, specifying how and when citizens can participate in politics," and, as Tracy Burch points out, "determining the balance of power and influence among citizens."[28]

While much of the policy feedback literature focuses on policy stability and path dependence, there is a growing interest in understanding the ways in which public policies mobilize new interests and, in some instances, create opposition among the most disadvantaged—what Alan Jacobs and R. Kent Weaver refer to as the "self-undermining" effects of policy feedback.[29] Policies, they argue, can have "social consequences that reshape actors' preferences and capacities . . . in ways that diminish political support and expand opposition coalitions."[30]

This feedback occurs, Paul Pierson argues, through two main mechanisms: resource incentives and interpretation.[31] Below I illustrate how, through the rearrangement of government structures and the allocation of resource benefits and burdens, the municipal takeover of Flint generated instrumental effects, which in turn fostered particular interpretations of the policy and about certain actors' relative positions in the local political system.

Instrumental Feedback Mechanisms

Instrumental feedback effects derive from the policy tools and strategies outlined in the policy design. Here, the instrumental effects include allocation of benefits and burdens, as well as organizational restructuring.

Benefits and Burdens Policies distribute benefits and burdens. The allocation of economic or political resources, or benefits, creates positive feedback effects that mobilize constituencies and interests that seek to maintain the policy, thus leading to policy stability.[32] On the other hand, policies may also allocate burdens, in which case constituencies may mobilize in opposition, threatening the stability of the policy,[33] or they may acquiesce to the status quo by disengaging.[34]

EMs, for example, are given the authority to implement municipal takeover policy at the local level, distributing benefits and burdens to community stakeholders. While the "rationality project" attempts to minimize politics, this authority is political in that the EM has the capacity, within the confines of the law, to decide "who gets what, when, [and] how."[35] Unsurprisingly, those who benefited in some capacity from the municipal takeover, whether directly or indirectly, supported the takeover and attempted to preserve the changes made under emergency management, while those who bore the burdens disengaged or found alternative means for participating in the local political system.[36]

The allocation of benefits and burdens under the takeover, whether through a new government contract with the city or the termination of a collective bargaining agreement, is also mediated by how the process is, or is perceived to be, managed and administered. Policy implementation and administration are fundamental. Encounters with local government bureaucrats, including EMs, teaches citizens "lessons about the state" and, as such, "mark[s] them in politically consequential ways."[37] In other words, how the benefits and burdens are managed matters. When decisions are made behind closed doors, people notice. For example, Alexei, a Flint-based artist, speaking on the sale of a public asset to a private firm, stated: "It was all done completely behind closed doors. Whether or not it was the right decision..., the fact that it was done in that fashion really bothered me."[38]

Organizational Restructuring

Organizational restructuring is related in that changes to local government structures impact how communities participate in the governance of the city. Municipal takeover policy allows for EMs to restructure local government, creating short-term barriers to access for some members of the community. For example, traditional pathways of engagement, such as speaking during public comment at city hall meetings, are rendered meaningless. EMs, under Michigan law, also have the capacity to change and remove board members on various governing boards, providing opportunities to surround themselves and the EM team with like-minded community stakeholders. In Benton Harbor, for example, the EM reconfigured the city's planning commission.[39]

Longer-term structural changes are also put in place under the auspices of reducing costs and staffing. EMs may consolidate departments or eliminate offices all together. In Camden, New Jersey, the city's planning and development offices were consolidated, and the city's defunct redevelopment agency was "resuscitated."[40] In Flint, one of the first executive orders issued by EM Michael Brown was the elimination of the city Office of the Ombudsman and the Civil Service Board, which, while costly to run, served as checks on executive power and provided an important participation access point for city employees and residents (see Figure 3.1).

Changes in the institutional structure, whether temporary or permanent, mean that some community stakeholders have access to decision makers while others do not. Those stakeholders whose participation is barred or otherwise impeded will overcome this obstacle by expressing their discontent in other ways. Opposition interests may engage in political protest, or, as Robert Lake and colleagues found in the case of Camden, New Jersey, may organize community groups to oppose to actions undertaken by the EM.[41] In Michigan, union members targeted under the enhanced EM law sought to undermine the law by organizing a statewide ballot initiative to overturn it. Moreover, as takeovers remain in place for years, temporary protest movements may formalize, creating new community-based organizations through which community members can voice their concerns and advance an alternative political agenda, as was the case in Flint with the Democracy Defense League.[42]

Symbolic Feedback Effects

While it is true that policies may have a disparate impact on stakeholders through the allocation of benefits and burdens or the restructuring of local government, policies also have interpretive effects. Policies codify whose interests and values are legitimate, communicating to residents their degree of membership within the political community and thus shaping their civic identity.[43] Public policies shape both the "ability and desire" of citizens to engage with the political world.[44]

Responses to public policy are, therefore, informed by how policies are perceived and how people interpret the goals and targets of the policies. Anne Schneider and Helen Ingram posited that people construct meaning and interpret public policies based on their experience with the policy: because policies structure opportunities differently for different populations, they are therefore perceived differently.[45] From this perspective, it is important not only to understand how municipal takeover policy disparately impacts community stakeholders but also to understand how people interpret and make meaning out of the takeover.

For example, when asked to reflect on the decisions made under Flint's EM team, Shaun, a local community activist, stated:

> In some ways I feel like they are doing it to exclude people. It's just like, when you don't know what's going on, you're not going to participate. . . . Why do you want to spend

**EMERGENCY MANAGER
CITY OF FLINT
GENESEE COUNTY MICHIGAN**

ORDER No. 5

ELIMINATION OF THE OFFICE OF OMBUDSMAN

BY THE POWER AND AUTHORITY VESTED IN THE EMERGENCY MANAGER ("EMERGENCY MANAGER) FOR THE CITY OF FLINT, MICHIGAN ("CITY") PURSUANT TO MICHIGAN'S PUBLIC ACT 4 OF 2011, THE LOCAL GOVERNMENT AND SCHOOL DISTRICT FISCAL ACCOUNTABILITY ACT, ("PA 4"); MICHAEL BROWN, THE EMERGENCY MANAGER, ISSUES THE FOLLOWING ORDER:

On March 16, 2011, the Local Government and School District Fiscal Accountability Act, Public Act 4 of 2011, ("Public Act 4"), was enacted to safeguard and assure the fiscal accountability of units of local government; to preserve the capacity of units of local government to provide or cause to be provided necessary services essential to the public health, safety and welfare of citizens; and

Governor Rick Snyder appointed Michael Brown as the Emergency Manager for the City of Flint on November 28, 2011, and his contract was approved by the State Treasurer on November 29, 2011; and

Pursuant to Public Act 4, the Emergency Manager has broad powers in receivership to rectify the financial emergency and to assure the fiscal accountability of the City of Flint and its capacity to provide or cause to be provided necessary services essential to the public health, safety and welfare; and

Pursuant to Public Act 4, the Emergency Manager acts in place of local officials unless the Emergency Manager delegates specific authority; and

Figure 3.1 One of the hundreds of executive orders and directives signed by Flint's emergency managers. Executive Order No. 5, signed by EM Michael Brown on December 8, 2011, eliminated the Office of the Ombudsman, an act that angered many community residents and signaled a disinterest in engaging community concerns. (City of Flint.)

two to three hours trying to figure out what's going on when you've got to go look for a new stove because your stove blew, or whatever. You've got to get the laundry done. You've got to cut the grass. You've got to take the kids to soccer. You've got competing priorities. You shouldn't slam the folks [because] they have other priorities.[46]

> Pursuant to Public Act 4, the Emergency Manager may, at his discretion and notwithstanding any charter provisions to the contrary, eliminate departments of local government; and
>
> Pursuant to Public Act 4, the Emergency Manager may, notwithstanding any minimum staffing level requirement established by charter or contract, establish and implement staffing levels for local government; and
>
> Based on the foregoing, it is hereby ordered that the Office of Ombudsman established by Flint City Charter §3-501 through §3-517 is eliminated. All employees assigned to the Office of Ombudsman are terminated.
>
> This Order is effective immediately.
>
> This Order may be amended, modified, repealed or terminated by any subsequent order issued by the Emergency Manager.
>
> Dated: 12-8-11   By: *Michael K. Brown*
>   Michael K. Brown
>   Emergency Manager
>   City of Flint
>
> xc: State of Michigan Department of Treasury
>   Mayor Dayne Walling
>   Flint City Council
>   Inez Brown, City Clerk

As Shaun's comments suggest, government responsiveness to community concerns and an individual's access to government decision makers send a message to citizens about their "role in the community, their status in relation to other citizens and government," as well as their perception about the "extent to which a policy affected their lives."[47] Policy design (i.e., rules, tools, and rationales) sends important messages to stakeholders about the importance of their problems and how likely it is that their participation in policy making will be effective.[48] In this way, policies have the capacity to shape both internal and external political efficacy.[49] Municipal takeovers are based on the assumption that citizens are unable to govern themselves, something that is not lost on opponents of municipal takeover policies.

Deborah Stone's concept of the "causal story" fits well here, because it suggests that different stakeholders develop narratives, or "causal stories," around problems. Causal stories not only influence how we perceive a problem; they also inform solutions and thus are important politically:

> They have a strong normative component that links suffering with an identifiable agent, and so they can be critical of existing social conditions and relationships. They implicitly call for a redistribution of power by demanding that causal agents cease producing harm and by suggesting the types of people who should be entrusted with reform. And, they can restructure political alliances by creating common categories of victims.[50]

In the case of municipal takeovers, who tells the story, and which story they adopt—in other words, how they identify the reasons for the takeover—helps explain the formation of the takeover agenda and whatever backlash ensues.

Additionally, because symbolic effects are mediated by context,[51] how people make meaning out of the takeover is, in part, influenced by their actual and perceived position and role in local politics prior to the takeover. In Flint, historical realities regarding race and the role of unions are important to understand when examining how policies are interpreted.

Opposition stories centered on narratives of popular sovereignty, civil and human rights, and legacies of oppression. The city's fiscal problems, when they were addressed, were viewed by many as rooted in legacies of racism, failures of the state, and to some extent local mismanagement. The resolution proposed by the state and by municipal takeover proponents, however, was the primary problem. The EM—and municipal takeover law, more broadly—was stripping the city of community control.

On the flip side, for proponents of the policy, Flint's problems were primarily the result of community control, divisive local politics, and financial mismanagement. In 2002, reflecting on the first takeover, the *Flint Journal* wrote:

Who in Flint or Genesee County or anywhere else thinks much of Flint as a place to live, or to start a business? The city's name brings revulsion. That's not entirely fair, but that's the reality. An extraordinary action—and good luck—are needed to turn Flint's desperate situation around.

The council and [acting mayor] Earley aren't equipped or positioned to do it. Even a new mayor isn't the answer. Flint needs outstanding leadership from a pure manager without politics or history holding him back. Kurtz could be that person. He needs the council's unquestioned support, not a lawsuit blocking his way.[52]

The problem, the *Journal* points out, is internal, and thus the solution is "outstanding leadership from a pure manager without politics or history holding him back." Similar sentiments were argued by the Mackinac Center for Public Policy, a conservative think tank, in 2011. Michael LaFaive, director of the Morey Fiscal Policy Initiative at the Mackinac Center, arguing for competitive compensation for EMs, wrote: "If these cities had not fouled their own nest, it would not be necessary to compensate emergency financial managers at any level."[53] Both the *Journal* and the Mackinac Center illustrate how the causal story of internal mismanagement and/or negligence necessitates strong state invention.

But, as Keith, the member of Flint's 2011 EM team quoted earlier, points out, municipal takeover is not just about addressing local mismanagement; it is about saving the city:

> KEITH: You can't just say, "They created the problem; they have to live with it." A business in the private sector can go bankrupt. Yes, it goes away and employees get laid off. Maybe somebody comes in, somebody doesn't. If a city goes bankrupt? Guess what? The city is still there.
> AEN: Yeah, the people are still there.
> KEITH: These are people that, you know, they're not part of government. They're community, okay.
> AEN: Yeah.

KEITH: What do you do with them? I think that the whole notion, I mean . . . there's clearly a process in place for evaluating whether the city is in financial distress. There are numerous steps along the way, where local governments can have that awakening and convince the state that they've got it, they understand. But, failing that, an emergency manager can come in and do some things that would not get done locally. But it [e.g., an emergency manager] should not be long term. I mean, if it becomes long term, then local government goes away. This is a check and balance for cities that are not, that don't do what they should be doing.[54]

As Keith argues, the EMs are temporarily there to put out the fire because local officials have not done "what they should be doing."

Value Conflicts and Competing Interests

In the context of a fiscal crisis—especially under municipal takeovers—where emphasis is on fiscal stability, the policy agenda is biased toward economic interests.[55] Municipal takeover values technical rationality over the messiness of politics. The rules, norms, and values of this logic are evident in not only how Michigan's municipal takeover policy was designed (and redesigned) but also how the policy was implemented in Flint.

For many fiscally distressed cities, strong state interventions are most useful in addressing "short-term emergency problems,"[56] often doing "next to nothing" to address "structural causes of local distress."[57] In other words, municipal takeovers may have short-term success in balancing the city's budget but fail to address deeper structural issues, such as population decline, increasing poverty, economic disinvestment, or persistent racial and economic inequality. Municipal takeovers, as the most aggressive form of state intervention, are considered a necessary evil.[58] Yet placing emphasis on technical rationality at the expense of the democratic process requires that an EM team make significant trade-offs.

Reflecting on decisions like cutting police or parks, Keith noted that the EM's choices boiled down to balancing financial stability with public safety and quality of life. As quoted at the beginning of the chapter, he said, "It's not good. The end result, today, is that Flint's finances are stable and the level of service is incredibly low, and it does not bode well for fostering future growth.... If the house is on fire, you might not be able to rebuild the house, but you have to put the fire out."[59]

Shayne, a local community activist and opponent of the takeover, framed it more bluntly:

> To me, it's like a corporate raider coming into a failing business and liquidating all assets to balance a bottom line. That's it. No one—people, places, things don't matter. They even sold Santa Claus that used to be outside of city hall. Isn't that cold?[60]

The temporary suspension of local control and the ability to carry out sweeping policy changes with few or no checks and balances are viewed as essential to saving the city—or at least putting the fire out. But, as some opponents of the policy have asked: Who benefits? For whom is the city being saved?

4

Contextualizing the Flint Case

Race, Class, and Contentious Politics

BRUCE: Your question was Flint politics. I represented a pretty moderate ward but when I would get to city hall, you've got a dynamic there, especially at those meetings, which is just insane sometimes. I don't know what to say. One thing I wanted to mention was, I think, between White politics in the city and Black politics in the city. White politics is pretty tame, I think. Politics within the African American community is pretty intense, and that's where you get the hornet's nest.

I don't know that I could survive if I were African American and involved politically in the city, because it can be very, very cutthroat. These politicians go through much more than a White politician does. I had it easy, comparatively. I just had to deal with the hornet's nest aspect at times. They're in it every single day. You've got pastors and that whole piece of it, and it's a mess.

AEN: Are people angry? Or has it always been—

BRUCE: It's lots of positioning and ego and . . . I think that the African American community has been marginalized for so long and not allowed to participate in portions of community life. They've been contained.

That's the word I would use. They've been contained. They've developed their own internal leadership processes; part of that is the pastors. A big part of leadership in the African American community is religious, and it's in Christian churches and its pastors. They've had to create that leadership system because they weren't allowed to do it beyond that. The other piece of it is, if there are political positions that are in constituencies that are majority African American, there's an intense fight over those positions and there are rival camps all over the place. It's intense.[1]

In Flint, "politics" is often a bad word. Many residents perceive "politics," especially local politics, as confrontational and divisive, as the quotes above suggest. Legacies of redlining,[2] racial housing covenants,[3] and urban renewal have shaped Flint's contemporary politics.[4] As Bruce points out, for decades Flint's African American community has been "contained," and as a result, has developed its own "internal leadership processes." Much as the church served as the center of civil rights organizing due to exclusions from traditional White power structures, the church is the epicenter of Flint's Black politics.[5] For many, this internal organizing and leadership structure is an obstacle.

Francis, a nonprofit executive in Flint, noted:

It's very closed and it's very hard to permeate, and really the only way you get in is a link. You're kind of brought in by somebody. It's hard for newcomers to get in, and then if they're a newcomer to politics in Flint they still need to have some sort of family link or legacy to what's going on.[6]

Legacies of local social movements, including labor strikes and race rebellions, have informed Flint's contentious contemporary politics.[7] For example, one political activist, in a speech about the relationship between Flint's recent water crisis and emergency management, noted:

This is the Flint with a rich history. The sit-down strike put the unions on the map. The first city to elect [*sic*] an

African American, a Black for mayor. The first city to pass open housing. We are history makers and we set the pace on a lot of things. I am proud of us. We must remember who we are.[8]

History and context are important in understanding how policies shape politics.[9] While the primary focus of this analysis is recent history—focusing on the municipal takeovers of 2002 and 2011—the nature of local fiscal crises, as outlined in Chapter 1, necessitates a deeper historical understanding. More importantly, Flint's historical context matters because community responses to the takeover were mediated by both place-based and racial and economic identities.

This chapter centers on Flint's demographic, economic, and political history as a foundation for understanding the city's experience with municipal takeover. Understanding these socioeconomic factors is essential for identifying how and why Flint's experience with municipal takeover reshaped the city's political landscape.

The "Vehicle City"

Flint, Michigan, is located sixty-five miles northwest of Detroit, situated along the easternmost fifteen miles of the Flint River. Driving into Flint from the west, you pass through cornfields and the small towns dotting Michigan's rural midlands. Driving east from Grand Rapids on M-21 or south from the city of Saginaw on I-75, you might expect the city to look like other small towns throughout the region: mostly rural, not too many tall buildings—almost quaint to someone from a bigger city. But as you drive though Flint, the vestiges of a formerly prosperous city are evident: large brick Tudor homes and turn-of-the-century buildings give way to mid-century high-rises. The "Vehicle City" arches stretch across the brick street of Saginaw as you drive through downtown (see Figure 4.1).

Founded in 1819, Flint was a small town known first for its fur trade and lumber and later for production of horseless carriages. The rise of the automobile industry in the early twentieth century established the city as a major metropolitan center.

Figure 4.1 "Vehicle City": downtown Flint and Genesee County arches, 2011. (Printed with permission from Michigan Municipal League/mml.org, 2011; licensed under CC BY-ND 2.0: https://creativecommons.org/licenses/by-nd/2.0/legalcode.)

The Buick Motor Company was founded there in 1903, followed shortly by General Motors (GM) in 1908, itself an offshoot of the Durant-Dort Carriage Company. Flint became known as the "Vehicle City."

Flint flourished for most of the 1930s through the 1970s, with workers and bosses prospering alike. The growth of GM brought with it concerns over working conditions and pay. The first sit-down strike in 1936–1937, which took place at GM plants in Flint, lasted forty-four days and forced the company to recognize the recently founded United Automobile Workers union (UAW).[10] The UAW played a vital role in Flint's development and prosperity, improving working conditions and wages and making Flint one of the wealthiest cities in the country based on per capita earnings. At the end of World War II, Flint's per capita income was 30 percent higher than the national average.[11] Flint was referred to as "Fabulous Flint" and the "Happiest Town in Michigan."[12] In 1955, on the centennial of its official incorporation as a city, Flint held a parade featuring both GM spokesmodel Dinah Shore and then–U.S. vice president Richard Nixon. Flint was an "industrial marvel," with "more GM workers than any other city in the world."[13] With a peak population of nearly 200,000 in the 1960s, it was once the second-largest city in the state of Michigan, smaller than only Detroit.

Shifting Racial Demographics

With GM's manufacturing headquarters in Flint, the company's growth translated into Flint's growth. From 1900 to 1930 the population increased from 13,103 to 156,492.[14] "Tens of thousands of migrants flocked to the Vehicle City," drawn by high wages, especially after the company unionized in the 1930s.[15] In 1930 the city was still a majority native-born White city, and as Flint historian Andrew Highsmith points out, in the decades before World War II,

> a potent combination of private discrimination, federal housing and development initiatives, corporate practices, and municipal pubic policies converged to make Flint one of the most racially segregated cities in the United States.[16]

In the 1940s and 1950s, the city's Black population nearly doubled, hovering around 12,000 in 1947, with most establishing residency in the city's two Black neighborhoods, Floral Park and St. John.[17] Outside of these neighborhoods, according to Highsmith, "Black pedestrians and motorists faced near constant harassment by officers from the Flint Police Department."[18]

During the second great migration, which lasted from approximately 1940 to the 1970s, more than five million African Americans moved from the South to the North and Midwest. In Flint, the Black population boomed. From 1950 to 1970, the city's Black population went from 13,906 to 54,237, a 290 percent increase.

Explicit and implicit racism created community divisions along racial lines that still reverberate today. A recent report regarding the causes of the Flint water crisis, issued by the Michigan Civil Rights Commission (MCRC), states:

> We are not suggesting that those making decisions related to this crisis were racists, or meant to treat Flint any differently because it is a community primarily made up by

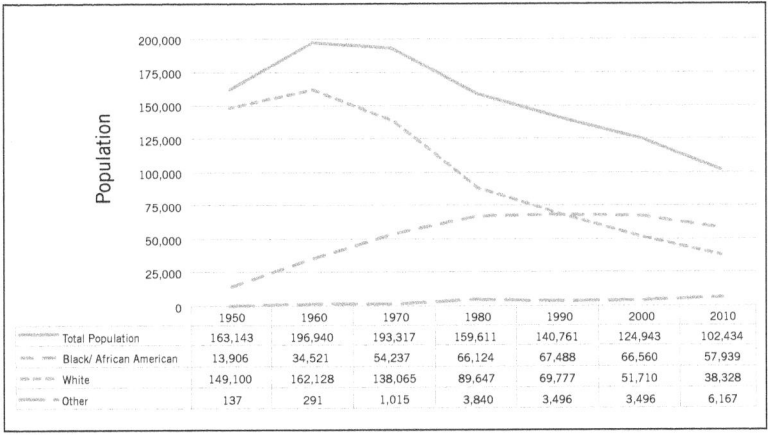

Figure 4.2 Flint population by race, 1950–2010. (U.S. Census Bureau, "QuickFacts: United States; Flint City, Michigan," 2010, http://www.census.gov/quickfacts/table/PST045215/00,2629000.)

people of color. Rather, the disparate response is the result of systemic racism that was built into the foundation and growth of Flint, its industry and the suburban area surrounding it. This is revealed through the story of housing, employment, tax base and regionalization which are interconnected in creating the legacy of Flint.[19]

GM policies and programs specifically created two classes of employees along racial lines. Prior to World War II, Blacks were excluded from most jobs, except for custodial and dangerous foundry positions. The GM Modern Housing division, which built homes in the city, was created to help alleviate a housing shortage, but the housing was available to only White employees.[20]

By the 1950s and 1960s Whites began to move out of Flint, as GM built more plants in the surrounding suburbs. As in communities across the United States, integration only encouraged White flight because Black home purchases in predominantly White neighborhoods brought down property values.[21] In 2000 Flint became a majority-Black city, with 53.3 percent of the population identifying as Black. The city's current racial makeup is 56.6 percent African American/Black, 37.4 percent White, and 6 percent Other (see Figure 4.2).[22]

Shifting Economic Conditions

Like many other industrialized cities, Flint's prosperity began to decline as the auto industry modernized, outsourced jobs, and shut down plants. In 1978 more than 80,000 Flint-area residents were employed by GM. By 2005, only 27 years later, the number had dropped 90 percent to 8,000, and by 2008 approximately 7,100 hourly and salaried employees remained.[23] In the mid-1980s GM laid off more than 30,000 employees, despite reporting record profits as a company. By the end of the decade Flint had fallen on truly hard times, depicted cinematically in Flint native Michael Moore's well-known documentary *Roger and Me.*

Ainsley, a former Flint resident, reflected on Flint's collapse, which they said began during the administration of Mayor James Rutherford:

> The beginning of the end for me was the Rutherford administration [1975–1983]. That was really when GM started pulling out. . . . Factories were closing, workers started losing their jobs, people started leaving *en masse,* and the schools started losing population. . . . The city and the schools couldn't deal with the shrinking city. . . . Dealing with a shrinking city and having to maneuver around that has been very difficult for Flint. . . . There's still huge amounts of money and pockets of money still left over from General Motors days . . . and like other cities there's a lot of super-poor. Thousands of people in poverty. You get a great divide.[24]

As GM jobs disappeared, the city's unemployment, poverty, and residential vacancy rates increased, while the overall population decreased and became less White. In 1982, in the midst of the GM layoffs, Daniel Zwerdling, an investigative reporter from National Public Radio (NPR), described the changes in Flint, calling it a "ghost town."

> To see what 25 percent unemployment does to a community, take a stroll down Saginaw Street to the middle of town. It used to be a lovely place, lined with old brick

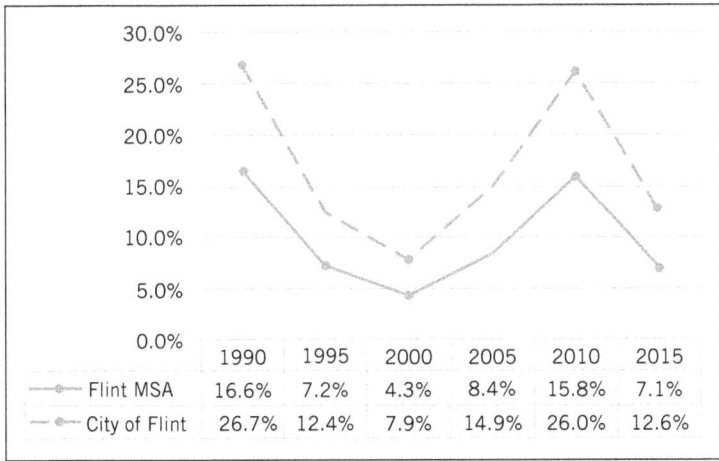

Figure 4.3 Flint unemployment rate, 1990–2015. (Flint MSA data retrieved from Bureau of Labor Statistics [BLS]; City of Flint data retrieved from Michigan Department of Technology, Management, and Budget.)

buildings, with the kind of turn-of-the-century masonry you don't see much of any more. Saginaw, the main street, is paved with bricks, and the sidewalks are shaded by awnings. But there is almost nobody and nothing here. Virtually every second store is boarded up with plywood. Some businesses have fled to suburban malls, the rest have simply folded.[25]

The mid-1990s brought short-term economic stabilization for the city—when both the unemployment and poverty rate dropped. But the end of the decade saw GM spending billions to build factories in Mexico, Brazil, and China, and shuttering more plants in and around Flint.[26] As shown in Figure 4.3, by 2010 Flint's unemployment rate was at 26 percent; more than ten percentage points higher than the unemployment rate of 15.8 percent in the Flint metropolitan statistical area (MSA), defined by Genesee County boundaries. In addition to the loss of GM jobs, the second-largest employer, the city of Flint itself, also shed jobs. The number of city employees decreased from 90,412 in 2001 to 49,500 in 2010.[27]

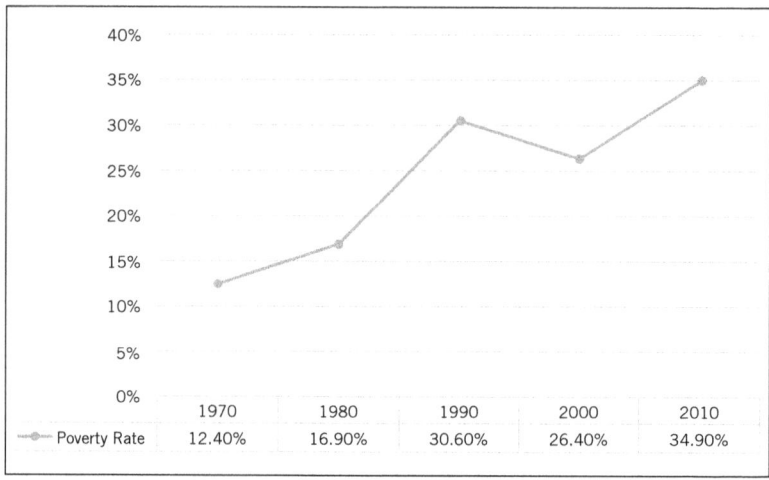

Figure 4.4 Flint poverty rate, 1970–2010. (U.S. Census Bureau, "QuickFacts: United States; Flint City, Michigan," 2010, http://www.census.gov/quickfacts/table/PST045215/00,2629000.)

Due in part to the first municipal takeover and continuing efforts to stem budget shortfalls, the size of Flint's government, in terms of employees, was nearly cut in half in less than a decade. With increased unemployment, Flint's poverty rate began to grow, as indicated in Figure 4.4.

While there was a slight improvement between 1990 and 2000, the poverty rate has generally increased, with the 2010 U.S. Census recording a forty-year high of 34.9 percent.

Flint has experienced fifty-plus years of population decline, with a peak population of 196,940 in 1960 dropping to 102,434 by 2010 (see Figure 4.2). In 2014 the U.S. Census Bureau estimated the city's population had fallen below 100,000 for the first time since the 1920s.[28] In 2015, when the takeover was lifted and local control was nominally returned to city officials, the population was estimated at 98,140, a 50.2 percent decrease from its height in 1960.[29]

GM's Environmental Footprint

While the overall population decreased, the percentage of residents who identify as Black and the number of households living below the poverty line increased. As outlined above, Flint has long been a racially and economically segregated city in which African Americans have disproportionately borne the burdens of economic decline.[30] This burden has also included environmental and health hazards associated with the introduction of leaded gas by GM, years of industrial pollution in the air, and industrial and agricultural waste dumping into the Flint River.

GM created leaded gas to compete with the Ford Motor Company in the 1920s. While leaded gas boosts octane levels and allows the production of faster and more powerful vehicles, its harmful effects on humans were known even then.[31] In addition, prior to the creation of the Environmental Protection Agency (EPA) and the Clean Air Act of 1970, Flint's residents suffered from heavily polluted air, especially in the Blacker and poorer areas of the city's North End.[32] Studies have shown poor communities and communities of color to be disproportionately victimized by environmental pollution, and Flint was a prime example of this dynamic.[33]

Concerns about the pollution levels in the Flint River began as early as the 1930s and 1940s, as fishing stocks decreased and some species of fish even disappeared altogether due to high levels of industrial waste dumped into the river. Several reports from environmental agencies at the state and federal levels (1955, 1960, 1974, and 1975) showed that the Flint River was highly polluted by raw sewage, phenol from GM plants, ammonia from wastewater facilities, and fertilizer runoff from farms.[34] However, it was not concern about the dirty water that prompted Flint to begin acquiring water from Lake Huron via Detroit in 1967, but the sheer volume of water needed to keep the booming city supplied. Concerns about pollution, illegal dumping, and the overall health of the river continued throughout the early twenty-first century as well.[35] There were no illusions as to the quality of the river water when the EM and local officials met to discuss using the Flint River as a water source in 2014; in fact, a 2001 report from the Michigan Department of Natural Resources indicated considerable public knowledge and distrust about the cleanliness of the Flint River.[36]

Flint's Political Stakeholders

Comprehending Flint's municipal takeover also means understanding local context and the key players in the local political system, the "who's who" of local politics. As Bruce's opening comments suggest and the preceding sections illustrate, Flint's political stakeholders have been shaped by legacies of racial segregation and economic change. While GM's dominance has faded and the UAW has lost its strength, other political stakeholders, deeply rooted in Flint's history, have gained prominence.

However, it is equally important to explore the emergence and evolution of Flint's "nominally powerless" stakeholders in order to "be more compatible with the typical approaches to democracy and social justice."[37] Moreover, a wider review captures how stakeholders vary in terms of their interests, framing, and interpretation of the takeover.[38] In other words, it is insufficient to focus on only those who have "power to afford the future," and thus a wider review should include groups and individuals to whom responsibility is owed. In order to understand the impact of EM rule in Flint, it is essential to understand the key figures and events that have shaped local politics and their current interests and larger motives.

Here I differentiate political stakeholders loosely by sector: business, nonprofit, and public (see Table 4.1 for a summary of the political stakeholder groups).

Business

As both the preceding and following sections highlight, Flint's business community has evolved over time. GM was once a significant presence in Flint. As GM's presence—physically and politically—has diminished, the strength of Flint's business community has weakened. However, as explored below, downtown businesses and developers have closely aligned interests with Flint's high-capacity nonprofits, making the distinction between sectors a bit blurry at times.

Nonprofit

Flint has an extensive nonprofit sector—from large nonprofits like the C. S. Mott Foundation, founded in 1926, and the United Way of Genesee County, founded in 1922, to smaller organizations like the Flint Democracy Defense League (DDL), founded

TABLE 4.1 FLINT POLITICAL STAKEHOLDERS BY SECTOR

Sector	Stakeholder group	Examples	Relative power	Use of power
Business	Major corporations	General Motors (GM)	Diminished	
	Downtown businesses		Moderate to significant	Many downtown businesses are aligned with Chamber of Commerce and/or Uptown Developments and Uptown Reinvestment Corporation.
Nonprofit	High-capacity nonprofits (universities, foundations, and development corporations)	Kettering University, C. S. Mott Foundation, Uptown Reinvestment	Moderate to significant	Power is manifest in the "development regime," a cadre of political stakeholders, including the C. S. Mott Foundation, the Chamber of Commerce, and the Uptown Corporation.
	Community-based and grassroots associations	Flint Democracy Defense League (DDL); Flint Rising; Concerned Pastors for Social Action (CPSA); churches	Marginal	Power is manifest primarily through contentious politics.
Public	Flint City government		Diminished	The powers of the local government are weakened by economic decline and are further diminished under the takeover.
	Political leadership		Marginal to moderate	Mayoral and city councilmembers have often been at odds, undermining each other's power. Recall elections disrupt political stability.

in 2011 in response to the municipal takeover. In response to the water crisis even more community organizations blossomed, including Water You Fighting For? and Flint Rising.

Nonprofit organizations range in size and scope. In this analysis, I focus on local, community-based organizations and associations, specifically on high-capacity nonprofits (HCNPs, or 501c tax-exempt organizations) and grassroots associations, as they offer a useful analytic lens for illustrating the role of nonprofits in Flint's changing political arena.

HCNP organizations can be local, but they are certainly not grassroots. This group includes community-based "anchor" institutions, like hospitals and universities,[39] as well as chambers of commerce, nonprofit economic development firms, or local private foundations.[40] These organizations are hierarchically structured, with boards of directors and paid staff. Moreover, these organizations are themselves embedded in the local, state, and regional political systems, be it through formal contracts, collaborative working agreements, or informal channels of elite influence.[41] Some have termed this close connection between high-capacity nonprofits and local political systems as the "nonprofit industrial complex."[42]

Grassroots associations, on the other hand, are community-based, social justice-focused associations of activists and residents who come together over an extended period of time to address a local social problem. These associations are nonhierarchical in structure. Some may provide services, but their work typically focuses on political advocacy and social change.[43] Grassroots activists may serve as the convening body for local social movements and community organizing,[44] often responding to policy threats by calling for community control.[45]

From loosely affiliated associations to neighborhood organizations to large, well-established nonprofits, Flint's nonprofit sector has provided a platform for individuals and communities to identify problems and propose solutions at the local level.

Public

The city of Flint was incorporated in 1855 and the city's present charter, which went into effect in 2018, was adopted in August

CITY OF FLINT
Ward Boundaries

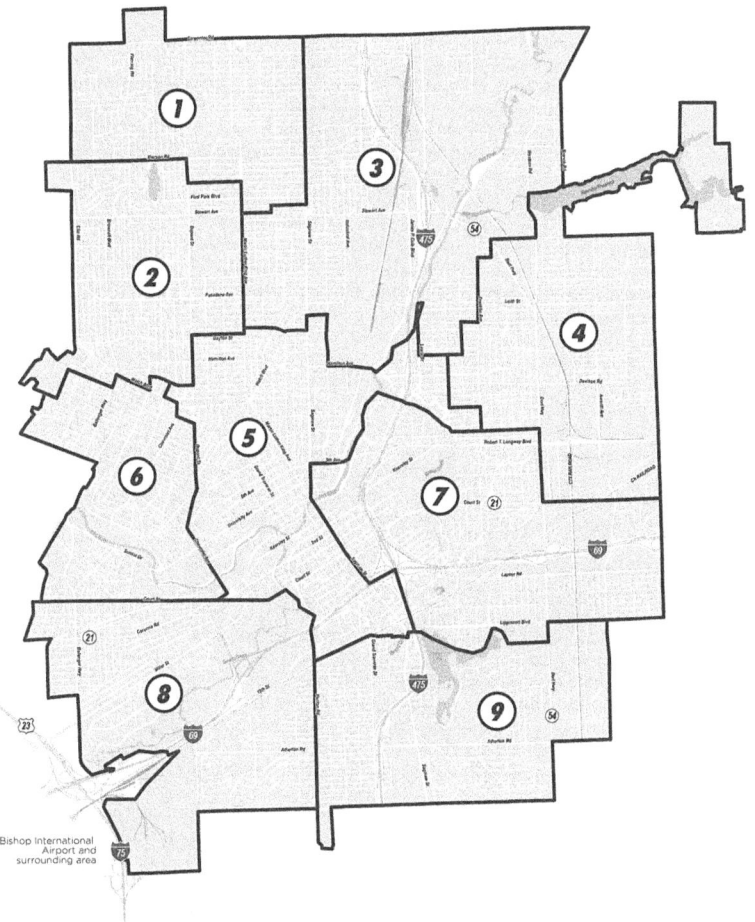

Figure 4.5 City of Flint ward map, 2012. (City of Flint; this map represents the 2012 map, which was redrawn after the 2010 census.)

2017.[46] The previous charter, which shifted the city to a strong mayor-council form of government, was adopted in 1974. The current charter also stipulates a strong mayor-council form of government. The city council is made up of nine council members, each serving one of nine city wards in staggered four-year terms, with no limit on the number of terms they may serve (see Figure 4.5). The mayor is elected in a nonpartisan election, every four years. As the chief executive of the city, the mayor has authority to appoint a city administrator as well as department heads.

The city of Flint is a general-purpose municipality that provides a range of services, including police and fire, water and sewer, streets and sanitation, parks and recreation, and community and economic development. The city is also the fiduciary for five other quasi-autonomous institutions: the Board of Hospital Managers, which manages and operates Hurley Medical Center; Flint Downtown Development Authority; Flint Economic Development Corporation; Flint Area Enterprise Community; and the Oak Business Center, a local business incubator.[47] In many respects, the city of Flint is set up and run like the vast majority of municipalities in United States, governed by local elected officials who oversee bodies responsible for providing basic government services.

Another important quasi-governmental political stakeholder in Flint is the Genesee County Land Bank Authority. Unlike a land trust, which holds land in a communal trust in order to enhance community control over land, a land bank serves as a clearinghouse for buying and selling land in order to return vacant or abandoned properties back to productive use.[48] In Flint, the Genesee County Land Bank was established in 2004 in order to "assemble and transfer land" for green space as well as residential and commercial development.[49] The idea for the Land Bank, however, was initiated under Dan Kildee (D-MI), who was then the county treasurer, in 1999. Given the authority's involvement in community development initiatives, specifically related to housing, land use, and commercial development; its ownership of nearly 9,000 city properties;[50] and its political roots, the Genesee County Land Bank plays an important role in Flint politics.

Flint Politics in Their Own Words

As several interviewees noted, Flint politics can be defined by the competing interests among different groups: Black versus White, North versus South, downtown versus neighborhood, rich versus poor, or labor versus management. Interview participants were in agreement that local politics can be divisive. However, some concluded that politics in Flint was no different than in other cities. Bruce, the former Flint City Council member representing the College Cultural Neighborhood on the city's south side, described Flint politics as a "hornet's nest that's been stirred up times a million. . . . It's a hornet's nest of competing interests and egos." When asked to describe Flint politics, other interview participants not only identified the tensions at play in the city but also fleshed out the major players, the key stakeholders, in local politics.

One such stakeholder is the Charles Stewart (C. S.) Mott Foundation, a legacy of GM industrialist Charles Stewart Mott. Mott, along with fellow GM executive William C. Durant, used his wealth and political power to establish many of the city's educational and cultural institutions, most notably the foundation that bears his name, which he founded in 1926 to address the problems that accompanied the city's growth.

Mott was also instrumental in the establishment of the Flint College and Cultural Center, which included what are now known as Mott Community College, the Flint Institute of Arts, Sloan Museum, Bower Theater, Dort Music Center, and Robert T. Longway Planetarium.[51] These institutions gave the College Cultural Neighborhood, for which Bruce served as council member, its name.

Mott was a wealthy Republican in a left-leaning union city who "believed deeply in the virtues of self-help, privatized charity, and laissez-faire approaches to social welfare." In response to the Flint sit-down strike, Mott reportedly said that the "workers deserved to be shot for illegally occupying the auto factories."[52]

The C. S. Mott Foundation has played a critical role in Flint politics since at least the mid-1930s, when Charles Stewart Mott and Frank Manely, a local educator, launched Flint's "community education" program to remake "city schools into neighborhood civic centers."[53] As Andrew Highsmith and Ansley Erickson point out, in order for its program to work, the C. S. Mott Foundation "forged a close bond with the board of education."[54] When the school program first began, Flint was a predominantly White city, but between the 1940s and 1960s the city's Black population grew rapidly and Black families began moving into previously segregated school attendance zones. Subsequently, "community education leaders responded by launching an active campaign to maintain racial segregation within local schools and neighborhoods."[55] Notably, when Flint's school zoning policy was struck down by the courts for its impact on Black residents, the C. S. Mott Foundation suspended the community education program.

The foundation also played an important role in the 1950s and 1960s, when it was involved in plans to try to expand the city of Flint's boundaries, as well as in 1975, when former Flint police chief James Rutherford ran for mayor and narrowly defeated incumbent Floyd McCree, the city's first Black mayor. This is when the foundation's downtown economic development agenda began to emerge. Rutherford took office as major economic development plans were being discussed.

A coalition of community leaders, including the Flint Area Conference, Inc. (FACI), a nonprofit organization of civic and business leaders working with public officials to promote economic development, the C. S. Mott Foundation, and "other civic groups," with support from Rutherford, put forward a "sweeping revitalization plan for the central business district."[56] The plans included the now infamous AutoWorld, a theme park devoted to the industry. According to Highsmith, "To help launch the enterprising plan, the Mott Foundation pledged $4.25 million in start-up grants, with the mayor and city council members offering their full support."[57]

The coalition's efforts to foster robust downtown economic development were unsuccessful, however. As GM continued to shut down factories and lay off workers, and as the city began to face White flight, increased unemployment, and rising poverty rates, the Rutherford administration attempted to stave off the city's mounting fiscal crisis by laying off more than three hundred city workers and cutting garbage collection services to twice a month. Of particular relevance to this part of Flint's story is the decision made by local elites to focus on downtown economic development while simultaneously cutting city services and jobs. Perceptions of these elites as interested in only downtown economic development were echoed in interviews.

The C. S. Mott Foundation continues to play a significant role in local political and civic life, particularly in the way it favors certain neighborhoods, including the College Cultural Neighborhood, which is home to some of the city's wealthiest residents and most of its cultural institutions. George, a long-time elected official, said of the C. S. Mott Foundation and the Chamber of Commerce, "These institutions play politics. They say they don't, but they do. They play big time."[58]

Brenda, a former resident and nonprofit executive, emphasized the important, though divisive, role the C. S. Mott Foundation plays in the city. Informally, through its funding, the organization has significant influence in determining what does and what does not happen in the city. She stated:

> One of the major players in this city is the C. S. Mott Foundation. They ultimately run the other foundations. So, I'm in a nonprofit. From the philanthropy point of view, if [Mott] likes it everybody else loves it. If [Mott] don't like it, hang it up.
>
> I look at cities like Detroit. I look at what the Skillman Foundation has invested inside of Detroit. They're very intentional. They have engaged the community and there are people that have critiqued that . . . but you cannot deny the dollars that they have intentionally put into Detroit and said, "We're going to focus on these communities." They didn't pick the nicest communities. . . . They were about building up Detroit from the grassroots up, not grass tops down.
>
> C. S. Mott Foundation doesn't get that model. That's not what they do. They prescribe what's going to happen.[59]

Drawing an analogy to a dysfunctional family, Jennifer, a community activist, noted, if "GM is the alcoholic abusive father, [the C. S.] Mott Foundation is the co-dependent, enabling mother."[60]

The C. S. Mott Foundation, which in 2016 celebrated ninety years of grant making with a cumulative $3 billion in grants,[61] and other political stakeholders have played a significant role in shaping not only Flint politics, formally and informally, but also the city's color line.[62]

Flint is and has historically been a racially segregated city, a topic that came up in nearly all of the four dozen interviews I conducted. When asked to describe Flint politics, Bruce, for example, notes that Flint is "still highly segregated," despite the presence of Black leaders such as Woodrow Stanley and Floyd McCree, who both served as mayor and are viewed as "titans of local politics."[63]

McCree was Flint's first Black mayor and one of the first Black mayors in the country. McCree was first elected to Flint's city council in 1958, in the midst of significant racial tensions in the city. In 1966 McCree was appointed to the position of mayor; he was not directly elected by voters but was elected by members of the city council. Highsmith suggests that McCree's appointment to mayor was more a symbolic victory than a significant shift in local politics and race relations in the city, noting that McCree's appointment "gave momentum to those organizing on the ground, but it didn't generate any power for the African American communities in local politics."[64]

James Sharp Jr. was Flint's first Black mayor, elected under the "strong mayor" charter, running against James Rutherford in 1983. Sharp served from 1983 to 1987, when he was defeated by Matthew Collier. Woodrow Stanley, however, was and continues to be a major presence in Flint. He served as mayor for almost eleven years, from 1991 until he was removed from office via recall election in 2002. Stanley began his political career in 1983, when he was appointed to the Flint City Council to represent the city's Second Ward. Under his administration, the city saw a momentary return to economic stability, with both unemployment and poverty rates declining. Stanley went on to serve on the Genesee County Board of Commissioners from 2008 to 2009 and the Michigan House of Representatives from 2009 to 2014. He was an outspoken critic of PA 4 (see Chapter 2) as it was debated in the legislature. Stanley continues to play an important, though divisive, role in the city, most recently helping to elect current mayor Karen Weaver.

In the chapter opening, Bruce argues that Flint's Black community, marginalized for so long, "developed their own internal leadership processes, [and] part of that is the pastors. A big part of leadership in the African community is religious and it's in Christian churches and its pastors. They've had to create that leadership system because they weren't allowed to do it beyond that."

Concerned Pastors for Social Action (CPSA) was established in 1969 by Dr. Avery Aldridge "to rid the community of local institutional racism, and to improve the relationship between community and the police."⁶⁵ The organization, representing mostly Black religious leaders, has been involved in local politics since its inception. In 1987 CPSA succeeded in pushing for Detroit Street to be renamed Martin Luther King Jr. Boulevard. While slow to respond to the municipal takeover initially, CPSA played a significant role, leveraging what political power they had—inside and outside the city—to bring attention to the water crisis. In coalition with the Natural Resources Defense Council, the Michigan ACLU, and Flint resident Melissa Mays (also associated with the community-based organization Flint Rising), the CPSA filed a suit against the state in federal court.⁶⁶

Other community-based organizations, such as the Flint NAACP and the Flint Area Congregations Together (FACT, now known as Michigan Faith in Action), have also served as organizing institutions for Flint's Black community, amplifying their interests to local political leaders. Janean, a local organizer, said of FACT in an interview, "Our pastors have them [EMs] on speed dial. They answer the phone on the other end, their cellphones, 'Hi, pastor. What can I do for you today?' They have the contacts."⁶⁷

Black community members who live in the North End of Flint, the area of the city north of the Flint River, are the most politically marginalized. Zach, a community activist and lawyer, notes:

> If there's a division that is readily apparent within the city limits, it is between the North End and the remainder of the city. The North End is overwhelmingly African American.... The North End is destitute compared to a lot of the areas of the county, certainly, and of the city as well. If you're going to an area of Flint that's by the cultural center, for example, you're looking at almost a different city altogether.... [T]he North End has its own interests.⁶⁸

Those "interests" include responding to crime, blight, and improving education and job opportunities for residents. North End residents that participated in interviews expressed skepticism about the city's downtown economic development agenda.⁶⁹

Francis expanded on this sentiment, noting that Flint's political leaders are just "figureheads, and we've had figureheads for a long time, powerless figureheads." Pointing to 1974, when the city was drafting its charter, Francis said that "they had already decided that this was going to be a university town."[70] Flint is home to three colleges and universities, including University of Michigan–Flint, Kettering University (formerly, General Motors Institute), and Mott Community College. Michigan State University also has a campus in Flint.

"They" meant the powers that be: The C. S. Mott Foundation, the Flint and Genesee Chamber of Commerce, and the city's economic leaders, who, as another respondent noted, have a "development agenda."[71] The emphasis on downtown development and the creation of the university corridor were viewed by many interviewees as evidence of the influence of the Mott Foundation and the Chamber of Commerce on local political decision making.[72] As Adrian noted, the perception that there is outside influence, on behalf of the C. S. Mott Foundation and the Chamber of Commerce, for example, in local government, "was heightened during the emergency manager period."[73]

Shayne, a community activist, further illustrates this point:

> I'll be blunt with you. There's Dayne Walling and the Uptown elitists who feel like, if you can't pay to stay, you can't stay. That's their approach. We are gonna shrink the city, take the assets, and our twenty-first-century developments can bump up. Meanwhile [a low-income housing development is] sitting empty right now with all those millions pumped into it. But, and then there's Karen Weaver, who represents the Black pastor community. She's into the churches, she does all that stuff with the Black [community]—you've seen it. It's a divide.[74]

Uptown was often used synonymously with downtown economic development interests, due to the prominent role of Uptown Developments, LLC, and its sister nonprofit, the Uptown Reinvestment Corporation. The two organizations were established in 2002 to develop downtown Flint with significant financial support from the C. S. Mott Foundation.[75] Uptown grew out of a revitalization group referred to as the "Uptown Six" that was focused on a pro-growth, development agenda. Troy Farah, a real estate developer and one of the founding members of the Uptown Six, noted that Uptown practices "real estate philanthropy," emphasizing that the organization is not looking for a "financial return on investment" but a "return on investment [that] is the economic impact on Downtown and the benefits to the community."[76]

The founding members and executives of the Uptown organizations, in addition to Farah, include other prominent businessmen from Flint: Phil Shaltz, who was instrumental in coordinating Michael Brown's appointment as city administrator in 2009, and Tim Herman, CEO of the Flint and Genesee Chamber of Commerce, member of the EM advisory team, and current board president of the Uptown Reinvestment Corporation.[77] Ridgway White served as a C. S. Mott Foundation executive on loan to the Uptown Reinvestment Corporation from 2009 until 2015, when he was named president of the C. S. Mott Foundation.

GM's influence in Flint did not end with Charles Stewart Mott and his foundation. GM also gave rise to the UAW. Drawing attention to Flint as a union town, Bill, a young Black nonprofit executive, offered the view that Flint politics in many ways mirrors the union-management relationship. Flint politics was born, he noted, out of an adversarial yet co-dependent relationship with GM. Employees relied on the company while using the unions to fight for what they needed.[78] Bill suggests that the relationship rests on the idea that people can fall in line when things are good, although they will fight when things go bad.

Unions were not only cultural and economic influencers; they also had significant power in local politics. "At one point the union endorsement was pretty much all you needed to get into office," Bill said.[79] Others echoed Bill's comments, further highlighting the connection often made between Flint being a union town and "a one-party city," in Zach's words.[80] Adrian, a local nonprofit executive, concurred: "Flint, it seems to be . . . pretty Democrat-leaning, tends to be pretty blue collar. . . . [T]he unions had a lot of political sway, and to an extent, that's still the case I think, but maybe not to the degree it used to be." Peter, a civically active resident from the College Cultural Neighborhood, also agreed, adding that Flint politics is run by the "Democratic Party and the UAW."[81]

The prominence of the UAW, and to a lesser extent the American Federation of State, County, and Municipal Employees (AFSCME), gave rise to a powerful union culture. The "union culture" sentiment was referenced repeatedly in my interviews. People needed the jobs that GM provided, but "at the same time, for individuals to be successful in large systems like that, [they] had to fight and advocate," Bill said. There is a constant push and pull between falling in line and fighting for a "fair share."[82] However, even as they noted the power of the unions, most of the people interviewed identified the C. S. Mott Foundation and the Chamber of Commerce as the most significant players, and ones that had made Flint politics "closed" or "inaccessible." Shaun, a local community activity and organizer, added, "Flint politics is a hot mess. . . . On paper, there's an opportunity for everyone to be represented. . . . [T]he actuality of Flint politics, we have low voting participation. There aren't a lot of people that come to meetings."[83]

While some interviewees observed the divisiveness, tensions, and apathy in Flint politics, a few were quick to point out the positive aspects of Flint's civic life. Liesel, a retired schoolteacher, praised what she called the ability to work together on issues: "No matter what their arguments are otherwise, if there's a need, this community steps up. . . . It's one of the things that I love about this community. If we need to step up, we'll step together."[84] Adrian commented that Flint values "underdog-ness,"[85] by which she meant the power that comes from being viewed as less-than, counted-out, or marginalized.

The city's history of marginalization and the implementation of the municipal takeover, however, have reinforced that "underdog-ness." Respondents were well aware of the ways in which state intervention laws influenced local politics. While high-capacity nonprofits associated with the development regime gained influence, others struggled to pay for the water that, as it turned out, was poisonous.

"It's been constant chaos," Carl, a former elected official, said.[86]

5

The "Development Agenda"

Implementing Municipal Takeover in Flint

> AEN: So what did the municipal takeover/emergency manager mean to you?
> JENNIFER: I mean, it was basically a Mott takeover.
> —JENNIFER, community activist,
> personal interview, July 2017

Since 2002 Flint has experienced two municipal takeovers, during which time four EMs were appointed and thousands of executive orders, resolutions, and directives were issued. Under the authority of EMs, the city of Flint went through significant changes. Policy implementation, as Donald Moynihan and Joe Soss have noted, "can reorganize power relations in a society, redefine terms of political conflict, mobilize or pacify constituencies, and convey cues about group deservingness."[1] In order to understand how such policies impacted politics, it is imperative to examine how the takeovers were implemented in Flint.

As discussed in the Introduction, municipal takeovers symbolize the "rationality project," wherein expert policy makers and implementers view policy through a market lens. From this perspective, the solution, and thus the policy design, is claimed to be directed at fiscal conditions and predetermined policy outcomes (e.g., a balanced budget and economic stability). Evaluation of the policy, therefore, focuses on whether those outcomes were achieved.

Municipal takeovers upset the existing political order by shifting the rules of the game. At the same time, these shifts create opportunities for longer-term change not necessarily envisioned by drafters of the policy. In Flint, even temporary changes to the rules, such as the consolidation of authority in the EM's office and its focus on economic issues, served to simultaneously isolate and exclude those perceived to be impediments to the city's economic stability and development. That included labor unions, adversarial elected officials, retirees, special-interest groups, and the public more generally. Whether this exclusion was intentional or not, it had consequences beyond the official period of emergency management.

In Flint, as in other cities,[2] the strategy adopted for balancing the city's budget focused on cutting services and staff and fostering local economic development. The city's "development regime,"[3] referenced in Chapter 4, was a major player in setting the EM's municipal takeover agenda. Flint's experience with municipal takeovers—particularly the 2011 takeover—provides an excellent opportunity to examine the ways in which politics and local political participation change under the implementation of aggressive intervention policy.

The Takeovers, 2002 and 2011

Municipal Takeover, 2002

In 2002 Flint residents pursued a recall election to oust the mayor, Woodrow Stanley, setting off a series of events that ultimately led to Flint's first municipal takeover in July of that year. Stanley had served as mayor for more than a decade, from 1991 to 2002, after serving eight years on the city council. While he was well liked in some parts of the city (his own Second Ward in particular), Stanley faced criticism for his handling of the city's finances and his ineffective attempts to address the city's ongoing economic woes.

Stanley's tenure as mayor coincided with huge changes in Flint. From 1990 to 2000 the city witnessed a significant shift in its population, shrinking from 140,761 to 124,943—an 11.2 percent decrease over the decade, as discussed in greater detail in Chapter 4. According to the *Flint Journal*, the city's "racial divide also continued, with whites leaving the city of Flint in droves and the county ranking as the 9th most segregated metropolitan area in the nation."[4] During that same decade, the city lost approximately four thousand manufacturing jobs, in part because GM moved its administrative division to Detroit and because Buick City, a major manufacturing plant in Flint, closed. In February 2000 Moody's Investor Services placed Flint's bond rating on the "watch list," indicating that it was a risky investment.[5]

Under the Stanley administration, the city had attempted to stave off the direct and indirect fiscal impact of increasing unemployment and depopulation on local government resources by laying off nearly a third of the fire department and moving to privatize garbage collection. These efforts, however, faced resistance from the American Federation of State, County, and Municipal Employees (AFSCME).[6] The city did manage, however, to sell off the IMA Sports Arena for $2.2 million to a local entrepreneur.[7]

In March 2002 Stanley, a three-term mayor, was recalled by voters. Darnell Earley, who served as city administrator during Stanley's time in office, was appointed interim mayor. In an interview with the *Los Angeles Times,* Stanley indicated that he had been "made the scapegoat for the downturn created by GM's painful withdrawal" and that the election had "reopened deep racial wounds in a place where Blacks live north of the Flint River, the Whites to the south."[8] In response to the mayor's recall and the financial crisis in the city, Earley noted, "The city should have made tougher decisions sooner."[9]

On March 13, 2002, only a week after the recall, State Senator Bob Emerson (D-Flint) sought a preliminary review of the city of Flint's financial condition under the Local Government Fiscal Responsibility Act, known as PA 72. The subsequent findings compelled the governor to appoint a Financial Review Team to conduct an assessment of the city's fiscal situation. As cited in the case *City Council of Flint v. State of Michigan* in October 2002:

> The review team concluded that city officials demonstrated an inability "to accurately monitor revenues and expenditures throughout a given fiscal year and to amend city budgets accordingly." The 2000 and 2001 financial audit reports indicated that "the city failed to maintain an accurate and timely general ledger, failed to perform timely

reconciliations of bank balances to the general ledger, and incurred an excess of expenditures over revenues."[10]

The review team found that the city had borrowed money from special purpose funds to supplement the general fund to the point that the city was no longer able to provide road maintenance and water and sewer service. Their report indicated that during the fiscal year ending June 2001, the city's general fund deficit had doubled from $13 million to $26 million. Moreover, the review team reported, "There was a surprising difference of opinion among city officials regarding what the general fund deficit will be for the current fiscal year ending on June 30th [2002]," concluding that the fact that "city officials could not even agree upon the magnitude of the accumulated deficit, let alone upon a credible plan for its elimination, was troubling and suggestive of an inability to resolve the serious financial problem confronting the city."[11]

On July 8, 2002, the Financial Assistance Loan Board appointed Ed Kurtz, former president of Flint-based Baker College, as Flint's emergency financial manager. The following day, on behalf of the City Council, attorneys filed an appeal with the Ingham County Circuit Court, starting a months-long legal battle between the city and the state regarding the legality of PA 72 and the use of EFMs. During Kurtz's tenure as manager, from July 2002 through July 2004, he issued "nearly 120 directives," according to the *Flint Journal*.[12] Actions undertaken by Kurtz included conducting a salary and wage study of top officials; implementing new procedures for hiring, travel, and spending within the city; closing city community centers and the Office of the Ombudsman; laying off city employees; and raising water rates by 11 percent. He also negotiated pay cuts with unions and contribution cuts with the city retirement board.

The appointment of Kurtz was met with mixed reviews. The *Flint Journal*'s editorial board praised the state for stepping in to address the city's fiscal concerns. The Mackinac Center, a conservative Michigan-based think tank, also supported the action, while criticizing the policy for not going far enough to address the issues facing Flint.[13] Others living and working in the city, however, were skeptical of the policy. Lawrence Ford, president of the Flint and Genesee Chamber of Commerce at the time, noted that he would have preferred no takeover but would work with "whoever [sic]" and that he hoped "it will be resolved and it will be resolved quickly."[14] Others leveled criticisms at Kurtz directly, suggesting that his appointment was "fueled by a larger power base that included the business community, the Mott Foundation and *The Flint Journal*."[15] (See Chapter 4 for a discussion of the C. S. Mott Foundation's historic role in the development of Flint.) City council vice president Johnnie Coleman seconded this criticism, concluding, "The White elite group has picked this receiver and their only concerns are downtown and City Hall, not the neighborhoods.... [T]hey literally took away our rights as citizens."[16]

Kurtz's term as EFM ended in July 2004, although the state continued to monitor the city's finances until 2006.[17] Kurtz was able to engineer a transition from a $26.6 million general fund deficit to a $6.1 million surplus by June 30, 2005.[18] He did so by cutting the pay of the mayor and city council; eliminating health, dental, and vision benefits for most city officials; closing city centers and various governmental offices; negotiating pay cuts with major unions; and laying off employees.[19]

In the seven years between the end of the first takeover and the beginning of the second, the city experienced a series of mayors (see Table 5.1) as well as continued economic hardship. Understanding what happened during that period is important to understanding the second takeover in 2011, because the choices made during each of the mayoral administrations provide evidence of the ongoing policy paradoxes, tensions between the market and the polis, and the power of the "development regime."

Near the end of Kurtz's term as EFM, voters elected Don Williamson as mayor. Williamson, as the *Flint Journal* reported, was a divisive character in Flint: "Some love him, some hate him, but everyone knows the mayor."[20] Williamson won the mayoral seat in 2003, surprising many people because he ran against the Democratic Party–backed incumbent and former mayor James Rutherford. Independently wealthy, Williamson was seen by many as a political outsider. The upset, which rejected the development agenda's candidate, foreshadowed the 2015 election, when Dayne Walling was replaced by Karen Weaver, who is the mayor at the time of this writing.

TABLE 5.1 FLINT MAYORS, 1975–2017

Mayor	Term	Elections (year: votes cast)	Notes
James Rutherford	1975–1983	1975: 20,679 to 20,474, against Floyd McCree 1979: 20,738 to 12,902, against Floyd McCree	McCree had served as mayor from 1966 to 1968. Rutherford worked in coalition with the "development regime" to push for a downtown development agenda.
James Sharp Jr.	1983–1987	1983: 21,718 to 20,467, against James Rutherford	Sharp was the first Black mayor elected to Flint under the 1974 strong-mayor charter.
Matthew Collier	1987–1991	1987: 22,874 to 19,509, against James Sharp Jr.	Michael Brown served as director of community development and government relations, and Tim Herman, CEP of Flint and Genesee Chamber of Commerce, served as director of finance under Collier.
Woodrow Stanley	1991–2002	1991: 25,946 to 17,686, against Matthew Collier 1995: 21,687 to 9,168, against Don Williamson 1999: 17,224 to 16,393, against Scott Kincaid 2002, recall election: 12,336 to 15,863	Stanley was removed from office by recall election on March 5, 2002, and replaced by his city administrator, Darnell Earley.
Darnell Earley	2002–2002		Earley served as temporary mayor from March 5, 2002, to August 6, 2002. He became state-appointed EFM in July 2002.
James Rutherford	2002–2003	2002: 11,239 to 4,712, against Arthur Pointer	Rutherford was elected to carry out the remainder of Stanley's term, though his powers were limited under EFM.
Don Williamson	2003–2009	2003: 13,906 to 9,228, against Floyd Clack 2007: 12,434 to 11,853, against Dayne Walling	Williamson served with limited powers under EFM until 2004. Facing recall election, he resigned on February 15, 2009.
Michael Brown	2009–2009		Michael Brown served as temporary mayor until August 5, 2009.
Dayne Walling	2009–2015	2009: 12,266 to 6,876, against Brenda Clack 2011: 8,819 to 6,868, against Darryl Buchanan	On the day of Dayne Walling's second election in 2011, the state announced another municipal takeover. Walling served with limited powers from December 2011 to April 2015; he was mayor when the water crisis was confirmed.
Karen Weaver	2015–	2015: 7,825 to 6,061, against Dayne Walling	Karen Weaver is the city's first female mayor.

Williamson declined his mayoral salary, opting instead to be paid $1 per year by the city, and was known for his engagement with community residents. Every Wednesday, for example, he set aside time so that residents could meet with him. Residents took this opportunity, even if it meant waiting hours for their turn.[21] In some instances, the mayor paid out of his own pocket to aid residents in need.[22] Williamson was not universally liked, however. Some saw him as the "combative, in-your-face, gruff Mayor of Flint."[23] According to Gordon Young, he once stated that the city council was "about as valuable as puke on brand new carpet."[24] In 2005 Williamson led the charge against his opponents on the city council, effectively getting them "booted" from their positions.[25] In February 2009 Williamson resigned from office under the threat of a recall election. Under his leadership, the city fell back into a budget shortfall of more than $8 million.

Despite being well liked in parts of the city, Williamson was the antithesis of the budget-focused technocratic management of Kurtz or the development-focused leadership of Rutherford.[26] Williamson, for all of his faults, paid attention to the needs and desires of the broader public, especially the less affluent Black communities in the North End of Flint. However, as Young pointed out, "Flint-style democracy, with its recalls and special elections, was costing the city a lot of money it clearly did not have."[27] After years of divisive politics and facing a recall election himself, Williamson resigned. But, just as he was set to leave office, he appointed Michael Brown as city administrator. At the time of his appointment, Brown was working for the Flint and Genesee Chamber of Commerce and had a reputation for financial acumen. Two weeks later, Brown was named the city's interim mayor, per the city charter, after the resignation of Williamson.[28]

Reflecting on Brown's short stint as city administrator, Bruce, the former city council member, said that he believed that Williamson's resignation and the naming of Brown as city administrator was prompted by business leaders known as the "Uptown Six."

> It's my understanding that Mayor Williamson had a city administrator, Darryl Buchanan, who had been a council member from the First Ward. He was Williamson's city

administrator. He demoted him or put him into another position. Williamson did that to Buchanan and brought on Mike Brown, I think, at the urging of Uptown. Phil Shaltz . . . in particular was working behind the scenes on that, is what I was told. They somehow convinced Williamson to resign and put Mike Brown in, as city administrator, knowing that he would be elevated to the position of interim mayor. I don't know all the details, but I'll bet you that that whole scenario was developed by the economic powers downtown and that's how Mike got in there that first time. Then when he left, he went back to the Flint Area Investment Corporation, which is funded by the C. S. Mott Foundation, primarily, and then slid back in as EM.[29]

Although Brown was in office for only six months, he made significant changes at city hall immediately upon taking office. Of particular importance to this analysis are the political appointments he made, as they further highlight the relationship between Brown and the local development regime discussed in more detail below. As mayor, Brown appointed eight new administrators, two of whom are notable: Duane Miller, former GM executive (now vice president of the Chamber of Commerce), was tapped to serve as governmental operations director, and Darryl Buchanan, a political adversary (whom he had just replaced) was made special projects director.[30]

During his short stint as mayor, Brown not only shook up city hall; he also submitted a deficit reduction plan to the state, which included eliminating forty-eight police officers, twenty-four firefighters, and thirteen other positions within local government.[31] As early as 2009 Brown was suggesting that the city needed to make significant cuts in order to avoid another takeover.[32]

Brown did not run for mayor in the August 2009 special election. Instead, Dayne Walling, a Flint native and Ph.D. candidate with a specialization in urban development at the University of Minnesota, handily won the election against Genesee County Commissioner Brenda Clack, taking "35 of the city's 60 precincts, including five predominantly black precincts."[33] The *Flint Journal* reported, "Walling arguably got more support from the Black community than former Mayor Don Williamson did in 2003 when he ran against Clack's husband, former state Rep. Floyd Clack."[34]

Walling's first term was aimed at creating what he called a "diversity coalition," in which he actively sought advice and input from constituents from across the city.[35] One of Walling's biggest contributions, initiated in 2009 but not launched until 2012, was updating the city's comprehensive master plan, which had not been revised in fifty years. "Imagine Flint," was a "blueprint" or "road map" for Flint's future. This master plan, adopted by the city council in 2013, included "sections on economic development, educational and public facilities, and services including public safety, transportation and mobility, infrastructure, environmental features and open space, and housing." It was intended to serve as a "policy guide" for city officials and city leaders for long-range planning, assuming that implementation would take place over the next twenty years.[36] The project was supported by the C. S. Mott Foundation with a $529,477 grant. In an interview with *Next City*, one of the foundation's program officers noted:

> Flint is already in the process of revitalizing. . . . The master plan is a reference for coordinating the resources in the city, and also pointing out the opportunities for raising the profile of assets and building on them. . . . Engagement will be key to getting projects implemented.[37]

As such, unsurprisingly, some viewed Walling's master plan initiative as a "Mott project." Jennifer, who was involved with the planning process, noted: "You know, it was always interesting to me during the master planning process that [Mayor] Dayne [Walling] would always be accompanied by a program officer of the Mott Foundation. Always."[38]

Municipal Takeover, 2011

Regardless of Walling's commitment to building a "diversity coalition," under his leadership the city of Flint continued to accumulate debt. In 2011 the city again found itself confronted with a municipal takeover. The "progress" made under Kurtz was reversed within three years: "Subsequent labor settlements, costly litigation, and declining revenues caused the City to return to a significant deficit position. By June 30, 2008, the City closed the fiscal year with a deficit in the General Fund of $6.8 million."[39] By 2011 the city was facing "severe financial pressure."[40] At the end of 2010 the city's general fund deficit was $14.6 million. Three of the city's special purpose funds were also in a deficit position: the building department fund, parks and recreation, and garbage collection. The city's property tax revenue, income tax revenue, and state-shared revenue had decreased significantly between 2006 and 2010, while expenditures kept increasing. In 2011, recognizing the financial condition of the city, the Walling administration asked the Michigan Department of Treasury's permission to issue a twenty-five-year $20 million stabilization bond in order to maintain operations. The state authorized $8 million.[41]

Walling's action in seeking bond funds to help Flint was not sufficient. After the state was notified of the city's fiscal condition by then–finance director Michael Townsend,[42] the Department of Treasury, acting under PA 4, began a preliminary review of Flint's financial condition. The preliminary review confirmed that the city had incurred cumulative deficits in many of its funds, had not followed its own deficit elimination plan, and had consecutive years in which expenditures exceeded revenues. The preliminary review also pointed out that the city's ability to pay its short-term obligations was "uncertain," the city's pension system was "less than 60 percent funded," and city officials had failed to reduce staff "in accordance with their deficit elimination plan."[43] Based on the findings, the Treasury Department reported on September 12, 2011, "Probable financial stress existed in the city of Flint and recommended the appointment of a financial review team."[44]

On September 30, 2011, Governor Rick Snyder appointed an eight-member Financial Review Team. Key among them were former Flint city administrator Darnell Earley and former Michigan state senator Bob Emerson (D-Flint), who had also been a former state budget director. The review team met during October and November 2011 to review the financial statements and reports from the city as well as conduct interviews with local officials. Interviews and meetings were conducted with both outside experts and a range of interested parties, including appointed city administrators and department heads, judicial officials, and local elected representatives.

These discussions, in combination with the findings of the preliminary review, convinced the Financial Review Team, pursuant to the rules set out in the law, that "conditions indicative of a financial emergency" existed in Flint.[45] In addition to Flint's financial deficiencies, the report also criticized the city for failing to put city charter review amendments before voters and failing to achieve concessions from the city's unions.

At the same time that the Financial Review Team was finalizing its report, politicians were vying to be elected mayor of Flint. Fewer than 20 percent of registered voters turned out to vote on November 8, 2011, further highlighting that Flint was plagued with low voter turnout even before the takeover. With 8,819 votes (56 percent), incumbent Dayne Walling beat his opponent Darryl Buchanan, who had 6,868 votes.[46] "The same day voters handed him a solid victory, the state handed Mayor Dayne Walling a stunning blow," reported local journalist Kristen Longley. That blow was

> a declaration of a financial emergency in Flint and a recommendation that an Emergency Manager take the reins. Now, Flint's newly re-elected mayor is under the shadow of a likely state takeover—the cash-strapped city's second in just under a decade. Walling could be stripped of authority to carry out the duties of his own office.[47]

Furthermore, Longley reported, "despite the Walling administration's budget cuts, including controversial police layoffs that led to an unsuccessful attempt to recall him last year [2010], the [Financial Review Team] panel said city officials haven't done enough to fix the structural deficit in Flint and recommended an outsider step in." Walling reportedly responded, "As mayor I have the difficult job of balancing budget realities with human realities."[48]

On December 1, 2011, Michael Brown, the city's first state-appointed EM, took office. Brown's reputation as city administrator and interim mayor in 2009 had made him an obvious choice and, once appointed, he wasted little time. Within the first week, Brown had eliminated the positions of seven political appointees, cut the salaries and benefits of the mayor and city council members, set strict guidelines for city procurement and the process for submitting resolutions and ordinances, and eliminated the Office of the Ombudsman and the Civil Service Commission.

Brown served as EM for only nine months, although he remained part of the EM team and returned to the position for four months in late summer 2013. Others who held the position were Ed Kurtz, former EFM in 2002; Darnell Earley, former city administrator under Woodrow Stanley; and Gerald (Jerry) Ambrose, a financial expert from Lansing. All, with the exception of Ambrose, were well known in Flint.[49] The actions they took are discussed more fully below, paying particular attention to issues and concerns raised by my interviewees.

During this period, Michigan legislators were determined to establish a policy that would permit the state to monitor and supervise the financial actions of a city when necessary. During Flint's 2002–2004 takeover, PA 72 provided the authorizing legislation. In 2011 the legislature passed the much more restrictive PA 4. When voters overturned PA 4 by referendum, PA 72 was reinstated. Then, within months, the legislature approved PA 436. The differences between PA 4 and PA 436 were insignificant, as members of the EM team reported. While the names and titles of the managers changed, the agenda, as set by Brown, was carried out. One of the team noted, "Look at all the different people that went through. What's amazing is, we never missed a step. That plan we submitted was executed."[50]

That plan was Brown's forty-five-day "Financial and Operating Plan," which was submitted to the state on January 15, 2012. In that plan, Brown laid out his goals:

- Long-term financial stability;
- An increase in revenue base to provide quality services to its residents;
- A reduction in government costs through negotiated union contracts, consolidation and shared services, and ongoing professional development of staff;
- Continue to maintain and modernize the infrastructure

of the city in alignment with the current population counts;
- To streamline the processes necessary for businesses to locate, and continue operations, in the city;
- To utilize the Master Plan to stabilize and then increase both the commercial and residential base of the city;
- To provide public safety services, focusing on reducing violent crime, commensurate with cities of comparable size and resources.[51]

Of particular relevance here are the last three goals. Emphasized above, they illustrate that the objectives of the takeover were not explicitly "financial" but were certainly aligned with the EM's interest in broader economic development and revitalization.

Brown's "team" included the Emergency Manager Core Team as well as advisory committee chairs and a citizen's advisory council. Many of Brown's advisors had ties to the business community or high-capacity nonprofits throughout the city.[52]

Brown's selection of advisors was unsurprising, given his longtime involvement with the C. S. Mott Foundation and the Chamber of Commerce. Brown's appointment, coupled with the people he selected to implement change, led to the same criticisms that had been leveled during his term as interim mayor of Flint in 2009. Many residents assumed, with some evidence, that Brown was appointed at the request of the local power players. Carl, a former local elected official, noted, "My understanding is that the governor and [state] treasurer, Dillon, consulted extensively with the Mott Foundation and the business community about how the intervention would be best executed in Flint." Those organizations, he continued, "really pushed for more of a local approach. Mike Brown had been a nonprofit executive in the community. He had worked for the City of Flint as Department of Community Development director back in the late 1980s."[53] Brown had seemed like the ideal candidate.

As a result of PA 4's repeal by popular vote and the reinstatement of PA 72, Brown stepped down as EM in August 2012; however, he continued to serve on the EM team as the city administrator under Kurtz.[54] Brown returned to the position of EM for a short time in the summer of 2013, after PA 436 went into

TABLE 5.2 FLINT EMERGENCY MANAGERS, 2002–2015

Manager	Dates	Title	Law	Governor
Ed Kurtz	July 2002–June 2004	EFM	PA 72	John Engler
Michael Brown	December 2011–August 2012	EM	PA 4	Rick Snyder
Ed Kurtz	August 2012–March 2013 March 2013–July 2013	EFM EM	PA 72/ PA 436	Rick Snyder
Michael Brown	July 2013–October 2013	EM	PA 436	Rick Snyder
Darnell Earley	October 2013–Jan 2015	EM	PA 436	Rick Snyder
Jerry Ambrose	January 2015–April 2015	EM	PA 436	Rick Snyder

effect. When he left, the governor appointed Darnell Earley to the post. Ambrose, the appointed finance director and a member of the EM team from the very beginning, took over from Earley in January 2015 and served in that role until the emergency was lifted in April 2015 (see Table 5.2).

Between 2011 and 2015, under these four state-appointed EMs, more than one hundred executive orders, resolutions, and directives were implemented. These directives included, among other things, shuttering city offices, laying off employees, restructuring collective bargaining agreements, selling city assets, and increasing fees.

Flint's development-focused interests, including but not limited to the C. S. Mott Foundation and the Chamber of Commerce, have long informed local politics. Under Flint's municipal takeovers, these high-capacity nonprofit organizations, along with their partners, had an opportunity to help shape the takeover agenda. Chapter 6 outlines how the newly aligned development regime's implementation of a policy that disparately allocated benefits and burdens informed people's understanding of both the policy and their roles in local government.

6

From Development Agenda to Development Regime

Allocating Benefits and Burdens and Interpreting Winners and Losers

In Flint, some groups benefited from the 2011 municipal takeover, while others lost out. Tasked with correcting the city's budget woes and armed with a newly revised law, the EM possessed sweeping authority; subsequently city residents saw city offices shuttered, employees laid off, collective bargaining agreements restructured, city assets sold, and water rates raised. These decisions, carried out under the state-appointed EM, reshaped the local political landscape in numerous ways, creating a new politics. This chapter uncovers and explains the longer-term instrumental and symbolic feedback mechanisms that played out in Flint's new politics, specifically changes in participatory access, allocation of resource benefits and burdens, and residents' perceptions of policy winners and losers.

Changes in Participatory Access

Under EMs, the organization and operation of Flint's government changed, and so did the rules of the game. The changes undertaken by the EMs, who gave short shrift to the political and social implications of their fiscal focus, created winners and losers among community groups. Some community residents and organizations gained further access to local decision making, while others were excluded.

Improved Access

Mike Brown was already well liked and well connected in Flint when he was appointed EM in 2011. Brown had previously served in elected office as a Genesee County commissioner from 1981 to 1984 and was appointed director of community development and government relations for the city of Flint under Mayor Matthew Collier from 1987 to 1991. He was also a former city administrator and interim mayor. Beyond his role in local government, however, Brown had led numerous nonprofit organizations, including the American Red Cross of Genesee and Lapeer Counties, United Way of Genesee and Lapeer Counties, and the Capital Area United Way. In 2008, before being appointed city administrator, he was the executive vice president for public policy at the Flint and Genesee Chamber of Commerce. After his short time at city hall, he founded and served as the director of the Flint Area Reinvestment Office, a program run by the United Way of Genesee County and funded by area foundations, including the C. S. Mott Foundation.

Outlining Brown's résumé serves two functions. First, it highlights the connections he had with the Chamber of Commerce and the C. S. Mott Foundation. It also shows Brown's focus on economic development, what one of my interviewees called his "development agenda." Unsurprisingly, those whom he selected as advisors, as described in Chapter 5, were also primarily development-oriented community stakeholders: representatives of the Chamber of Commerce, Metro Community Development, and the C. S. Mott Foundation.

Community members were not completely excluded from Brown's advisory roles. The Citizens Advisory Committee, for example, included representatives from area churches, as well as city council members that represented the North End. The members of the Advisory Committee, as required under the law, "shall be one representative of the City's elected officials, one representative of the Flint business community, one citizen of Flint, and up to two more persons with interest in and knowledge of the Flint community."[1] The initial members selected for the council included Flint City Council member Delrico Loyd, representing the First Ward; community member Kenyatta Dotson; and the Reverend Latrelle Holmes. The council also included Mayor Dayne Walling and president of the Chamber of Commerce Tim Herman. The power and influence that the council as a whole was able to wield was unclear from interviews and government documents.

There were other, smaller ways for community leaders to be involved as well. For example, a representative from Concerned Pastors for Social Action (CPSA) sat on the committee to hire City Administrator Natasha Henderson. However, alongside CPSA member Rev. Alfred Harris were representatives from the Michigan Department of Treasury, the EM finance director, the mayor, a council member, and a businessperson. While this was an important appointment of a moderately anti-EM community leader, it also suggests that these appointments were not authentic means of participation but token nods to an important political constituency—namely the Black faith community.

Restricted Access

The first and most often criticized element of municipal takeover is the suspension of the city council's and the mayor's decision-making authority. For example, many of the early criticisms of Michigan's emergency manager law focused on the suspension of representative democracy.[2] Giving the EM sole power to make decisions on behalf of the city was viewed as undemocratic by opponents. As noted in the Introduction, proponents of the policy have responded with assertions that the policy is only temporary, that the governor is democratically elected, and the EM reports to the governor. Unaddressed, however, was the issue that the Flint City Council, in particular, was an important venue where both union and Black community interests could be heard. The elimination of local officials' authority effectively cut local unions and many Black political leaders out of the agenda-setting process.

Residents were also isolated from meaningful participation in decision making. The first "community roundtable" meeting after Brown's appointment took place weeks after he took office in December 2011. The meeting, which focused on crime, was by invitation only. In attendance were "community leaders from local churches, the Genesee Regional Chamber of Commerce, the Charles Stewart Mott Foundation," as well as local groups such as the Flint NAACP and local schools.[3] Frances Gilcreast, the local NAACP president, noted there was an "elephant in the room" at the meeting, acknowledging the lack of resident voices, particularly since the law is a "disenfranchisement of the community."[4] Also in attendance, though not invited, were local protesters holding signs reading "EM Law = dictatorship" and "Don't remember the vote for Mr. Brown?"

Brown did hold a series of community and neighborhood forums in February 2012. At those meetings, Brown presented attendees with information on the city's fiscal condition and warned that there would be cuts to city services to address the budget deficit before taking questions from the audience.[5] Many residents felt as though the process was a farce and not intended to be more than information sharing.

More importantly, though, Brown eliminated two important mechanisms for residents to bring their concerns to the city in a formal manner, the Office of the Ombudsman and various citizen councils.[6] The Office of the Ombudsman was an ongoing point of contention. Ed Kurtz, for example, had previously closed the office under his term as EFM. Because it cost nearly $325,000 each year, others (including Mayor Walling), also advocated for the elimination of the office.[7] Others, including former city council member, ombudsman, and attorney Terry Bankert, were advocates for the office, calling the Office of the Ombudsman the "'good government' thing to do."[8] Moreover, an ombudsman's office is stipulated in the Flint City Charter. The office had subpoena powers to investigate the grievances of city residents regarding city agencies. In essence it provided an important check on executive power, giving local residents the opportunity to formally lodge complaints against the city. This mechanism for engagement and transparency was eliminated.

On August 8, 2012, hours before the State Board of Canvassers placed the repeal of PA 4 on the ballot, Brown, in a flurry of decisions, eliminated each of Flint's Citizen District Councils: Smith Village, I-475 Neighborhood Development, and Flint Park Lake. The Citizens District Councils advise the city on local grant-funded development projects. The community development corporations, with which they are linked, serve as liaisons between neighborhood interests and city officials. In the same executive order, Brown also consolidated two quasi-governmental units, placing the Flint Area Enterprise Community under the Enterprise Economic Development Corporation, and removed and replaced appointees on Flint's Historic District Commission, Downtown Development Authority, and the Local Officers Compensation Commission.[9] In response to this rush of directives, the *Flint Journal* reported that city council members were dismayed, with city council member Bernard Lawler calling the move to get rid of citizens' groups a "'slap in the face' to the citizens of Flint." "'It's pretty disappointing because those residents, those CDCs, have been hanging in there for years,' Lawler said. 'There was total disregard for the work they've been doing over the years.'"[10]

It should be noted, however, that the elimination of the councils was supported by Mayor Walling, who noted that the reduction in the size of the city's Department of Community and Economic Development necessitated the elimination of the citizens' groups. He was quoted in the press saying, "The city's Department of Community and Economic Development staff is at a lower level than in years past and the focus now is on the citywide master plan.... Without dedicated federal funds for those specific areas, it's more appropriate those organizations incorporate as nonprofit groups, separate from the city."[11]

While more indirect, the elimination of these councils and the reshaping of various commissions also meant less involvement from neighborhood constituents in developing, or at least informing, the local development agenda. In many ways, the EM used his authority to cut or change various civil boards in the name of expediency. What does this say about the value of participatory governance? What message did this send to community residents about the value of civic engagement? Protesters continued to demonstrate outside of city hall, holding signs that read, "EM Law = Dictatorship" (see Figure 6.1).

Just as the EM has the power to eliminate citizen boards and remove or replace citizens serving in other appointed positions,

Figure 6.1 Local community members with "EM Law = Dictatorship" sign at "Our Voice Is Silent" demonstration on April 4, 2014. The protest took place after EM Darnell Earley changed the public speaking time during city council meetings from the beginning of the meeting to the end, an act that many viewed as a means of silencing community voices. (Printed with permission from Nayyirah Shariff.)

he or she also has the power to create new ad hoc committees. The Blue Ribbon Committee on Governance was created under Darnell Earley in January 2014. The twenty-two-member committee was tasked with evaluating Flint's governing structure with a focus on ways to improve the city charter.[12] Members were appointed by Earley and included a range of interested parties and experts: nonprofit executives, attorneys, the president of Kettering University, county commissioners and administrators, faith leaders, members of the Flint planning commission, as well as Chamber of Commerce CEO Tim Herman, former EM Ed Kurtz, EM advisor and program director at Metro Community Development Diana Kelly, and Mayor Walling.[13] All but three of the members lived in Flint.[14] The process was facilitated by Eric Scorsone and Mary Doidge, faculty members at Michigan State University and advisors on Michigan's EM law.

Much like the elimination of the Office of the Ombudsman, the creation of the Blue Ribbon Committee on Governance was viewed by many as an indicator that decisions were made "behind closed doors." Bill, a nonprofit executive, highlighted that the group included a range of key stakeholders, "representing institutions, community groups, faith leaders, elected officials. It was a pretty diverse group." However, he continued, "the fact that it [the Blue Ribbon Committee] was a closed meeting [and] it wasn't an open meeting" drew skepticism and concern from community residents.[15]

"If you want to set up a group that sounds elite, just call it the 'Blue Ribbon Committee,'" said Adrian, another nonprofit leader.[16] The committee met privately from January through June 2014. However, the committee was committed to engaging with the community and hosted three workshops in May of that year, drawing community members from across the city.[17] Attendees expressed a range of concerns about the process. "Are these sessions just to rubber stamp the decisions already made?" one asked.[18] Another attendee spoke about the larger issue of the EM undermining democracy, noting, "This public input is a smoke screen."[19] "How do you enact democratic reform when a majority of the population chooses not to participate?" asked another.[20] Others voiced concerns regarding the EM's emphasis on governance rather than financial concerns, represented by a statement made at a meeting in May: "Seems like a disproportionate amount of energy is being given to the issue of governance without dealing with other important issues like city finances, water bills, etc."[21]

On June 30, 2014, the committee submitted its findings and recommendations to the EM. Six recommendations were made: the shift to a hybrid form of council-manager government with an elected mayor and an appointed city manager; a charter commission's reconsideration of the city council system; ongoing training for all city council members; the shift to having city-appointed officials report to and be hired by the city manager (with the exception of the city attorney and city clerk); elimination of the Civil Service Commission and removal from the charter of the Office of the Ombudsman; and adoption of multiyear budgeting, strategic planning, and long-term financial forecasts.

On the basis of these recommendations, Earley, using the authority granted to him under state law, placed five of the proposed charter amendments and a proposal to conduct a charter review, as recommended by the Blue Ribbon Committee, on the November ballot.

One member on the committee, Elizabeth Jordan, took copious notes at the committee meetings and disseminated them to other stakeholders in the community, reporting:

> As those who read the Journal's coverage of the last City Council meeting on the subject could attest, many people have strong feelings about the Blue Ribbon Committee. What I hope is not lost in the emotion, however, is that it is the Flint voters—not the Blue Ribbon Committee—who get to decide this vote. As a community, there are ways we have been politically disempowered. To treat the questions we face about our charter as a decision that someone else has already made (either by refusing to vote or voting all up or all down without due consideration of the merits of each proposal) would be to give up the very real power we do have. The Blue Ribbon Committee made recommendations, but it is the people of Flint who will decide.[22]

Nearly thirty thousand Flint residents cast ballots on November 4, 2014.[23] Voters passed some of the proposals but overwhelmingly opposed the elimination of executive offices, the Civil Service Board, and the Office of the Ombudsman (see Table 6.1). The results of the November election provided further proof that the general public, or at least the voting public, was opposed to the elimination of the Office of the Ombudsman. However, Earley refused to reestablish the office after the election, noting, "There are no plans to hire an ombudsman."[24] This was in direct contravention of ballot results, though legal under the terms of municipal takeover.[25]

Two other changes made just before Flint's financial emergency status was lifted in April 2015 included the creation of the Receivership Transition Advisory Board (RTAB) and the appointment of a contracted city administrator. Both the RTAB and the new city administrator, Natasha Henderson, are further exam-

TABLE 6.1 CHARTER AMENDMENT AND REVIEW BALLOT QUESTIONS AND RESULTS, 2014

Proposal	Result	Total votes	% Support-oppose
1. Shall there be a general revision of the city charter?*	Pass	20,328	56.10%–43.90%
2. Shall there be a reduction in the number of principal staff appointed by the mayor for legal counsel and administrative services from no more than 10 to no more than five?	Pass	20,709	59.65%–40.35%
3. Shall there be a requirement that the annual budget presented to the City Council be accompanied by a message explaining the budget, to provide for multi-year financial plans and revenue projections, and the establishment of a budget stabilization fund?	Pass	20,736	67.37%–32.63%
4. Shall the requirement for specific executive departments be eliminated?	Fail	20,455	45.29%–54.71%
5. Shall the Civil Service Commission be eliminated?	Fail	20,740	28.39%–71.61%
6. Shall the Office of Ombudsman be eliminated?	Fail	20,955	36.99%–63.01%

Source: Genesee County Election Division.

* Some of the recommendations, including the recommendation to change the form of government, require the election of a charter revision commission. The other five amendments could be adopted without a charter review.

ples of how changes under municipal takeover can last beyond the city's fiscal emergency. Both were tasked with upholding the changes made under the municipal takeover and, in the case of the RTAB, serving a supervisory function over the city council. According to Flint's RTAB website:

> As of the end of April, 2015, the city of Flint moved from being under the control of an Emergency Manager to home rule order under the guidance of a Receivership Transition Advisory Board (RTAB). This board will ensure a smooth transition by maintaining the measures prescribed upon the Emergency Manager's exit. The Mayor and City Council have resumed their defined roles with regard to City business, yet major financial and policy decisions will

be reviewed by the RTAB to ensure that they maintain fiscal and organizational stability, as directed under Public Act 436.

The Emergency Manager was appointed by the Governor under Public Act 436 to oversee the management of the city during financial crisis. The job of the EM was to bring long term financial stability back to the city by addressing any and all issues that threatened the city's financial solvency. Four different individuals served as Emergency Manager from December 2011 to April 2015.[26]

While some viewed the RTAB and the city administrator as a continuance of nonelected management, one of my interviewees saw the RTAB, in particular, as a step in the right direction and evidence that PA 436 was an improvement over PA 4: "I think the state as a whole is a winner, because 436 has the opportunity for the governor to employ a receivership transition advisory board with no particular end date. I think that's one of the strongest items that was included in 436."[27]

Parallel Access

The municipal takeover of 2011 temporarily suspended the governing authority of local elected officials, rendering local elections and public comment at city council meetings mere symbols of participatory engagement. To be fair, public comment at town hall or city council meetings is nominally influential during times of political normalcy.[28] Yet, the suspension or dissolution of participatory access under the policy has important implications. What are alternative pathways for participatory access?

Given the policy goal of local fiscal stability, the implementation of municipal takeovers is often coupled with other economic development and/or planning initiatives.[29] In the case of Flint, Mayor Walling began the city's master planning process, which became known as "Imagine Flint," when he first took office in 2009. The city had not adopted a master plan since 1960 but had experienced significant economic and demographic change since that time. In an interview Walling stated, "When I came into office, there wasn't a single urban planner on staff."[30] In 2010

Walling proposed to the city council that the city hire a planning officer and rebuild the city's planning department, but limited resources caused the city council to deny the request. So, in 2010, the city applied for and won a $1.5 million HUD grant that was matched by an additional $1.5 million in local support, the largest of these funders being the C. S. Mott Foundation.

In his 2011 state of the city address, Walling announced the grant. The planning process began in earnest in June. But in November 2011 the city was notified of its financial emergency, and in December the city was placed under state control. Because the three-year funding was coming from outside support, the planning process was allowed to move forward with Walling as the lead. "In some ways, the master plan process allowed Flint residents, who no longer enjoy locally elected government, to have a voice that is denied to them under emergency management."[31]

Walling, who was eager to make the process as participatory as possible, convened a twenty-one-member steering committee, which "included the co-chair and chair of the planning commission, two city council designees, and the representatives from each of the city's nine wards. Plus, business, faith, and civic/community organizations and key partners like the land bank which owns a lot of property in the city."[32] After conducting its initial "existing conditions report," the steering committee organized a series of community talks in December 2012 and January 2013. Hundreds of community residents attended. As Walling put it:

> There was a real appetite for this process. Hundreds of people showed up at these initial sessions. And then, in order to coalesce all of the diverse feedback from multiple meetings, we decided to have one large community summit. We contracted . . . with America Speaks . . . a national civic engagement company. . . . [They] worked with us on a one-day summit. . . . More than five hundred people came out.[33]

Pressed on whether this was partially the result of the presence of an EM, Walling stated, "There's a core group in every community that naturally wants to be involved in shaping their future and, when one path is taken away, there's energy available to go in a different direction," adding, however, "I suspect there would have been a large turnout regardless [of the municipal takeover]."[34]

In her analysis of the link between planning and municipal takeover in Michigan, Carolyn Loh argues that planners play an important role in "providing a parallel citizen participation process that may be able to restore some level of meaningful voice of disenfranchised stakeholders."[35] Community activists interviewed for this book viewed the planning process as serving dual purposes: (1) to provide a means of participatory engagement in the planning process and (2) to offer a platform to express anger and frustration about the takeover.

Adrian, a local nonprofit executive, compared the participatory master planning process to city council meetings at the time:

> I think there was a commitment [to civic engagement and social equity] because it's inherently important and good to do that, but it became more significant as . . . [it] was a powerful means for engaging residents who didn't necessarily have the same kind of opportunity in other city processes at the time.
>
> Even at city council there was a decision at a point by an emergency manager to put the public comment period at the end of the agenda, which other than maybe giving people an opportunity to voice their agreement or disagreement with a decision that's already been made, it sort of circumvents at the point of public comment that you believe part of public comment is to inform and educate people before they make a decision.[36]

There were others, however, that were more skeptical of the participatory nature of the planning process. For example, Jennifer, a community activist who was involved in the planning process, noted, "Dayne would always be accompanied by a program officer of the Mott Foundation. Always."[37]

Suspicion that the process was not truly participatory was shared by others as well. One resident indicated that their employer discouraged opposition to the planning process because the C. S. Mott Foundation was funding both the planning process and their organization. Whether the Mott threat was real or not, some community members felt as if the process was participatory in name only.

Allocation of Resource Benefits

Often supporters of the municipal takeover acknowledged that while the policy benefited city residents most, it placed significant burdens on city employees and retirees. Morgan, a member of the EM team, for example, noted that while changes to retiree pension options were "a tremendous benefit for the city," "these [changes] were a big impact to [retirees]. . . . [T]hese are huge hits to people."[38] None of the supporters, however, admitted that some of the decisions made by the EMs benefited specific groups in the community, an issue that routinely came up in interviews with other community members.

Some groups did benefit from the takeover. This is not to say that they did so in a nefarious or illegal way; instead, their close connections to the EMs and the power in the city made some stakeholders feel fewer of the burdens and more of the benefits. The benefits were captured by those closest to the EM, especially Uptown Developments, LLC. (See Chapter 5.)

Because of its access to the EM and the ability to help set the policy agenda, it is unsurprising that two of the more controversial decisions made during the 2011 municipal takeover revolved around the sale of two city assets that benefitted members of the development regime, specifically Uptown Reinvestment Corporation, Inc.: Genesee Towers and the Flint Farmers' Market. These decisions were divisive because many viewed them as unfairly benefiting local elites. Additionally, the sale of the assets to Uptown Reinvestment Corporation, Inc., further reinforced its important role in Flint politics—the institution is now responsible for what many residents view as an important public good: the Flint Farmers' Market.

Genesee Towers was first built in 1968; by 2013 the building had been abandoned and had stood empty for over a decade. Poor construction and years of neglect made the building a public safety concern. After years of legal battles with the property owner during the Williams administration, the Michigan Court of Appeals upheld a previous arbitrator's ruling that the city take ownership of the property and pay the owner $6 million.[39] In 2010 a judge ordered the city to assess Flint taxpayers for the cost of the legal debacle, placing an extra 6.751 mills on each property owner's tax bill, a fee of approximately $150, on average, for each homeowner.[40] Then, in August 2012, Michael Brown signed a development agreement with Uptown Reinvestment Corporation to transfer ownership of Genesee Towers for one dollar.[41]

Adrian captured the sentiments of many of the community members I interviewed regarding this decision, noting, "We had a boatload of additional money that we had to shell out, each and every person [in the city] for this building [Genesee Towers], and then [Brown] give[s] it away for a dollar for a plan that had not been publicly discussed or vetted or commented on."[42]

The purchase of the towers was part of a larger plan by Uptown Reinvestment Corporation to demolish the towers and create an urban plaza.[43] Part of the plan, developed by Uptown and supported by the EM, was to move the Flint Farmers' Market, which had been managed by Uptown since 2002, to a new building that it owned. The action effectively privatized the market. Adrian noted, as part of the deal to purchase the towers, the city basically "signed, sealed, and delivered the demise of our old farmers' market, which was publicly owned, [with] the promise of a new farmers' market that would be privately owned, all of which was done completely behind closed doors. Whether or not it was the right decision, the fact that it was done in that fashion really bothered me."[44]

Alexei, a local artist, shared Adrian's sentiments. "I like the new Farmers' Market," he said, but the decision to sell public properties concerned him in terms of its "being a trend. . . . I'm not saying all development is evil, but [it is] a little shifty in terms of who is making the decisions and who it profiting from them. I think that was significant."[45]

Allocation of Resource Burdens

While some community stakeholders benefited under municipal takeover, significant resource burdens were incurred by community residents across the city. The Reverend Reginald Flynn, an active member of the group Concerned Pastors for Social Action, argued that Flint's increased fees felt like "taxation without representation."[46] Between 2011 and 2015 retirees, active union members, and the public more generally saw increased costs, including rising healthcare costs, cuts to pensions, and increased costs for municipal services.

Drawing on their broader authority under PA 4, Brown and his successors attempted to address the costs associated with the city's collective bargaining agreements and so-called legacy costs. While some of the unions—AFSCME Local 1799, P.O.L.C.-Flint Police Sergeants Union, the Flint Police Captains and Lieutenants Union, and I.A.F.F.–Flint Firefighters Union—came to the table and negotiated agreements,[47] others opted out. Both the Flint Police Officers Association (FPOA) and AFSCME Local 1600 "refused to agree to any of [the EMs'] proposed concessions."[48] In April 2012 the EM requested that the state treasurer agree with his request to modify the collective bargaining agreements without approval from the unions.

In addition to modifying the collective bargaining agreements, the EM significantly cut health insurance options for retirees, including for non-union retirees and for members of each of the city's unions: P.O.L.C.-Flint Police Sergeants Union Retirees, P.O.L.C.-Flint Police Captains and Lieutenants Union retirees, FPOA Union retirees, Flint I.A.F.F.–Flint Firefighters Union retirees, AFSCME Local 1600 retirees, and AFSCME Local 1799 retirees.[49] Brown also modified a settlement agreement from Ed Kurtz's term as EFM in 2002 with the United Retirement Governmental Employees (URGE) regarding prescription drug coverage, prompting URGE members to file a lawsuit against the EM.

According to court documents, retirees would be required to pay an additional $100 per person per month because of the change. Changes to the retiree health-care plans also shifted costs from the city to retirees, increasing retiree "deductibles from $50 ($100 per family) to $1,000, and increasing the co-pay maximum from $1,000 to $2,500," resulting in an estimated $3.5 million a year in savings for the city.[50]

In addition to modifying union collective bargaining agreements and modifying health-care insurance coverage for current and former employees, the EM eliminated the positions of 115 city employees and implemented a 20 percent salary reduction for remaining employees. The cuts to staffing levels and reduction in pay and health-care costs "result[ed] in approximately $20 million to be put toward deficit reduction."[51]

Beyond the impact on city employees and retirees, the EM team simultaneously reduced municipal services and increased fees. In his deposition for *Welch v. Brown*, Ambrose, Brown's appointed finance director, noted:

> It was necessary for [the EM team] to increase the fees for water and sewer rates by approximately $15 million. It was necessary for [the team] to impose increased fees for garbage collection netting approximately one and a half million dollars. It was necessary for us to impose a street light assessment resulting in additional revenues of $2.85 million.[52]

Each homeowner was assessed the streetlight fee, which increased each year, starting at $66 in 2012 and growing to nearly $71 by 2014. The trash collection fee, which replaced a 3-mill waste collection tax, was $143 per household. Such user fees are illustrative of the neoliberal rationality frame, wherein coercion (e.g., fees) is one of the primary solutions to providing public goods, and the primary users shoulder the burden.[53]

Under Michigan's municipal takeover law, an EM cannot raise taxes. Therefore, in addition to applying assessment *fees* to residents' property taxes, Brown also proposed a 6-mill tax levy to fund police and fire. The millage, placed on the November 2012 ballot, increased property taxes to pay for "about 53 police and firefighters," eliminating the city's reliance on grants from foundations and the federal government.[54] Voters approved the millage, "bringing Flint's total level to within 1 mill of its maximum 20 mill limit."[55]

In addition to increasing costs, city residents experienced declines in the quality of services—especially with regard to their water. As part of a decision agreed to under Kurtz's tenure, the city of Flint switched from Lake Huron to the Flint River as its source of drinking water, beginning the debacle that is now the Flint water crisis.

In an effort to save $5 million in less than two years,[56] the plan was implemented under Darnell Earley, who called the plan and its cost-saving measures, "a 'monumental change' for the city."[57] The cost savings were not redistributed to residents, who continued to see their water rates increase and the quality of their water decline. After the switch, city officials were "flooded with complaints."[58] More than a year later, during my stay in Flint, protestors held regular vigils outside of city hall, holding containers of brownish, murky water that came from their taps. In the fall of 2015 the crisis finally gained national attention when Virginia Tech professor Marc Edwards, at the request of Flint activists, conducted a collaborative study of Flint's river water with Flint activists and reported high lead levels.[59] A few weeks later a second expert, Dr. Mona Hanna-Attisha, a researcher at Hurley Medical Center in Flint, demonstrated there were high lead levels in the blood of Flint children.[60]

The municipal takeover of Flint has had real consequences in regard to the allocation of resources, both physical and intangible. Those close to the EM and in-line with the development focus of the agenda received increased access to benefits. On the other hand, those removed from or distant from formal power structures—the polis—were faced with decreasing access and increasing financial burdens. Moreover, the process of the takeover was implemented with little transparency, increasing the perception, whether true or not, that the development regime was intentionally consolidating its power in order to push through its agenda.

The development regime framed the problem as economic and fiscal instability, and thus responded with financial analyses from outside experts, the development of fiscal policy outcomes, and an economic development agenda. This approach, in line with Deborah Stone's ([1997] 2011) "rationality project," excluded, whether intentionally or not, the perspectives and insights of the polis. As such, "EMs have proven to be a divisive solution," wherein the authority to outsource services and abolish collective bargaining "takes a page right out of the right-wing play book . . . pushing out poor residents to make way for developers."[61]

To further explore the dichotomy of the market and the polis, the following section examines the powerful symbolic effect of the takeovers on individuals, groups, and organizations. Moreover, I highlight the ways in which citizens and community organizations responded to each of the takeovers, identifying how some individuals and groups sought new pathways for political engagement.

Making Meaning of the Takeovers

As the preceding discussion of Flint's municipal takeover makes clear, the approach to resolving Flint's fiscal problems was guided by the "rationality project" (i.e., determining the financial causes of city failure and fixing them and, where necessary, removing political obstacles). What this view of takeovers avoids is any meaningful acknowledgment of politics; or, rather, the rationality project hides politics under the guise of rationality, which, practically speaking, simply elevates one set of values (efficiency and effectiveness) above all others (equity, equality, liberty). In fact, if local politics are even discussed, it is because of local fiscal distress. Basing the "success" of the takeover solely on fiscal and economic policy outcomes ignores the perspective of the polis.

To be sure, community responses to the EM were more nuanced than a simple "support" or "oppose." In presenting and discussing a more nuanced perspective, the following analysis relies on forty-eight interviews conducted with Flint residents, representing a range of political interests and perspectives. Where direct interview data were unavailable, or were incomplete, the analysis draws on opinion articles and letters to the editor in the local newspaper, the *Flint Journal*. There was great variation in how people felt about and made meaning of the takeover. There were leaders that fully supported the intervention, but many others that voiced concerns about the policy. These ambivalent community leaders felt that it was a "necessary evil," acknowledging that something had to be done to address Flint's dire fiscal situation, but they also voiced discomfort with the suspension of local democracy.

Reflections on the 2002 Takeover

During the interviews conducted with community leaders over the summer of 2015, most respondents had little memory of specific actions undertaken by EFM Kurtz unless those actions had affected them directly. One respondent, Shaun, recalled the closure of the city's community centers. Shaun was a volunteer and a tutor at a center when it closed in December 2002.

> We had a self-esteem program for the girls. I got some of my friends together, and we paid for them to go on trips and stuff. . . . We have like a hundred kids coming in a day to use this facility that was in a neighborhood right across from the public housing area and some apartments. It's like, we got this good thing going on. We got the kids involved, and it was like basically [ages] five to thirteen. We have these kids, and now they're just kind of scattered because they have no place to go. That was kind of like my first interaction [with municipal takeover]. I was like, "What the hell is going on with this?"[62]

More often, however, community leaders remembered general elements of the 2002 takeover. Whether it was the limitations of the policy due to the inability of the EFM to renegotiate debt or cancel contracts, or the loss of a job or a place to volunteer, community leaders tended to view the 2002 takeover in relationship to the 2011 takeover: it was shorter, the problem was bigger, and, as evidenced by the 2011 takeover, it wasn't successful in the long term.

When asked to compare the 2002 and 2011 takeovers, Wilson, a former city employee and active member of the Flint community, said:

> You're talking about apples and oranges. Number one, [in] 2002, you're talking about almost a $37 million deficit. That was a real deficit. That was a real one. Compared to an $8.5 million deficit, for which there really was only $3–4 million of an actual general fund deficit. Back then

[in 2002], you're talking about almost all of that was really a general fund deficit. The two are not comparable. What I will say is, here's where the two are similar: back then it disenfranchised the people [and] all decisions were made unilaterally.[63]

Some community members, however, were displeased with the 2002 intervention. Yet, as the following letter to the editor from the *Flint Journal* suggests, there was "no public outcry," much to the author's chagrin. In a scathing critique, Bela Jobb, a now-retired die maker at GM, referred to the EFM as "führer Ed Kurtz":

He is an appointee of the governor, who has the "power" to remove the representatives duly elected by the citizens of Flint if they don't agree and cooperate with him. . . . Here is a man who is probably used to pulling down a six-figure salary as a desk jockey, telling our police and firefighters, who risk their lives in the performance of their jobs, the public works employees who risk their health and safety, and all the other city employees that they have it too good.[64]

Jobb's long letter pointed to other problems with Kurtz.

Some may see him as having the courage to "take the bull by the horns" and slash jobs or cut wages and benefits, but he's just behaving in true administrative fashion and taking the easy way out. It is much easier to blame and cut the workforce, wages or benefits than it is to reduce waste, cut overhead, increase efficiency or do any number of other things to reduce costs.[65]

Jobb also held great contempt for city leaders, pointing to "poorly executed protest by City Council" and union leaders, noting that the announcement from Kurtz to "set aside and break union contracts ratified by both sides and replace them with 'contracts' of his own . . . should have produced a public protest from the head of every local of every union at least in the city of Flint, who should then have involved their respective regional or national offices."

Jobb's opinions were held by others. Another local resident and city employee, D. L. McPhail, writing to the *Flint Journal,* characterized Kurtz's lack of engagement with employees as a slight to union workers. "Any management textbook or study of successful private enterprise firms will clearly tell you to ask the front-line lower level people actually doing the work how they would improve things," he wrote, noting that both GM and the "supposedly inefficient U.S. military" paid attention to suggestions from those with experience. "Never once in my 10 years as a Flint employee has any member of management ever asked my opinion or a co-worker's opinion about how to reduce waste, cut inefficiency, or boost output."

McPhail suggested that rather than hire "an outside efficiency expert to come in and 'find the waste,'" Kurtz should "have a candid 10-minute meeting with one or two 'real people,' such as a firefighter, waste collector, meter reader, or city hall clerk, and really listen to them, they'd tell him honestly and truthfully where the waste is."[66] Of course, these efficiencies, even if realized, would not have addressed the fiscal crisis, which required immediate cutting of costs. Nevertheless, it is not an either/or approach, and such criticism of the EMs for their short-term perspective suggests also that residents and public employees want a voice in the process.

Reflections on the 2011 Takeover

While the 2002 takeover drew little response, the 2011 takeover was met with a range of emotions. Some community members were supportive of the takeover strategy, while others took to the streets to protest the "death of democracy." Still others were ambivalent, concerned by the suspension of local democracy but eager to have the state step in and offer support. Interviewees represented all three groups.

When asked about one of the key criticisms of the law and whether it was indeed an "affront to democracy," Morgan, a member of the EM team, responded:

I never saw it as the end of democracy. I thought that was a ridiculous response. Michigan Home Rule Act allows the governor to have oversight and responsibility for the cities that are created under the Home Rule Act. The governor and the legislators who created PA 4 were directly elected.[67]

Patrick, another member of the EM team, likened state intervention in municipal affairs to federal-state relations. "If a state is violating the law, the feds can step in," he said, going on to argue that the state has an obligation to intervene.

In this case, the governor is elected by all the people of Michigan. The state has an obligation, whether it's Flushing, Michigan, or Grand Blanc or Flint, to step in and say, "We've got to right the ship here." To me, that's part of democracy, too. If the statewide elected official is not doing his job or her job to manage the affairs of the state, then the people can act on that. I think again, one can say that democracy was taken away from folks, but I think the way the system works in this country is you have different levels of government, and different levels of democratic involvement.[68]

This perspective is unsurprising as it aligns with the evolution of municipal takeover policy in Michigan and, more broadly, the evolving and often contentious relationship between municipalities and states.

It is important to note, however, that most supporters of the takeover recognized the cost placed on city residents and employees. Keith, a member of the EM team, said that you cannot fix

the financial problems of the city without affecting the employed and retiring. Now is that because of the Emergency Manager or is that because of a situation that arose that required [the] Emergency Manager be there? It's clear the Emergency Manager coming in has to make those decisions. Those decisions are not academic[;] they're real decisions that really affect people. . . . I mean it's necessary

for survival for the city . . . [t]hat the employees lose—
one can argue the employees lose because the government
structure failed.

Keith then drew comparisons to the private sector, saying
that when businesses go bankrupt, "employees get laid off."
Implying that employees go elsewhere, he continued: "If a city
goes bankrupt, guess what? The city is still there. What do you
do with [the people]?"

Keith's conclusions were particularly insightful regarding the
effects of long-term intervention.

> There's clearly a process in place for evaluating whether
> the city is in financial distress. There are numerous steps
> along the way for local governments to convince the state
> that they've got it, they understand. Failing that, an emer-
> gency manager can come in. [But] if [the intervention]
> *becomes long term, then local government goes away.*[69]

Keith's sentiments about the value of state intervention were
echoed by Jeffrey, a former elected official, who noted that the
takeover was needed to "take the politics out" of the decision-
making process: "The first Emergency Manager [Michael Brown]
tried to give the appearance that he was getting input from the
community and that sort of thing, but I think when it boiled
down [to it] he didn't really give two rips about what the community thought."

Jeffrey continued:

> [Brown] was going to come in and make those decisions.
> . . . He had the authority to do it. He needed to come in
> and make those decisions. Maybe one of the good things
> about the law [was that] it allowed him to take the politics
> out of those decisions and just come in and do what he
> thought was right for the community. . . . Sometimes the
> community doesn't know what's best for the community.[70]

Martin, a local nonprofit leader, also was of the "something
needed to be done" mind-set. He noted:

It's a very unpopular opinion but I actually feel like having an emergency manager here was necessary because the politics are so bad in Flint that you couldn't make things happen. You couldn't make real change happen unless you were a part of whatever that group was that was running things at that particular time. With the emergency financial manager in place, they kind of dictate, "Well, you're going to do X, Y or Z despite who got appointed where to do what job. This is the way it's going to be." That helps to break that cycle a little bit. Yes, it's true. It is disenfranchising people. I understand that part totally and philosophically, I can agree with that position. I also know how dysfunctional [the] city was.[71]

For proponents and those on the fence about municipal takeovers, Flint's internal political chaos was reason enough to bring in the EM. From the time Mayor Stanley was recalled in 2002 until the takeover was lifted in 2015, the city saw six mayors cycle in and out of public office, and four EMs. Political infighting between the city council and the mayor further underscored the tensions.

Flint's political dysfunction, however, was no excuse, opponents argued, for appointing an EM. As Jeffrey alluded, most people saw the EM's outreach efforts as a charade. Carl, another former elected official, stated, "I think there were concerns that there was the appearance of citizen involvement but that it wasn't tied to a decision-making process."[72]

In response to hearing that the city council would not appeal the appointment of an EM in 2011, Nayyirah Shariff, a vocal opponent of the EM law and one of the founders of DDL, said she felt betrayed. "I feel like Flint is the bastion of civil rights. . . . We have a legacy that we need to protect, and what happened tonight is not in alignment with that legacy. Why roll over and play dead and give up your power?"[73]

Later, in a 2014 op-ed in the *People's Tribune,* Shariff wrote:

> Democracy doesn't work without transparency and accountability. So the first thing that the Emergency Manager did was get rid of Flint's ombudsman, even

though the Charter [that] Walling talked about requires the ombudsman. Judge Damon Keith said, "Democracies die behind closed doors." The new emergency manager's Blue Ribbon Committee meets behind closed doors, planning Flint's future in secret. The mayor doesn't care about the charter's open meeting requirements, and his own city attorney, one of the few employees the Emergency Manager kept on, says that Flint's residents don't have any right to be in those closed door meetings. So much for democracy.[74]

Much of the opposition narrative about municipal takeover emphasizes the political consequences of austerity politics. Aaron, a former member of one of Flint's community boards and longtime resident, reiterated concerns that Flint's takeover emphasized austerity measures at the expense of the community:

> An emergency manager's [job] is to balance the books. It's not to put in place a long-term plan that will result in rebuilding the fundamentals that are necessary to maintain a livable community. It really doesn't matter how good the person is, because they're not in a position . . . to coordinate all the information, it's too high cost to gather all that information at the lowest level. . . . It's austerity, and austerity is a mistake. You don't disinvest in a place that has problems, you invest in a place that's having problems. When you disinvest you undercut the obvious things that make a place worth living in.[75]

Skeptical of the city's development agenda, Brenda, a local nonprofit leader, stated that the takeover highlighted that local leaders "don't put a lot of stock in the people that are here and [don't] invest in the people that are here. . . . People have to matter more than money."[76] Skepticism came from having sat in meetings with decision makers, hearing them make statements like: "'We're going to go for the easy wins. We're going to go for the easy victories. Dealing with the [less affluent, predominantly Black] north side of Flint and east side of Flint is not an easy win. It's not an easy victory so we're not going to deal with that.'"[77]

A few of the interviewees noted that their initial suspicion was that the takeover was politically motivated. For example, after reviewing the financial information on the city, Aaron noted, "There were problems there, but . . . it was not enough to justify this." That led him and others to suspect "it was a conservative state government doing the kind of thing it does to pull the teeth of places that don't vote for Republicans."[78]

It should be noted that municipal takeovers have been carried out by both Democratic and Republican state administrations. In Michigan, both Democratic and Republican governors used their authority to implement takeovers of local governments. However, it was under a Republican governor and legislature that Michigan revised its EM law and further strengthened the powers of state-appointed managers. It was under a Republican-controlled legislature, with the backing of conservative think tanks like the Mackinac Center, that PA 4 and later PA 436 were adopted. It was under Governor Rick Snyder, a Republican, that the policy was implemented in cities throughout the state.

"I guess the bottom line is that most folks really felt they were stripped of any influence on the major choices for the city," said Casey, a local nonprofit leader and community activist.[79]

7

Defending Democracy

Responding to the Municipal Takeover

> AEN: So, I'm gonna transition a little bit to emergency managers and municipal takeover. In 2002 was the first takeover. Were you—in what capacity were you involved, or paying attention to local government at the time, and would you—
> CRYSTAL: I wasn't.
> AEN: That's a consistent comment, by the way.
> CRYSTAL: Yeah, I know. I wasn't paying attention. At that time, I was not paying attention. I didn't start paying attention until I started noticing the effects of it.
> —CRYSTAL, community activist,
> personal interview, July 2017

It was Valentine's Day 2015, and more than fifty protesters lined the streets outside Flint's city hall in subzero temperatures. One of the protesters, a member of the Flint Democracy Defense League (DDL), held a sign that read: "Down with Water Rates and Up with Democracy."[1] The DDL is a grassroots group that developed in response to the city's municipal takeover. It is also a prime example of the long-term effects of Flint's takeovers.

Municipal takeovers, by design, are intended to be temporary and limited. Once the crisis is abated, the city is supposed to return to its ex-ante political status. In reality, changes to the city governance structure and the manner in which community members interpret the takeover have a long-term political legacy.

As such, the use of municipal takeover creates a "policy paradox," as discussed in Chapter 3, in which politics are eschewed and economic rationality is emphasized over democratic principles of community control, participation, and deliberation in the hope of achieving short-term fiscal stability.[2] These value conflicts help us understand why and how Flint's takeover gave rise to new opposition organizations focused on "defending democracy." After all, policies not only allocate benefits and burdens; they also affect how we understand politics, our role in the political process, and our perceived relative value as members of society.[3]

This chapter focuses on grassroots and participatory responses to the takeover in two areas: grassroots mobilization and charter review. I begin with a review of how the Flint DDL framed the takeover and mobilized opposition through contentious politics—particularly protest. I then outline how the charter review process also served as a platform for dissent. Though formal in nature, these forums for participatory engagement provided an important way for the grassroots community, including opposition leaders, to inform local decision making.

Grassroots Mobilization and Protest

In Flint, residents who felt excluded from local decision making during the 2011 takeover formed the DDL. Shaun, a local activist, reflecting on the DDL's work, noted:

> In Flint, all of our organizations are charitable non-profits . . . [and] the majority of them either receive some sort of funding from Ruth Mott or C. S. Mott. They're pretty much the big names in town. We don't really have, I would say, I don't want to call them fringe groups, but like anarchist, socialist [organizations]. I'll say the left wing. We didn't have any left-wing organizations who would kind of be like the watchdog to raise [a] red flag over this stuff.[4]

Thus, the DDL emerged to serve in this capacity. The DDL developed out of a number of different movement-based and organizing efforts, including both the Occupy Movement and Stand Up for Democracy, which served as a statewide coalition to repeal PA 4. At the time of the takeover, there were two major community-organizing entities in Flint: Concerned Pastors for

Social Action (CPSA) and Flint Area Congregations Together (FACT, a PICO-affiliated organization).[5] Both of these organizations, however, were faith-based.

Establishment organizations were slow to respond to the takeover. For example, Shaun noted:

> We had, I would say, the establishment groups who you would think would be just-not-quite-right with [the municipal takeover], [but] who are silent or closet supporters of what was happening. . . . [For example], the Democratic Party did not come out against the Public Act 4 until [community organizers] had already got it on the ballot and fought to keep it on the ballot. . . . The UAW did no more than like lip service. In Flint, some [groups] were closet supporters because our first emergency manager [was] . . . Mike Brown.[6]

The DDL is not formalized or incorporated, instead it functions on a volunteer basis, holding semi-regular meetings and sponsoring and/or attending organized protests. "We don't do hierarchies; we are all members," one member wrote on their Facebook page. As an organization, its membership "ebbs and flows." Currently, the organization has eighty-one followers of their closed-group Facebook page, but the majority of the group's work is carried out by a core group of four to six people.

Framing the Opposition Movement

Frames are used to define a problem, identify its causes, pass judgment on what might have caused the problem, and offer solutions.[7] Frames help the target audience understand the motivation behind a group's stance, informing people's interpretation of an issue.[8] For example, proponents of municipal takeover focus on budgets, efficiency, and numbers, whereas opponents focus on democracy, rights, and accountability. Deborah Stone argues that symbols are used by political actors strategically to "define a problem in a way that will persuade doubters and attract support for their own side in a conflict."[9]

Framing is an active exercise; it is, in a sense, a marketing strategy to get one's point across. It is also a way in which activists create a sense of identity with each other and mobilize participants.[10] A common framing strategy through which groups define problems is through telling stories. Stone argues that political problems rely on causal stories, or narratives, that political actors create in order to gain traction for their interpretation of and solutions to a particular problem.[11] She further describes two frameworks in which these causal stories live: the natural world and the social world. The natural world creates problems, but these are not any person's fault; causation of natural events is accidental and not deliberate. The social world, on the other hand, is created by the actions, and inaction, of humans; problems are seen as consequences of these deliberate acts.[12] Political problem solving then becomes an exercise in framing the issue as either natural and unforeseeable or manmade and able to be changed through better planning. Groups on either side of a policy issue may choose to frame the narrative in one way or the other to gain traction. The Flint DDL became adept at doing this because it grew out of a response to the 2011 takeover.

Community organizers at heart, the DDL framed the municipal takeover around symbols of democracy—community control, democratic accountability, and voting rights—as well as legacies of oppression. The DDL collaborated with a wide range of organizations, from neighborhood associations to statewide coalitions. The group, made up of committed community organizers and residents, sought to build or join coalitions aimed at overturning municipal takeover and addressed what it viewed as an "affront to democracy." For example, it joined forces with Stand Up for Democracy, the organization that led the statewide ballot initiative to repeal Michigan's EM law in 2012 by knocking on doors and collecting signatures (see Chapter 2).[13] PA 4 was repealed by referendum, due in part to the DDL's efforts to educate voters, gather signatures, and create public outcry.[14] Even after PA 4 was successfully repealed and PA 436 was signed into law just months later, delivering a setback to the organization, it continued to present at neighborhood meetings, write editorials in progressive newspapers, and organize protests.

Emerging out of a deep concern for local democracy and community control, DDL activists viewed the EM as a threat to democracy and a mechanism for oppression. Drawing on interviews and readily available public documents and videos, I highlight below how the DDL framed the municipal takeover.

Democratic Principles
Community activists often talked about and framed the issue of municipal takeover in the context of democracy:

> In Flint, democracy is dead.[15]
>
> These managers have these powers: They replace your democratically elected, local government. When they come to town the mayor, and your city commissioners step aside. Their power is usurped by the manager. They have the right to change your collective bargaining agreements. Now, the emergency manager can sign a paper and say "Okay your healthcare is gone," just by signing an order. They call them orders, we call them edicts.[16]
>
> Now they say we will be under a dictatorship, that one man has all of the power. Not so. It will not happen. . . . [I]t is voter suppression.[17]

But the most common theme that runs through the narratives draws on the normative value of popular sovereignty: emphasizing that duly elected local officials were removed and replaced by illegitimately appointed officials. Emphasis is placed on the value of local control and representative democracy. It was not uncommon for people to discuss the EM as a "sham," undermining the powers of local elected officials, or "usurping" power.

Related to the issue of local control and representative democracy is the issue of transparency and accountability. Concerns over transparency in the policy process (e.g., agenda setting) are evidenced in DDL member Alec Gibb's commentary on the "secretive so-called Blue Ribbon campaign":

> [It] was appointed by Flint's Emergency Manager. And although it was closed to the public, prominent local

businessmen were invited to attend and give input, most notably representatives of the Mott-affiliated Uptown Development Corporation that has benefitted so much from EM rule in Flint.[18]

Community activists often voiced concerns about how decisions were made behind closed doors and how access to decision makers was limited.

To further emphasize the loss of democratic access and accountability, activists compared the use of state-appointed managers and their authority over local government as a form of fascism, dictatorship, and oligarchy. Claire McClinton wrote:

> With every new and draconian order issued, be it raising water rates, gutting police and fire services or selling precious public assets, Flint residents are growing enraged and aware as the Emergency Manager shows himself for the corporate shield that he is, led by Michigan's Governor Rick Snyder. Meanwhile, Emergency Managers establish a culture of fascism even after they leave, as demonstrated by the recent arrest and charges against Reverend Pinkney of Benton Harbor. . . . The Flint City Council meeting held several days after the "Silent Protest" was met with jeers and chants of "Democracy Now" and "Dictatorship" by an irate public.[19]

These comparisons to fascism were used to highlight how the EM not only removed local elected officials but also placed significant burdens on Flint residents in the name of "getting things done." As Shariff pointed out:

> Don't be fooled: when the emergency manager leaves, our democratic rights will not be automatically reinstated. Instead we will get a transition advisory board, one that Rick Snyder will pick for us and there is no timetable. That means members of the board can serve indefinitely. Anything that the mayor and city council do is subject to a veto. The name has changed, but the game is the same. A rigged, lucrative game for oligarchs is not a democra-

cy. But if we start demanding our rights back, well there are people that might lose some money. So the emergency manager is trying to rush through his "seven point" plan. He says if we want our rights back, we better agree, and we better follow the so-called "advisory" recommendations of his Blue Ribbon Committee.[20]

Expediency, Shariff highlighted, is the antithesis of democracy. While the activists may be extreme in referring to municipal takeover as fascist, the details of the statements are important. These quotes highlight the long-term impact of municipal takeover, noting that it is not simply a concern over the suspension of local elected officials but the longer-term consequences of "selling precious public assets" and implementing a "transition advisory board." Moreover, it highlights and recognizes that municipal takeover policy benefits only some, namely the "oligarchy," of which the transition advisory board is representative.

Oppression
Another theme that arises from the narratives of community activists is that of race. It is important, as it is a symbol used to both mobilize opposition and critique policy. McClinton noted:

> The first message is that the original Emergency Manager law, signed by Governor Snyder, was driven by the perception that Black elected officials are dysfunctional, incompetent, and corrupt, and cannot be trusted to manage the affairs of the city. This narrative helps to explain, in part, why despite comprising 13 percent of Michigan's population, over 50 percent of African Americans [sic] live under Emergency Managers. Under this scenario, the state hopes to keep the city of Flint under state control for as long as they want, playing the Race card, while preparing to take over even more cities, townships, and school districts.[21]

The quote captures the reality of municipal takeover: municipal takeovers disproportionately affect people of color, Black residents in particular,[22] and are viewed by many critics as vehicles to undermine local Black elected officials.[23]

Figure 7.1 City Council Member Wantwaz Davis attending the Water Rate Protest, which he organized, on July 14, 2014. (Printed with permission from Nayyirah Shariff.)

As cited previously, McClinton also linked the EM and Flint's water issues with race and the city's history of civil rights and labor activism. At a rally in August 2014 (see Figure 7.1), McClinton noted:

> This is what Flint looks like. This is the fighting Flint. This is the Flint we used to have. This is the Flint we have forgotten. This is the Flint with a rich history. The Flint sit-down strike put the unions on the map. The first city to elect an African American, Black for mayor. The first city to pass open housing. We are history makers and we set the pace on a lot of things. I am proud of all of us here today. We must remember who we are. . . . [L]et's be clear there is no daylight between the emergency manager and our right to water.[24]

The DDL used symbols and metaphors to frame the takeover as a threat to democracy and a perpetuation of oppression. In addition to organizing and speaking at protests or writing op-eds, the members of the DDL were also engaged in coalition building. While establishment organizations may have been slow to resist the takeover, the DDL's message resonated with other community activists and organizers.

Coalition Building among Community-Based and Grassroots Organizations

The DDL had allied with numerous local, regional, and statewide organizations over its short lifetime, including Detroiters Resisting Emergency Management, the ACLU of Michigan, Water You Fighting For?, Concerned Pastors for Social Action, and in some instances FACT and Flight Neighborhoods United. When the water crisis gained international attention, members of the DDL gave interviews to Rachel Maddow, Amy Goodman, and a host of other progressive journalists and news outlets.[25]

The group built networks outside of Flint as well. First through Stand Up for Democracy, which focused on municipal takeover, and later with activists—water warriors—from across the country.

In April 2014, when Flint's third EM, Darnell Earley, ordered Flint's water supply be switched from Lake Huron to the Flint River, the organization again helped mobilize a coalition of policy opponents. As concerns over water quality and the cost of water escalated, the DDL launched a water bottle distribution program and developed a Water Task Force.[26]

How Do You Work with a Fascist?

During an interview, one of the community organizers stated that they would often be told "you need to learn how to work with him [the emergency manager]," and the organizer would think "How do you work with a fascist?" The members of the DDL saw the municipal takeover as just that, a takeover of *their* government by suppressing dissent (through the removal of citizen advisory boards and so on) and seeking to control the local political economy (à la top-down economic development). As policy feedback literature suggests, how community members make meaning out of the municipal takeover has implications for political participation and action. Symbols of democracy—including accountability and civil rights—as well as a focus on oppression—particularly around race—were powerful tools for mobilizing residents.

While an analysis of municipal takeover focused solely on the suspension of representative democracy is insufficient, the values placed on these principles are a powerful tool for an organized, sustained resistance. Community activists viewed the state intervention and state-appointed EM as a threat to civil rights, an attack on Black elected officials, and a dismissal of their voice. As a result, these community activists organized and established the DDL, which has continued to serve in coalition with other activist groups and as a watchdog organization even after the end of the EM's term and during the water crisis.

Moreover, the DDL's early efforts during the takeover were instrumental in bringing state and national attention to the water crisis. As McClinton acknowledged in a 2016 interview with *Sojourners* magazine, "One of many watershed moments leading up to media attention [around the water crisis] was the community meetings to mobilize residents. There were demonstrations in the dead of winter organized by grassroots groups."[27]

Much of the same narrative and symbols used by the DDL about the municipal takeover continue to come through its framing of the water crisis. The persistence and outspokenness of the DDL and many other Flint residents opened the door for prominent outside voices to join the movement. The sheer volume of national attention that the water crisis has received certainly affirms the efforts of the community in their public fight for justice.

Participatory Resistance? An Alternative Pathway for Engagement

As outlined in Chapter 6, some have argued that the city's planning process offered an alternative pathway for meaningful participatory engagement; others have been more skeptical. Another, less explored, pathway for engagement came in the form of the city's charter review process, which was set in motion on November 4, 2014, when city residents voted to carry out a review for the first time since 1974.

Flint's Charter Review Process: Local Elections, Participation, and the Process of "Resistance"

A city charter is a legal document that, in many ways, determines the shape and character of a city. In Michigan, the Home Rule City Act, Act 279 of 1909, gives local governments the power to determine how and by what means to govern. The charter not only outlines the form of government (e.g., a strong mayor); it also provides the legal framework for ensuring accountability, transparency, and—of particular importance to many Flint residents—community control.

In November 2014 Flint voters rejected proposals to simply amend the 1974 charter by eliminating the Office of the Ombudsman or decreasing the number of executive offices, as put forth by the Blue Ribbon Committee on Governance. Instead, residents voted to support revising the charter, a process that entailed electing a board of commissioners to conduct a comprehensive two-year review of the city's governing document.

According to the Home Rule Act, once the charter revision was approved by voters, commissioners had to be elected within sixty days. Commissioners had to be at least three-year residents of the city and not employed by the city.

After years of EMs, who had the power to disregard the city charter, residents were optimistic about the chance at government reform and charter change or were simply frustrated with the status quo. Regardless of their motivations, on May 5, 2015, nine commissioners were elected to Flint's Charter Review Commission: Cleora Magee, chair; John Cherry, vice chair; Victoria McKenze; Charles Metcalf; Heidi Phaneuf; Jim Richardson; Marsha Wesley; and Barry Williams. Brian Larkin was also elected, but was replaced by Quincy Murphy, when Larkin stepped down after being appointed head of Flint's Planning and Development Department.

For two years elected commissioners met to discuss best practices, research forms of government, and listen to residents across the city to revise the outdated document. The commissioners tackled challenging issues: Should the city move to a city manager form of government, as recommended by Darnell Earley's Blue Ribbon group? Should the city reduce the number of wards, as recommended in 2010 by Mayor Walling? How could the charter address the pressing concerns about government transparency and accountability voiced by city residents?

The commission sought to "involve citizens" and get "out into the community," meeting regularly for two full years, hosting twelve Community Advisory Committee meetings and eight large-scale community forums at venues throughout the city. A citywide referendum on the changes the commission proposed was set for August 2017.

Importantly, the commission did not work under the process of majority rules but instead sought consensus. Their process was one of listening, discussion, and deliberation. The commissioners welcomed difficult dialogues and open, transparent debate about the future of the city. As Cleora Magee noted: "We worked really hard and we went through a lot with each other." She continued, "We had some hard decisions to make. We went through some hard times trying to come together on things, but we came to a consensus. . . . And this is the document we have come up with."[28]

The commissioners set out to meet four goals: to make the local officials, be they elected or appointed, more accountable to city residents; to increase transparency; to promote greater public involvement in local decision making; and to thereby create a more effective local government.

The new charter took into account some of the deep concerns expressed by residents—especially those concerns related to democratic accountability, transparency, and—of course—water. As the commissioners noted in numerous community forums that preceded the August 2017 vote, the new charter bars "raiding the water and sewer fund," a troubling practice that led to high water rates and poor infrastructure. Also, while the new charter does impose more transparency and accountability mechanisms on both the mayor and city council, the commissions opted to keep the city's strong mayor and nine-ward system intact. Moreover, the charter made some minor but important adjustments to the city attorney's office, the Office of the Ombudsman, and to administrative reporting requirements, as well as the budget process. One of the most important changes, in my view, is the change in the election cycle, transitioning all city elections to gubernatorial election years with the intent of increasing voter turnout. At their core, the changes were proposed to enhance community control.

At a city council meeting on July 24, 2017, city council president Kerry Nelson voiced reservations, noting that even if the new charter passed, little would change because the Receivership Transition Advisory Board (RTAB) was still in place. Nelson was highlighting that implementation of the proposed city charter would likely be postponed until after the RTAB was dissolved. Per EM Order 20, from April 29, 2015, which was amended and adopted, the RTAB would, on January 22, 2016, "ensure that the City is in full compliance with Public Act 436, all Emergency Manager Orders, local ordinances, and applicable state and federal laws"—meaning that all decisions made by the EM, such as the elimination of the Office of the Ombudsman, would stand unless specifically addressed by the state-appointed oversight board.

Despite this hurdle, the charter passed overwhelmingly, with more than 60 percent of the ballots supporting the new charter. The eighty-three-page document, which included language on ethics standards, pension obligations, and mechanisms for resident participation, both symbolically and practically reaffirmed the city's right to local control and, symbolically, its autonomy from the state. The charter reaffirmed community residents' power to not only vote on their representatives but also shape how those representatives make decisions.

8

From Fiscal Emergency to Public Health Emergency

Differing Responses to the Flint Water Crisis

Co-authored with
AMANDA D. CLARK

The language and symbols developed by the Flint Democracy Defense League (DDL), community organizers, and residents in response to the municipal takeover became a powerful springboard for the community response to the water crisis. The themes of suspension of democracy, oppression, dictatorship, and racism become central to how the community made meaning of the crisis and how they felt enabled to respond.

Claire McClinton, one of the founders of the DDL and a former labor organizer, stated:

> In their zeal to transfer the Flint water system to bondholders and other corporate interests—a Michigan city was poisoned. We have to publicize and shine the light of day on the fascist offensive going on in Michigan. . . . The backdrop is that Flint is the home of GM, and also the home of the great sit-down strike that established collective bargaining with GM. Flint was a game changer within the labor movement and the acceleration of unionization nationwide. . . . [W]e have become a throwaway disposable class—a class where people's lives don't matter anymore.[1]

Here, McClinton draws on symbols of democracy: the *threat to* democracy from fascism as well as Flint's historical significance in the labor movement. McClinton also ties the water crisis to the value conflict between financial interests (e.g., bondholders and corporate interests) and the people (e.g., "a throwaway disposable class," whose lives do not matter).

Kary Moss, the executive director of the Michigan ACLU, echoed this last point in an article in the *Detroit Free Press,* calling for a repeal of the emergency manager law:

> The suspension of democracy in these largely African-American communities makes this a civil rights issue. We can now see the dire consequences. The absolute powers granted the emergency manager enabled him to stay the course in contravention of complaints about the water and adverse environmental reports, subverted the scientific processes, and led to the manipulation of that data to achieve the desired results.[2]

For residents and organizers, the water crisis, which led to residents turning off the tap and loading up on cases of bottled water (see Figure 8.1), is yet another example of a disturbing recent history of the abuse of power; one that continues to portray the people of Flint as a throwaway population. The water crisis was an extension of the municipal takeover. But not everyone framed it that way.

Much like the interpretation and response to the takeover, the reaction to the water crisis varied considerably, and given Flint's political environment, the responses diverged along a common pattern. Of particular relevance were the different responses that emerged from the high-capacity nonprofit organizations affiliated with the development regime (see Chapter 6), particularly the C. S. Mott Foundation and the Flint and Genesee Chamber of Commerce, and local grassroots associations, such as the DDL.

While all groups spoke in terms of helping the community recover from the crisis, the narratives surrounding the crisis unfolded along two distinct paths. The development regime, for the most part, did not discuss the origins of the crisis or the bal-

Figure 8.1 Sign for water pickup in Flint, Michigan, 2016. (Photo by Lance Cheung [USDA, 2016].)

ance of power that created the situation in which the decision to use untreated Flint River water was made. The development regime was also very forward thinking in their public messaging: themes included "moving Flint forward" and concentrating on the positive. Grassroots groups, on the other hand, were very vocal about why the crisis happened, including discussions of the suspension of local democracy in the EM takeover, the constant pressure on the state to put profits over people, and the need to hold state and local officials responsible for the crisis and its impacts.

In the Flint water crisis, we see this process play out by comparing the rhetoric used by member organizations of the development regime and grassroots activists. The development regime organizations were careful to not assign blame to any particular entity when discussing the crisis. Many of the published documents from development regime organizations tended to describe the water crisis as a natural or surprising event. An article published on the C. S. Mott Foundation website, for example, emphasizes the chemical differences in the water, rather than sociopolitical causes. Using a quote from biologist Joseph Leonardi of the Michigan Department of Natural Resources, the article notes:

"The issue with the (lead in Flint's) drinking water stemmed from the Flint River having natural differences in chemistry compared to water from Lake Huron," Leonardi said. "The river water itself was not to blame."

The Flint River contains chlorides (some of which likely come from road salt), but the water does not pose direct threats to fish, wildlife or people who use the river. *Chlorides cause problems in drinking water* mainly because they corrode metal in the pipes and plumbing fixtures that transport water into homes.[3]

The focus is on mitigating the effects of the water crisis in a reactive way; there is little discussion about what might have caused the crisis in the first place, nor is there any focus on the topic of criminality. The discourse of the development regime was tied very closely to the official narrative, possibly due to the close political ties and financial relationships between the government and local business.

On the other hand, grassroots activists were very concerned with the why and how of the water crisis. They were also more willing to not only assign blame to people within the governmental power structure but also ask for justice and punishment for the crime that was committed. These groups had no deep financial or social ties to the city power structure. These were everyday citizens, impacted by water crisis in very real ways: financially, medically, and psychologically.

Framing of the Water Crisis

How issues are framed informs who is included and who is not. The rhetoric used in press releases or public statements provides insights into how groups perceive (and experience) power and oppression, and how problems are understood within that context. Patricia Hill Collins, drawing on feminist standpoint theory, notes that

> group location in hierarchical power relations produces shared challenges for individuals in those groups. These common challenges can foster similar angles of vision

leading to a group's knowledge or standpoint that in turn can influence the group's political action.[4]

Stated differently, group standpoints are situated in unjust power relations, reflect those power relations, and help shape them. High-capacity nonprofit organizations (e.g., the development regime) and grassroots activists in Flint, as highlighted throughout this book, gleaned power from different sources. The development regime at the onset of the water crisis was in a position of relative power, helping shape the development-focused takeover agenda. On the other hand, grassroots activists gleaned their power through their framing strategy and coalition-building efforts (see Chapter 7).

While both groups were embedded in the Flint community, the two groups differed in how they assigned blame and framed the water crisis. The development regime's concerns were framed in a manner consistent with their interests in economic development—often emphasizing the importance of moving the city forward. On the other hand, grassroots activists framed the water crisis as a continuation of the harms experienced over decades. Comparing the causal stories and framing strategy deployed by these two groups in response to the water crisis further illustrates the differences between the high-capacity nonprofit organizations and the grassroots groups.[5]

In Flint, development-focused nonprofits were careful to not assign blame to any particular entity when discussing the crisis, focusing instead on mitigating the effects of the water crisis in a reactive way. In general, these organizations focused little attention on what might have caused the crisis in the first place, nor on the topic of criminality. On the other hand, grassroots activists were very concerned with the why and how of the water crisis. They were also more willing to not only assign blame to people within the governmental power structure but also to ask for justice and punishment for the crime that was committed.

Identity and Power

High-capacity nonprofits and grassroots activists often perceive their status in the community in very different ways. HCNPs frame their concerns as emanating from their identity as members of the existing governance structure, and from the perspective of a predominantly White, relatively affluent local political elite. On the other hand, grassroots activists are very aware that not only is their power limited but their concerns—historically scaffolded by legacies of racial injustice and discrimination—are in direct opposition to the power structure.

Race, Class, Gender, and Power

The intersection of race, class, and gender is an important theme, associated with and forming the foundation of the causal stories told by grassroots activists. The movement in Flint was led by women, mostly women of color: Nayyirah Shariff, Bernadel Jefferson, and Claire McClinton; and mothers like LeeAnne Walters and Melissa Mays. Grassroots activists also included neighborhood association leaders, faith-based organizers, and angry residents. Some were outspoken on the history of systemic racism in Flint. Other activists expressed their belief that the community of Flint was not considered worthy of help by those in charge because of the high rates of poverty in the area. Grassroots activists framed the crisis as the haves versus the have-nots. Melissa Mays, from Water You Fighting For?, referred to the crisis as a case of "environmental racism," though she emphasized that the issue extends beyond race.[6]

McClinton also tied the crisis to one of class by pointing out that once workers are no longer needed in the factories, they become "disposable" and "a throw-away class whose lives don't matter."[7] The imagery of worthlessness, disposability, and expendability is common throughout the grassroots documents when discussing elite attitudes toward the citizens of Michigan and, particularly, Flint.

Gender was also a prominent theme—both in terms of the organizers' identities as well as in how they framed the movement. In many ways, traditional roles of mothers and caregivers gave many of these women a sense of shared identity. In addition, the lack of respect the women received at the hands of government officials, from the mayor of Flint to the governor of Michigan to the administrators at the Environmental Protection Agency (EPA), further fueled the desire of these women to right the wrongs that had been done to them and their families. Mays noted:

> My message is that this has been a motherrun movement. When you cross our babies, no. That's not going to happen. Go with your gut. Because when you think there's something wrong, that's because there probably is. And you can stand up against the government. It doesn't matter what your background is. You can make a difference and make your voice heard. No one would be doing anything now if it wasn't for a bunch of moms getting mad.[8]

Careful attention to the intersecting identities of the citizens (including gender, race, and class) of Flint and how the water crisis impacted each in a different way set the grassroots activists apart from the HCNPs. In fact, this was identified in 2016 by the National Women's Law Center, when it declared the Flint water crisis to be an intersectional feminist issue:

> An intersectional feminist movement is one that shines a light on the complexities of how issues interact and impact marginalized people. Low-income women of color, as well as undocumented immigrants, and their families are the ones who are hardest hit by this crisis. Its effects will have long lasting and, for many, irreversible impacts on the health and lives of the people of Flint. For all of these reasons and more, the Flint water crisis is undeniably a feminist issue.[9]

Equality
On the other hand, HCNPs created a narrative of equal suffering for all residents of Flint. This adherence to a color-blind, and class-blind, strategy is in direct opposition to the grassroots activists. Here the HCNPs are not explicitly telling racial stories, but their focus on "the past is the past" and the natural and unfortunate causes of the water crisis runs parallel to this narrative. Moreover, their lack of discussion around structural oppression and emphasis on equality further scaffolds the color-blind racism of HCNPs.

The phrases "all Flint residents," "Flint families," and "community" are used throughout the HCNP documents. These statements paint a picture of a community suffering together while HCNPs look to serve everyone equally. In a public service announcement from University of Michigan–Flint (UM-Flint) for the Big Ten Network, Dr. Martin Kaufman is seen stating, "This is about coming together as a community. We're in it until people can take a drink from a tap and not worry what the water quality is."[10]

Interestingly, much fanfare was made regarding the move back to Detroit water in October 2015, as if the move was something extraordinary and done magnanimously on behalf of the residents of Flint, ignoring the fact that the state forced the move away from Detroit water in the first place. The Mott Foundation offered $4 million to reconnect the water, citing that "the move to Detroit water is expected to carry public health benefits."[11] In addition, the HCNPs often tied economic success of the business sector with recovery from the water crisis. As George Wilkinson, group vice president for the Flint and Genesee Chamber of Commerce stated:

> No doubt, the water crisis has been catastrophic but we will continue to work diligently with community stakeholders to turn this setback into an opportunity for economic revitalization.[12]

This focus on the needs of the elite business community and the importance of wealthy philanthropists over the people were echoed in other statements. For example, in the UM-Flint chancellor's 2016 State of the University address, she stated:

> The public health crisis is a gut kick to a community that is working to create a positive future. The sustained investment of business people and philanthropists reinforces the hope and efforts of many who have been laying the groundwork for Flint's economic future.[13]

While a healthy economy is important to a community's long-term success, a singular focus on investment opportunities at the same time that people are suffering from the effects of lead-laced water and dying from Legionnaires' disease illustrates how HCNPs differed greatly from grassroots activists in prioritizing their concerns.

Causal Stories

The causal stories offered by the two groups differed in important ways as well: grassroots activists tended to focus on root causes of the crisis, particularly as they related to principles of democratic governance and social inequality, while HCNPs focused on technical failures. We explore each in turn, as their framing of the problem—the cause—informs their interpretations of possible solutions.

Deterioration of Democracy and Social Inequality
Given the political context in which the crisis unfolded, it is unsurprising that many of the grassroots activists focused on the status of democracy in Flint and the balance of power between citizens and the state as they identified causes of the crisis. The focus on the deterioration of democracy in Flint, and Michigan more broadly, starts with the EM law. The application of the EM law has been linked to racism, discrimination against the poor, and a drive to privatize public assets. The roles of the EM law, the EM, and the state, which suspended local control, are all at the center of this narrative. For example, grassroots activists emphasized the idea that the citizens of Flint had lost their voice involving civic matters, specifically the subversion of democracy in Flint.

Even though the decision to stop buying water from Detroit was billed as a needed financial savings, little consideration was placed on the potential impact, financial or otherwise, on people's lives. As Shariff, an activist with the DDL, stated:

> [Governor] Snyder has been trampling our democracy for years really, ever since he's been in office, and specifically since Flint has had an emergency manager in December 2011. And our City Council wanted to go back to Detroit (water), and our emergency manager, Jerry Ambrose, said

it was inconceivable because it was going to cost too much money. And the culture of the emergency manager is money trumps everything. It's more important than people's lives.[14]

Similarly, McClinton argued that the financial crises themselves were created by neoliberal economic policies that forced production overseas and, combined with technological automation, led to a large class of workers who have been "shut out of the process of production." Rather than helping those workers, EMs have been put in place to "impose dictatorship on the people" to silence their dissent.[15]

The Flint City Council, early in the crisis, voted to return to Detroit water but was overridden by the EM. Mays expressed her anger at the lack of accountability and the silencing of the people:

> I feel betrayed by my state government, the Michigan Department of Environmental Quality, and every single person put into place to protect us from exactly what they did to us. I am furious that they took away our voice with the undemocratic Emergency Manager Law.[16]

Tony Palladino, a local resident and community resident connected to Camp Promise, echoed this comment in an interview with a journalist, stating "I want to thank you for being here, because actually the only thing that's getting filtered in Flint now are our voices."[17]

For many within the grassroots movement, the appointment of EMs in Michigan was part of a larger process to privatize all public space and services to squeeze every bit of profit out of the system:

> The poisoning of the people in Flint shows what happens to workers who are no longer needed. As robots replace workers, our democracy is going by the wayside to protect the profits of a corporate ruling class as it coldly discards anything that won't make a profit, including people.[18]

Scholars and activists alike acknowledge that the EM law has had a disproportionate impact on communities of color;[19] and, as such, the water crisis, too, was clearly associated with racial and economic inequity. Much of this framing is captured in the Michigan Civil Rights Commission's 2017 report, which found evidence of systemic racism in Flint and states "we believe the underlying issue is historical and systemic, dates back nearly a century, and has at its foundation race and segregation of the Flint community."[20]

Technical and Governmental Causes
On the other hand, fewer than 10 percent of the HCNP documents (five of seventy-two) that we analyzed discussed themes related to the status of democracy in Flint. Of the five, only three directly mentioned the need to bring citizens back into the conversation in a meaningful way; the other two documents only referenced the need to improve communication with the public. UM-Flint cautioned that agencies should be more open to "findings about water quality reported by citizens and scientists,"[21] while the C. S. Mott Foundation called for "promoting community engagement" and "local decision-making" as it announced a large pledge to help the community.[22]

However, these comments do not address the deeper concern of the lack of democracy in Flint. In addition, none of the HCNPs mention the EM law and its impact on citizen participation in government decisions. In fact, the takeover was supported (if unofficially) and beneficial to many of the city's HCNPs. As noted earlier, the members of the city's "development regime" benefited by helping shape the city's political agenda under municipal takeover. This partnership between local public officials and the political power elites within the HCNPs began decades before the city's recent economic decline. For example, as discussed in Chapter 4, the Mott Foundation played a critical role in the 1950s and 1960s as the city sought to expand its boundaries.[23]

Additionally, the foundation played a significant role in shaping the city's color line vis à vis its community schools initiative by "creat[ing] new programs and policies that hardened and institutionalized patterns of racial separation, academic disadvantage, and social inequality";[24] moreover, when, in 1975, the federal government ordered desegregation of Flint's schools, the Mott Foundation canceled its long-standing financial commitment to the community's school system.[25] An HCNP with enough local power to pull its support to ostensibly weaken federal mandates on desegregation illustrates the embeddedness of the HCNPs in the governing power structure.

In the early days of the crisis, many lauded the efforts of government officials in returning the city back to Detroit water. Mott Foundation president Ridgway White stated, "It's heartening to know so many people are working at so many levels to bring safe, clean water back to Flint."[26] Many of the HCNPs varied with regard to identifying the causes of the crisis. While many educational institutions, such as UM-Flint, provided a platform to discuss various causes, others either avoided discussions of cause or focused on the technical issues related to the water crisis, such as water infrastructure and water distribution. In a UM-Flint blog post from July 2016, the water crisis is framed as a technical failure, noting: "The City of Flint has been experiencing a lead-in-water crisis for over 27 months due to improperly-treated water flowing through city pipes."[27]

Rather than focus on the cause, many HCNPs moved forward immediately with technical solutions. A press release from the Flint and Genesee Chamber of Commerce quotes CEO Tim Herman:

> We know from talking to local business owners and residents that the only way to restore confidence in the city's lead-contaminated water system for the long term is to begin removing lead service lines in the city's system as soon as possible.[28]

The causal stories of both groups lead to very different prescriptions for handling the water crisis. HCNPs focused on returning to a pre–water crisis environment by returning to Detroit water and replacing the (now damaged) lead service lines leading to people's homes. The grassroots activists focused on the fact that if the people (through their representatives on the elected city council) had been given a voice, the crisis would have never happened in the first place. This is not to say that the grassroots activists were not concerned about replacing lead services lines, but they wanted to emphasize that their concerns ran deeper, connecting the issue of water to the process of democracy rather than technical fixes. The gap between these two causal stories ensures, at the very least, a lack of understanding between these groups, which could impact their ability to work with and trust each other.

Justice, Restitution, and Moving Forward

The third and final major theme that we identified in our comparison of the two groups is related to identifying the cause of the crisis itself and if those actions were in fact criminal and deliberate. None of the HCNPs in Flint mentioned the word "criminal" or "crime," or indicated the suspicion of any deliberate intention to do harm by state or city officials. However, grassroots activists and groups regularly identified the criminal nature and deliberateness of the actions taken during the water crisis, especially the actions (or inactions) of the state. Positioning these frames in either the natural world (unplanned, unfortunate, and requiring reaction) or the social world (deliberate, intentional, and requiring proactive changes to the system) changes the causal story and creates tension between the two groups in addressing the issue.

HCNPs relied heavily on the premise that the crisis was something to be dealt with or responded to and then the community should move forward. There was a significant lack of concern for assigning any blame to any entity for the crisis itself or obtaining justice or making restitution to those hurt by the crisis. Organizations focused on the response to, not the causes of, the crisis. United Way CEO Jamie Gaskin compared the crisis to previous weather-related events; again, a framing indicating the crisis was a natural and unforeseeable event.[29] The Mott Foundation offered advice for combating lead poisoning in children by "eating foods rich in iron, calcium and Vitamin C."[30]

In addition, there was an almost uniform theme of moving past the crisis before most had even begun to deal with the consequences:

The Flint & Genesee Chamber of Commerce on June 14 will convene business executives from across Michigan to help craft a vision of the post–water crisis Flint.[31]

> While helping Flint residents meet immediate needs related to lead contamination, we also must think ahead about how to help the community emerge from the crisis.[32]

The Flint Chamber of Commerce was the organization most dedicated to the message that Flint must move on. Citing the need to attract and support business, the chamber implored residents to share positive stories of Flint, even in the midst of utter chaos. As early as April 2016, just three months after the initial emergency declarations were made, the chamber released statements asking Flint residents to use the hashtags #FlintFwd and #Choose Flint.[33] In addition, a campaign entitled Moving Flint Forward was announced with a charitable fund dedicated to "address immediate and long-term business development" concerns.[34]

These requests seem jarringly out of place when comparing grassroots documents from the same month as protesters marked the two-year anniversary of the switch away from Detroit water with little to no discernible change in people's day-to-day lives. Palladino, whose wife, Leah, was arrested at a town hall meeting just days before, was quoted as saying:

> I'm going to say something none of you are going to like to hear, but it's true. Flint lives don't matter. Listen to me: Flint lives don't matter. . . . This is the city of Flint that's dying. We need to take back our city.[35]

Although there was not total agreement on whether the state meant to do harm or was just negligent, most activists agreed that the covering up of the crime after the state learned of the water testing results negated the benefit of the doubt any had allowed the state. As Melissa Mays stated:

> I don't think anybody set out to intentionally poison us, but the minute you knew that our water was poisoned, you didn't tell us and that's criminal. You covered it up. People have died, so you need to go to jail.[36]

Others supported these thoughts as well. For example, Bernadel Jefferson noted:

> The whole city has been hurt. The whole city has been damaged. This is a travesty. This is a crime. This is . . . this needs to be fixed.[37]

Unlike the HCNPs, the grassroots activists framed their causal story as one of the social world, allowing them to assign blame and ask for justice. The use of the word "poison" and the idea that officials were "killing the people" of Flint were common terms in the grassroots documents. In her testimony before the U.S. Congress, LeeAnne Walters, the mother of four children whose tap water was twenty-seven times the EPA limit for lead, stated:

> The people in Flint and I'll stand with the people in DC, who suffered their own lead crisis a decade ago, because we now know the horror of poison running through our taps and the negligence of the agencies paid to protect us.[38]

Many grassroots activists and people in Flint were looking for not just accountability from officials but also restitution for the damages caused by those decisions. Residents were paying for increased medical costs, bottled water, and filters. The grassroots activists also pointed out that, to add insult to injury, officials were requiring them to pay for poisoned water they couldn't use; water rates in Flint had been some of the highest in the nation even before the crisis. Mays outlined some of the concerns:

> We live 41 percent at or below the poverty line, so paying those really high water rates on top of paying for the damages that the water has done to your body and your home is just unaffordable.[39]

Citizens who refused to pay their water bills on principle were threatened with water shutoffs, visits from Child Protective Services, and, ultimately, tax liens placed on their homes.

The causal story presented by both groups guides each to

radically different solutions. The HCNP response was technical and neutral, framed as something that could be addressed through replacement water lines and the distribution of bottled water. Moreover, the HCNPs spoke of moving forward and focusing on positive stories. Negative stories—such as the disproportionate burden felt by persons of color and people living in poverty that are linked to legacies of policies that facilitate racial and economic segregation—would only hurt business interests, including tourism, and so forth. Grassroots activists, however, were asking for restitution or, at the very least, accountability for the consequences of government negligence to make them whole before they could move forward. The grassroots activists insisted that those in power admit that their decisions caused the water crisis, rejecting the premise that it was a natural or unforeseen event.

Defining the Problem and Assigning Blame

The decision to change Flint's water supply flowed from the EM's directives, ostensibly to save money, but was ultimately the consequence of numerous bad decisions for which many parties are to blame. Yet, the residents have experienced a series of traumas, and, for many grassroots activists and residents, these include both the municipal takeover and the water crisis. Reflecting on the recovery, Shariff compared the trauma of the water crisis to the trauma of rape:

> There were a lot of people propping up this narrative that the water was safe to drink. Now they are in charge of our recovery. So you have this trauma. It is almost like you were raped. You call the police to handle your rape and your rapist is taking your case and documenting what happened. Your other rapist is the prosecutor and your other one's the judge.[40]

Similarly, McClinton points out, "The pretext that was used to even get these EMs in motion was that these minority cities are incapable of handling their finances."[41] This sentiment was echoed by Jefferson: "No, the reason why they chose Flint is because it is predominantly a city of color, over 65 percent are people of color, so we were expendable."[42]

The imagery of being treated as worthless, disposable, and expendable is common throughout grassroots narratives—both in response to the municipal takeover and the water crisis. Such frames highlight one of the tragedies of the myopia of the rationality project: its blindness to the polis—the human and the political—leaves policy makers and decision makers open to brutal attacks on their character. How local community-based organizations define social problems, assign blame, and offer solutions is integral to mobilizing their constituencies. In the case of the Flint water crisis, we examined two different groups: high-capacity nonprofits and grassroots associations. We found that each group approached the crisis relative to their embeddedness in the local political power structure. Their framing strategies were mostly in direct opposition to each other: the development regime situated the crisis in the natural, reactionary model, while grassroots activists relied on putting the crisis directly in the social model, requiring systemic change and justice for victims.

The grassroots associations used intersectional frames that served to identify differences among community members, while simultaneously identifying the power and privilege that underpin the systemic oppression of Flint's people. The activists drew on narratives of past exploitation and collective power in their framing of the problem. In this way, they both identified how local power structures shaped their individual experiences as well as ways in which those shared experiences provided a platform for solidarity.

On the other hand, the development regime, comprising mostly HCNPs, created a narrative of equal suffering for all residents of Flint. This adherence to a color-blind, and class-blind, strategy was in direct opposition to the grassroots associations. Here the development regime was not explicitly telling racial stories, but their focus on "the past is the past" and the natural and unfortunate causes of the water crisis ran parallel to this narrative. Moreover, their lack of discussion about structural oppression and their emphasis on equality further scaffolded the color-blind racism of the development regime.

Conclusion

Summary Findings, Implications, and Recommendations

Municipal takeover policies claim to eschew politics. These policies, which rest on the principle that local government is broken, suspend local democracy in an attempt to fix local fiscal problems. Fear of municipal bankruptcy, economic contagion, and credit downgrades are among the most common motivations for intervening in local municipal affairs. In this way, municipal takeovers are quintessential policy paradoxes, wherein market thinking and solutions are privileged over the needs of the polis, yet have important political consequences.[1] Proponents of municipal takeover seek expediency, efficiency, and fiscal stability, the hallmarks of the "rationality project." Democracy, on the other hand, is messy, and politics is complex.

Despite politicians' claims to the contrary, the municipal takeovers of Flint were political and had significant local political consequences. State intervention not only suspended the authority of local elected officials in the short-term but also reshaped the local political landscape in the long term, empowering some community interests, marginalizing others, and prompting some to seek new ways to engage in the political system through political protest and community organizing.

The implementation of the policy, by a series of state-appointed managers, interrupted politics-as-usual. While some argued that municipal takeovers were only temporary, thus implying that the political impact too would be only temporary, the tools and strategies utilized by the emergency managers are political. To borrow Howard Lasswell's phrasing, municipal takeovers determine "who gets what, when, [and] how."[2] Additionally, the implementation of the policy by the development regime is illustrative of how top-down decision-making structures the "allocation of values." In this context, the development regime was closely aligned with the values of the rationality project, eschewing—to their own detriment—the values of the polis.[3]

A policy-centered, interpretive approach was adopted for this research project. Drawing on the rich theoretical contributions of the policy paradox framework and policy feedback theory, I identified both instrumental and symbolic policy effects and the dynamics through which those feedback effects operated. Under a series of state-appointed managers, more than one hundred executive orders, resolutions, and directives were implemented. These directives included, among other things, shuttering city offices, laying off employees, restructuring collective bargaining agreements, selling city assets, and increasing fees. Cumulatively, these decisions reshaped the local political landscape by allocating resource benefits to some, while creating burdens for others, and restructuring local government, in some instances literally removing points of participatory access for city residents. In addition to these instrumental effects, the policy and subsequent implementation had a symbolic effect, which conveyed important messages to community stakeholders and residents about their value and position in the city.

The policy history of municipal takeovers highlights the value conflict between state intervention and local autonomy that has shaped the variation in state responses to local fiscal crises. These tensions, which serve as further exemplars of the policy paradox, underscore the historical development of municipal takeover policy across the country and in Michigan in particular. In Michigan, the municipal takeover policy evolved over time, becoming more aggressive in its approach.

Flint's case is particularly powerful for examining the impact of municipal takeovers. The city had also been placed under receivership and appointed an Emergency Financial Manager in 2002. The powers of the EFM in 2002 were more limited than those provided to the EMs from 2011 through 2015; thus, Flint's experience with municipal takeover in 2002 was decidedly different from the takeover in 2015. The second takeover granted much greater power to the state-appointed manager in an attempt to straighten out Flint's fiscal situation. These increased powers targeted perceived drains on local resources, and were often aligned with conservative, neoliberal politics. For example, in PA 4 and PA 436, EMs were given the authority to nullify collective bargaining agreements and retiree health-care agreements, which was advocated by Michigan's free-market think tank, the Mackinac Center for Public Policy.[4]

The tools and strategies of the policy are important in both instrumental and symbolic ways; the comparison between the two takeovers is useful from an analytic perspective. However, most of the data collected, both in terms of documentary data and interview data, focus on the takeover between 2011 and 2015. Where appropriate, however, I highlight how the 2002 takeover influenced both the strategy and the perception of the 2011 takeover.

With this project, I demonstrate that community stakeholders associated with the development regime, such as the Chamber of Commerce, the C. S. Mott Foundation, and the Uptown family of corporations, benefited under municipal takeover. These organizations have deep roots in Flint and have long been involved in local politics.[5] Under the municipal takeover, and with the appointment as emergency manager of Michael Brown, who had worked with and/or for executives at each of these institutions, these organizations were able to help shape the EM's agenda, particularly as it related to economic development. For example, Tim Herman, the CEO of the Flint and Genesee Chamber of Commerce, was appointed to the EM's Citizens Advisory Committee.

More importantly, this project illustrates how the development regime obfuscated the values of the polis (e.g., values of social equity, political equality) in its pursuit of efficiency and fiscal stability. The paradox of this myopic focus is that the city is facing a continuing public health crisis, further loss of population, and related financial challenges. In other words, the ostensibly apolitical policy had real political consequences, the fiscally focused takeover led to additional financial stresses, and the "color-blind" responses to urban fiscal distress and the water crisis led to further racial tensions and deep public distrust.

Implications

The financial crisis and takeover of Flint draws our attention to ongoing conflicts over state responses to urban fiscal crises. Is fiscal stability to be pursued at the expense of social equity, balancing budgets at the expense of helping people who live in a troubled city? Flint is hardly alone in experiencing financial stress—local governments across the United States, as they have throughout modern history, experience increasing costs and shrinking revenues, what Peter Dreier, John Mollenkopf, and Todd Swanstrom refer to as the "iron cage of municipal finance."[6] From city to city the proximate causes vary, from loss of state revenues to rising costs for public services and underfunded public pensions, to outright fiscal mismanagement. But the difficulties are similar and tend to affect poor and minority communities the most, creating acute dilemmas of social equity.

When policies are put in place with a narrow focus on the bottom line, potential social and political impacts are often overlooked, in some instances blinding administrators to harm.[7] Isolating local elected officials and community residents from public policy decisions that directly and indirectly affect them has long-term consequences. Opponents organize opposition and file lawsuits, and residents express distrust and anger with local and state government. Additionally, the impact of the municipal takeover in Flint has broader implications, as other states looked to Michigan as they considered strengthening their municipal takeover policy or adopting municipal takeover legislation.[8] On the other hand, the water crisis and international attention focusing on the EM may require not only Michigan but other states to reevaluate their intervention strategies. As Eric Scorsone has said, "The words 'emergency manager' are almost too toxic."[9]

Consequences of Municipal Takeover

- Redistributed and consolidated power. The beneficiaries of municipal takeover, in most instances, are not the residents, who, for example, might see their water bills rise or their land taken by eminent domain, but rather a handful of prominent local elites. As such, restructuring cities, done under the auspices of municipal takeover, has served to redistribute and consolidate the power of local governing regimes.
- Less access among residents to key decision makers, even after the municipal takeover is lifted. In Flint, Michigan, the state-appointed manager eliminated the Office of the Ombudsman and citizens advisory boards and temporarily shortened public comment at city council meetings.
- Anger, resentment, and distrust of local government. Municipal takeovers have been called the "death of democracy," highlighting the importance we as a nation place on local representative democracy.
- Increased racial tensions. The process of temporarily suspending the decision-making powers of local elected officials, in the name of "getting things done," also has a symbolic impact that is racially charged. In 2013 in the state of Michigan, nearly half of the state's African American population lived in cities under state control. The suspension of their duly elected local officials was seen by many as an affront to their hard-won civil rights and voting rights.
- Only short-term fiscal stability. By definition, a city is not released for municipal takeover until it is financially stable. However, even with draconian measures, some cities, like Detroit, Michigan, wind up filing for municipal bankruptcy; some end up back in receivership years later, as was the case in Flint, Michigan; and some continue to request aid from the state to fill budget shortfalls, like Camden, New Jersey.
- Unintended mobilization of new opposition coalitions. One of the important findings of this research project

is that the municipal takeover policy unintentionally mobilized new opposition coalitions, creating new pathways to political participation.
- Threats to public health and well-being. Although a worst-case scenario, the case of the Flint water crisis highlights the damage that can be done when decisions are made based on budgetary concerns and without regard to potential harm to residents.

Recommendations

As illustrated in this study, the municipal takeovers place a significant burden on residents, which outweighs the benefits of purported fiscal stability. However, my research, as well as that of other scholars, suggests that municipal fiscal emergency policies can be improved by placing greater emphasis on social equity.

- First, eliminate the use of state-appointed managers. As Chapter 2 highlights, there are multiple approaches to state intervention, with municipal takeover being the most aggressive and extreme. In part, this is due to giving sole authority to an unelected, state-appointed manager. This policy approach values the technical-rational approach to top-down decision-making that obscures the voices of community residents and thus fosters resentment, anger, and distrust among many community residents. In Flint, residents who opposed municipal takeover identified both the instrumental and symbolic meaning of having a state-appointed manager govern the city.
- Second, the tools currently in use for emergency management must be modified. Municipal takeovers are most often implemented in cities on the verge of municipal bankruptcy. Cities like East St. Louis, Illinois, or Camden, New Jersey, have high unemployment and poverty rates and have experienced years of economic disinvestment. These cities have high demand for services, but low property and income tax revenue to support these demands.[10] Most scholars and community residents would agree that municipal bankruptcy should be avoided, and that the

social and economic problems plaguing the city must be addressed. However, the tools and strategies provided for in municipal takeover policy emphasize budgets. Putting the "fiscal house back in order" often requires draconian cuts to resources and services and does little to address structural causes of problems, such as high unemployment and poverty, population decline, crime, or failing schools.[11] Moreover, these cuts are done under the auspices of an un-elected, state-appointed official, which undermines strongly held beliefs regarding democracy, popular sovereignty, and community control. The policy toolbox, so to speak, should be retooled to focus on prevention by addressing the root causes of the cities' fiscal crises. In Michigan, this can be done, in part, by amending the state's revenue-sharing structure or removing limitations on local government taxation powers. In other words, we need to focus on a prevention model, rather than an emergency model.

- Additionally, another way to think about prevention, rather than emergency, from a participatory perspective, is to look at policy tools that give community members an active role in addressing the fiscal concerns of the city. There are existing models—adopted in other cities, including post-bankruptcy Vallejo, California—that are founded on the principle of "empowered democracy"[12]—programs such as participatory budgeting, which give citizens the power to identify community needs and allocate government funds accordingly. Such programs, though in their infancy in the United States, provide a model for fiscal decision-making that seeks to increase trust in local government and foster a "renewed political culture in which citizens ... serve as democratic agents."[13] While such a model is unlikely to be adopted during a fiscal crisis, such programs provide evidence that there are ways in which local budgeting and knowledge of local finance could be improved and resistance to local fiscal policy actions may be reduced.
- Most important, policies should be designed to foster democracy, not undermine it. One of the key issues

identified in this book is the myopia of the rationality project—specifically, a lack of meaningful transparency and accountability to residents and a narrow focus on short-term goals with little regard for long-term political consequences. I recognize that in a crisis situation, democratic participation and deliberation are often eschewed in preference of immediate crisis response and mitigation. However, mechanisms of accountability and transparency, rather than a disingenuous invitation for the public to participate that tends to accompany takeovers, should be leveraged. As Deborah Stone points out, politics can be understood as disputes over interpretation. Lack of clarity, information, and access to decision-making bodies, coupled with legacies of social and political isolation, shaped Flint residents' interpretations of the municipal takeover. Residents asked "to whom was the EM accountable?" and overwhelmingly they came to perceive the EM as accountable to the state, the creditors, and the development regime.

Democracy is messy, yes. But decreasing access to local decision makers increases distrust among residents and provides openings for local elites to control or shape the agenda. Putting measures in place to ameliorate this problem would go a long way toward diminishing the lack of access to local power. In other words, deliberation and inclusion are essential to making laws aimed at addressing fiscal crises more socially equitable.

Appendix 1

Research Design and Methodology

To examine how municipal takeover policy created a new politics, I adopted a policy-centered single-case research design.[1] As Jacob Hacker, Suzanne Mettler, and Joe Soss have pointed out, in a policy-centered analysis, "policy serves as the focal point for a broader analysis of how political forces shape governance and how government actions reshape the society and polity."[2] In other words, this research project centers the concepts of policy design and policy implementation. Thus, we can unpack the policy paradox of municipal takeovers by using the policy as an analytic lens and using Flint, Michigan, as the site of investigation.

This book uses the Flint case to examine how a takeover unfolded, what choices were made, and how community residents and community leaders made meaning out of and reacted to the experience. Flint was selected for its analytic and practical utility. After decades of White flight, economic disinvestment, and neoliberal policies, Flint, like many other deindustrialized cities, faced a staggering structural deficit.[3] And under the auspices of fixing Flint's fiscal emergency, Michigan placed the city under emergency financial management. I argue that municipal takeover policy affected political strategies by creating both instrumental and symbolic effects related to how people interpreted the strategies, targets, and goals of the policy.

Because there has been limited analysis to date about the political impact of municipal takeovers, my research focuses on theory building to identify the conditions and causal mechanisms that, when activated, have the capacity to reshape local politics. I have drawn on theoretically grounded propositions about how municipal takeover policy is likely to change local politics through instrumental and symbolic mechanisms. In other words, as the theoretical framework discussed in the book makes clear, choices made by the EM team, as implemented through hundreds of directives and executive orders, had differing impacts on different members of the community, and whether or not particular residents were directly impacted by an executive order, their position within the local political system framed how they perceived or interpreted the EM's actions.[4]

Case Study Research Design

Given the nature of the question, this book draws on the rich methodological and epistemological traditions of social constructivism and neo-institutionalism by using a policy-centered case study research design. This research design is appropriate for two reasons. First, the political impact of the takeover, the dependent variable of interest in this analysis, was not known prior to my investigation. As Jason Seawright and John Gerring put it, my "puzzle of interest . . . lies within the case."[5] In this way, the research was exploratory. Second, I am not testing a theory, but identifying the political outcomes and building a theoretical explanation to support my findings.

Much like policy analysis or program evaluation, I am interested in the impact of the municipal takeover policy. Unlike traditional policy analysis, however, I am not interested in testing and evaluating intended outcomes, prescribed by the "rationality project." Instead, I investigate the intentional or unintentional impact on the polis.[6] Therefore, I adopted a policy-centered research design, where the policy serves as the "focal point" for a wider investigation of how policy shapes politics.[7] Such an approach is particularly amenable to qualitative research designs, as it requires in-depth, process-oriented, and context-specific investigation.[8]

Finally, the policy paradox framework and social construction theory draw on a constructivist-interpretive epistemology that maintains that our reality and understanding of the world are socially constructed.[9] The ways that people made meaning out of the takeover (e.g., whether they saw it as a necessary evil or the "death of democracy") matters in how they responded to the decisions made by the EM. Investigating how community members interpreted the takeover demands a research design that emphasizes depth over breath and complexity over parsimony.

Two other, more personal, reasons make the case study research design useful for this study. Both are practical in nature and draw on a postpositivist mentality. First is my commitment to engaged research, wherein the researcher seeks to engage and empower community members through the articulation of their views, concerns, and beliefs.[10] During my interviews, for example, many of the participants were eager to share their thoughts, good and bad, about EMs, in hopes that their contribution would serve to inform policy makers, government officials, and other community leaders.

The second reason is guided by my interest in informing future public policy debates regarding municipal takeover. The single-case research design allows me to delve deep into the stories, narratives, and experiences of municipal takeover in Flint, while recognizing that Flint is not isolated in its experience. As Daniel Carpenter points out, "There is value in studying a singular case, not because it represents so many others but because it influences so many others."[11] This argument is surely true in the case of municipal takeover legislation, where one state looks to others to draft legislation.[12] Therefore, the results of my case will not only empower Flint's residents but also serve as a warning to residents in other municipalities facing financial exigency of some sort.

Data Collection

The data collection process utilized here emphasizes data triangulation. Data triangulation is necessary in single-case research design to provide convergent evidence and strengthen construct validity. Therefore, this book draws on data from a variety of sources, including (1) documentary evidence, which included not only government documents (budget reports, progress reports, executive orders, and meeting minutes) but also newspaper articles, television and radio broadcast footage, and Facebook; (2) observation and field notes; and (3) semi-structured interviews with community leaders, residents, and activists.

Documentary Evidence

Documentary evidence was collected throughout the research project. However, the process began with the "soaking and poking" phase, a qualitative method often used as a preliminary step in case study research.[13] As the name denotes, this stage emphasizes the need to become familiar with the topic, examining how the issue has been presented to date and looking for possible relationships among the variables. In this case, the soaking and poking phase was carried out between November 2012 and March 2015. Throughout the two-plus-year time period, I reviewed and compiled a significant number of documents and raw data: newspaper and magazine articles from the *Detroit Free Press,* the *New York Times,* the *Los Angeles Times,* the *Flint Journal, Slate Magazine,* and the *New Yorker;* scholarly articles on the issue of fiscal distress and local democracy; research, dissertations, and books about Flint, including but not limited to *Demolition Means Progress* (Highsmith 2015), *Teardown* (Young 2013), and *A Town Abandoned* (Dandaneau 1996); and Flint-based social media posts and blogs.[14]

Documentary content also included such local government records as EM executive orders, quarterly budgetary reports, statements of the EM, city council meeting minutes, "Imagine Flint" planning reports,[15] and election result data from the Genesee County Clerk's Office.[16]

The preliminary soaking and poking phase of the research project culminated in a short trip to Flint in March 2015, where I carried out five preliminary interviews with long-time residents and community activists. I spent a weekend in Flint meeting with people and walking and driving around the city.[17] These interviews and observations were useful in further identifying target interview participants as well as familiarizing myself with the city's neighborhoods and landmarks. Familiarizing myself with the city proved important during the interviews, as participants often referenced specific neighborhoods or landmarks in the city.

During my brief four-day trip to Flint, I met with people from a prominent anti-takeover group as well as a former employee of the city of Flint. My goal during these preliminary interviews was to get a sense of what was happening in Flint from the perspective of engaged community activists, identify gaps in my knowledge of the Flint case, begin building relationships with people in the city, and better understand how the research project could benefit the community. It was, and continues to be, my hope that this research is practical and collaborative, where appropriate. The preliminary interviews and observations aided in the development of my interview guides, discussed in more detail below, and served as a key element in the stakeholder analysis. The preliminary meetings were not recorded or coded, but notes from the meetings were included in the field notes.

Observation and Field Research

It was important to familiarize myself with the city and become known and trusted by leaders in the community.[18] Fieldwork for this project was carried out during two distinct time periods: June–November 2015 and June–September 2017.

I immersed myself in the community: conducted interviews, attended community meetings and public events, and lived in the city. I got coffee from local shops, spent time in the city library, walked through area parks, shopped at the Flint Farmers' Market, and rented rooms and apartments in various neighborhoods across the city. To supplement my interviews, I periodically attended and/or observed political events, such as city council meetings and political protests, which were aimed at Flint's water crisis.[19] Additionally, I documented my experiences and observations via field notes. My field notes were not coded or formally analyzed but instead served as initial impressions of the situation.[20] These notes served two purposes: (1) They helped me make sense of, and document, what I was seeing when engaging in participant observation. (2) They later aided in the interview coding process.

Semi-structured Interviews

For this project, I conducted both formal and informal interviews. Interviews were conducted from June to November 2015 and again from June to September 2017. In total, fifty-seven interviews were conducted, of which forty-eight were transcribed, coded, and used in the analysis. Of the interviews not included in the analysis, two were conducted with former Flint residents whose research focuses on Flint. These two interviews were used to inform my background knowledge of the city, aiding in "putting together the pieces of the puzzle," but were not included in the interpretive analysis.

Two other interviews were with community residents who wished to be involved but did not wish to be recorded for the interview. The remainder were informal, nonrecorded interviews conducted over the course of my fieldwork. These informal interactions took place at city council meetings, at charter review commission meetings, and over lunch. The comments were captured in my field notes but are not used in the interview analysis.

Interview participants were initially selected on the basis of a preliminary stakeholder analysis, discussed in more detail below, and then using purposive, snowball sampling, I recruited others to participate in the interviews. Ultimately, I identified the following groups for semistructured interviews:

- Local elected officials, including mayors and city councilors
- City employees and appointees
- Emergency (financial) managers and key advisors
- Receivership Transition Advisory Board (RTAB)
- Labor unions, including the UAW and AFSCME
- Community organizers and grassroots activists
- Neighborhood associations
- Faith communities, including Black churches
- County government
- Members of local government planning and advisory boards
- Genesee and Flint Chamber of Commerce
- Flint-based anchor institutions, including Hurley Hospital, UM-Flint, Mott Community College
- Community and economic development agencies, including public and private entities
- Local business owners and executives
- Foundations, including Community Foundation of Greater Flint, Ruth W. Mott and C. S. Mott Foundations
- Nonprofit executives and program managers
- Journalists and scholars with expertise on Flint politics (note, these individuals were not included in interview analysis but offered important insights regarding their own work in Flint)

Interview Participants

Among the forty-eight interviews that were transcribed, coded, and used in the analysis, seventeen participants were Black (35.4 percent), twenty-nine participants were White (60.4 percent) and two participants were Latinx (4.2 percent).[21] While this does not reflect the population of Flint, where 56.6 percent of the population identifies as Black or African American (U.S. Census 2010f), the larger proportion of White participants reflects the nature of Flint's business and nonprofit elite, who are disproportionately White. Additionally, due to the nature of snowball sampling, White community leaders often referred other White community leaders and residents. As noted in more detail in Chapter 4 ("Contextualizing the Flint

TABLE A1.1 INTERVIEW RESPONDENTS BY RACE AND TAKEOVER OPINION

	White	Black	Latinx	TOTAL
Support	4 (13.8%)	2 (11.7%)	0	6 (12.5%)
Oppose	13 (44.8%)	13 (76.5%)	2 (100%)	28 (58.3%)
Ambivalent	12 (41.4%)	2 (11.7%)	0	14 (29.1%)
TOTAL	29	17	2	48

Note: Interview participants' opinions of Flint's municipal takeover varied by race and ethnicity. Racial identification was determined by observation or self-identified at the time of the interview and was not explicitly asked as a part of the interview.

Case"), while the city is a majority-Black city, many city institutions, the Chamber of Commerce and Mott Foundations (both Ruth Mott and C. S. Mott), for example, are predominantly White institutions.

Interview participants who identified as Black came from all areas of community leadership, however. Black interview participants represented public, private, and nonprofit interests, but were disproportionately opposed to the takeover (thirteen of the seventeen interviewees explicitly opposed the takeover).

Interview participants were also disproportionately men. Of the forty-eight participants, only eighteen (37.5 percent) of the respondents were women. While gender was not a primary variable of interest in the initial investigation, gender became much more significant as the water crisis unfolded, as women disproportionately led efforts to address the crisis. Moreover, it did create a concern with regard to the confidentiality of the informants. As such, I gave many of the respondents gender-neutral pseudonyms and used the gender-neutral plural pronoun to refer to an individual respondent in an attempt to mask their gender and, therefore, identity.

Interview Guide

Interview requests were sent to key stakeholders asking them to participate in the study. Interview requests were also sent to state-level officials, including individuals in the governor's office and the Michigan Department of Treasury, but the requests were either referred to local-level representatives or were unanswered.

The interviews were semistructured, with open-ended questions that centered on three main areas: the individual's organizational affiliations and "relationship" with the city of Flint, the individual's perception and involvement in local government and politics, and the individual's perceptions of and involvement with the municipal takeover. A fourth section was added to the interview guide in 2017, which focused on the Flint water crisis. The interviews were conversational, and I encouraged the interviewees to tell stories about their civic and political involvement in Flint to encourage authenticity in their responses. The purpose of the interviews was twofold: (1) to fill in the gaps about Flint's takeover, particularly with regard to how, when, and by whom, decisions were made and (2) to identify the differences in how community leaders talked about the takeover, focusing on symbolic and ideational differences among individuals.

All interview participants, regardless of whether or not they were elected or appointed officials, were offered confidentiality. Some interview participants asked for their names to be included. Therefore, the interview participants' identities were masked except where explicitly requested by the participant. Interview participants were assigned pseudonyms, and their places of employment or service (if a volunteer or appointee) were removed from their transcriptions. In the analysis, individuals are identified generically as "local nonprofit executive" or "community activist." Interview participants were also given the option to review their transcripts. However, most participants declined this offer.

Locations for the interviews were determined by each participant, emphasizing both comfort and convenience. Most were carried out in person in a public setting or in interviewees' places of employment, although some were conducted in the interviewee's home or by phone.

Data Analysis

The research project follows an iterative process of data collecting, coding, and analysis. As the preceding sections suggest, the data collection process was adjusted as new details about the case were discovered. This section highlights the primary tools and procedures of analysis: stakeholder analysis, process tracing, and interpretive analysis.

Descriptive Analysis and Contextualization

Contextualization, Dvora Yanow notes, involves organizing data in a way that emphasizes the "thickly contextualized renderings of social realities."[22] The context of Flint, which has experienced all iterations of Michigan's municipal takeover law, for example, was important in case selection. Additionally, Flint's economic history and political history are significant contextual factors in understanding the impact of the takeover. For example, Flint was home to the first union sit-down strike, which catapulted the UAW to becoming a major political player at the national level. The union culture in Flint, nurtured over the years, was identified by interview participants as one of the major reasons why the community responded to the takeover in the way that it did.

The descriptive analysis of the city's economic and political history drew heavily on the data collected and reviewed during the soaking and poking stage of data collection. I used census data and reports from "Imagine Flint,"[23] the city's planning initiative, to lay out a demographic profile of the city. I then used newspaper articles, urban histories, and memoirs to discuss the city's political history.[24]

Process Tracing
I also examined the changes in local governance and changes in modes of participation over time, drawing on the tools of process tracing: thick description and *sequencing*.[25] I focused on the time frame between 2001, the year before the first takeover, and 2016, the year after the most recent takeover was lifted. Process tracing also helps identify the mechanisms that are situated between "some structural cause and its purported effect" by "assembling bits and pieces of information into a pattern."[26] In other words, I use thick description and sequencing to build a theoretical explanation for how municipal takeovers reshape local democracy.

Using both coded interview transcripts and documentary evidence, I first developed a time line from 2001 to 2016 (provided in Appendix 3) of events related to the city's fiscal stability and municipal takeovers. I then used the interview transcripts to identify key triggering events that the participants in the first round of interviews (thirty-five community leaders in total) identified as "important." These included the following:

- Elimination of the Office of the Ombudsman, the Civil Service Board, and Citizens Advisory Committees
- Selection and appointment of the Blue Ribbon Committee of Governance
- Creation and appointment of the Receivership Transition Advisory Board
- Selling of city assets, including the Detroit water pipeline, Genesee Towers, and Flint Farmers' Market
- Increased taxes and service fees, including streetlight assessment, water and sewer rates, and 6-mill tax levy
- Modifications of collective bargaining agreements with local unions
- Employee layoffs
- Closure of community assets, including community centers
- Water quality (e.g., lead contamination and bacteria) was later added, as the crisis unfolded after my initial fieldwork was concluded.
- I overlaid the sequencing evidence with data from interview participants and news reports about community responses to gauge changes in power and participation. I examined likely shifts in stakeholder power as well as modalities of participation with voter data, documentary evidence of engagement (e.g., news articles and reports of political protest), and interview transcripts to evaluate changes in the patterns of participation, including group formation (grassroots organizing). By placing the events, elections, and protests that developed in response to the municipal takeover onto the time line, I was able to identify causal mechanisms that explain how the changes (e.g., shifts in power and participation) were the result of the municipal takeover.

Interview Coding and Analysis

Interview transcripts served as the primary data source for this research project. Forty-eight of the interviews were recorded, transcribed, and coded. The data were then analyzed to identify key variables of interest, including how local governing structures and arrangements changed; instrumental effects, such as who benefited and who was burdened by the policy; and changing patterns of participation, such as the development of grassroots organizations. The data were then triangulated with other sources of data, such as newspaper articles and government reports, to verify the accuracy of the information.

Another important use of the interviews, however, was to examine the variation in interpretive effects. To uncover these effects, I drew on interpretive techniques often used in discourse analysis to identify themes in the interview transcripts. Coding and analysis was done using a phenomenological approach. According to John Cresswell, "a phenomenological study describes the meaning for several individuals of their lived experiences of a concept or a phenomenon."[27] The purpose of the phenomenological approach is to search for meaning in the data. The method is well suited to exploring Anne Schneider and Helen Ingram's social construction theory, which suggests that we create, in part, our knowledge and understanding of the work through collective agreement.[28] Schneider and Ingram argue that "different realities based on different beliefs, expectations, and interpretations may exist among different groups."[29] How different groups frame an issue is indicative of their different realities. In other words, the differences in how community leaders framed the underlying problems of the city and the municipal takeovers of Flint provide insights into how they understood, interpreted, and thus were affected by the takeover.

The data analysis process was conducted in steps. First, I read through the transcribed interview texts to identify "significant statements."[30] This also served as a means of further familiarizing myself with the data. At this time, I took margin notes (codes) regarding initial themes in the text. I considered these initial codes antecedents to broader analytical themes, which informed the second read-through. Many of the initial codes were derived from Deborah Stone's policy paradox framework. For example, I identified references to "efficiency" and "finances" as well as references to "democracy," "equity," or "equality."[31]

During the second read-through I identified and formalized the themes and codes and identified the relationships among various themes. This time I focused on two elements of the respondents' interview transcripts: (1) their interpretation or perception of the policies' target population/outcome and (2) their perception of who "wins" and who "loses" under municipal takeover. I was able to identify a correlation between those who supported municipal takeovers and their emphasis on economic and fiscal outcomes, for example.

Both the first and second read-throughs focused on looking for specific ideas, symbols, or analogies that characterized the respondents' perception of municipal takeover. The third and final read-through focused on identifying the symbolic effects that served to motivate and mobilize different forms of engagement. In the final read-through, for example, I identified how the issues of race, voting rights, civil rights, and union power informed the opposition's perception of the takeover, and thus their response.

Appendix 2

TABLE A2.1 STATE STATUTES ASSOCIATED WITH STATE INTERVENTION

State	State statutes
CT	Connecticut deals with fiscal distress in an ad hoc manner. Four special acts have been enacted to address local fiscal emergencies in the state: LCO 4532 (Waterbury); SA 92-5 (West Haven); SA 88-80, 89-23, 89-47, 90-31, 91-40 (Bridgeport); and SA 93-4 (Jewett City)
FL	Florida Statutes, Ch. 218 § 503, Financial Matters Pertaining to Political Subdivisions
IL	Illinois Municipal Code 65 ILCS 5/Art. 8 Div. 12, Financially Distressed City Law Illinois Municipal Code 50 ILCS 320/Art. 1, Local Government Financial Planning and Supervision Act
IN	Indiana Code § 6-1.1-20.3, Distressed Political Subdivisions and Distressed Unit Appeal Board
MA	Massachusetts deals with fiscal distress in an ad hoc manner. See MA Session Laws: Chapter 58 of the Acts of 2010 and Chapter 169 of the Acts of 2004.
ME	Maine, 30-A M.R.S.A. § 6101-6113, Municipal Finance Board
MI	Michigan Public Act 72, Act MSA 141.937, Sec. 7. (a) 1988, Michigan Local Government Fiscal Responsibility Michigan Public Act 4, *MSA* 5.2771 et seq. (2011), Local Government and School District Fiscal Accountability Act Michigan Public Act 436 of 2012, Local Financial Stability and Choice Act

(continued on next page)

TABLE A2.1 STATE STATUTES ASSOCIATED WITH STATE INTERVENTION *(continued from previous page)*

State	State statutes
NC	North Carolina Statutes 159.1–159-180
NH	New Hampshire, N.H. Rev. Stat. § 13:1 through 13:7
NJ	New Jersey, N.J.S.A. 52:27D-118.24 to 118.31, Special Municipal Aid Act New Jersey, R.S. 52:27-1 to R.S. 52:27-66, Municipal Finance Commission New Jersey Local Government Supervision Act, Title 40, Municipalities and Counties New Jersey Revised Statutes 52:27BBB and 52:27BB, Municipal Rehabilitation and Economic Recovery Act
NM	New Mexico Audit Act, N.M.S.A. 1978, § 12–6-1 through 12–6-14 and N.M.S.A. 1978, § 6-1-1 through § 6-1-13, § 10–5-2, and § 10–5-8
NV	Nevada, N.R.S. 354.655 through 354.725 Nevada Revised Statutes 354.655 to 354.725, Local Government Budget and Finance Act
NY	NY Unconsolidated Law Ch. 22 § 5, New York State Financial Emergency Act for the City of New York. New York deals with fiscal distress in an ad hoc manner. New legislation is passed for each municipality to establish an emergency financial control board.
OH	Ohio Revised Code Chapter 118, 133, 34, and 375.49, Local Fiscal Emergencies. *Note:* If a fiscal emergency is declared, a Financial Planning and Supervision Commission is formed for each distressed locality, or the state auditor becomes the financial supervisor if the locality has fewer than 1,000 people.
OR	Oregon, O.R.S. § 203.095–100 and § 287A.630
PA	Pennsylvania, PA ST 53 P.S. § 11701.101–712, Municipalities Financial Recovery Act and Intergovernmental Cooperation Authority Act
RI	Rhode Island Statutes, Title 45, Ch. 45–49, Budget Commissions
TN	Tennessee State Code Title 9, Chapter 13, Part 2, Emergency Financial Aid to Local Government, Law of 1995 Tennessee, T.C.A. § 9–13–301 to 302, Financially Distressed Municipalities, Counties, Utility Districts and Education Agencies Act of 1993 Tennessee, T.C.A. § 9–21–403, Local Government Public Obligations Act
TX	Texas Local Government Code § 101.006, Receivership for Payment of Debts. *Note:* Municipalities that cannot pay their debts can voluntarily request that a receiver be appointed by the court.

Appendix 3

TABLE A3.1 KEY EVENTS FROM FLINT'S MUNICIPAL TAKEOVERS

Date	Event/order/directive/action	Details
1988		
	Public Act 101 takes effect.	PA 101, Local Government Fiscal Responsibility Action, is adopted. The legislation is aimed at preventing court intervention and putting control back in the hands of state legislature. Hamtramck is the first city to be placed under an emergency financial manager (EFM).
1990		
May 15	Public Act 72 takes effect.	PA 72, Local Government Fiscal Responsibility Action, goes into effect.
2000		
February	Flint added to bond watch list.	Moody's Investor Services puts Flint's bond rating on a watch list, indicating that Flint is a risky investment.
February	Flint City Council concerned over finances, discusses state intervention.	City council members vote 7–2 to send a letter to the state regarding Flint's finances, but they never send the letter.
June	Mayor's budget rejected by council.	City council rejects Mayor Woodrow Stanley's budget, noting problems with projections and inaccurate information.
August	Mayor sues council.	Mayor Stanley sues city council over the budget struggle, ending in a compromise to lay off 100 city employees.
2001		
June	1999–2000 audit completed.	The 1999–2000 audit is completed 5 months late. Auditors cite the debt at $14.7 million.
August	Recall petition	Recall petition filed against Mayor Stanley.
December	Recall signatures submitted.	More than 13,000 signatures are submitted, enough to hold a recall election.

(continued on next page)

TABLE A3.1 KEY EVENTS FROM FLINT'S MUNICIPAL TAKEOVERS *(continued from previous page)*

Date	Event/order/directive/action	Details
2002		
January	Recall certified.	Recall petition certified. Election set for March 5.
February	Mounting debt	Auditors note the city's debt now at $28.4 million. Debt forecasted to reach $32.4 million by June 30.
March 5	Stanley recalled.	Voters recall Mayor Stanley, and City Administrator Darnell Earley becomes acting mayor.
March	Bob Emerson meets with city council and UAW.	State Senator Bob Emerson (D-Flint) meets with UAW Region 1-C leader Cal Rapson and city council president Scott Kincaid to discuss the decision to investigate Flint finances.
March 13	Senate Resolution 184	Senate Resolution 184, sponsored by Senator Robert (Bob) L. Emerson, the state senator for the district that includes the city of Flint, seeks a preliminary review by the state treasurer of the city of Flint's financial condition.
March 21	Special election postponed.	The state legislature passes a bill to postpone Flint's election to replace Stanley, giving time for a state review team to complete its work.
March 27	Governor Engler appoints review team.	Governor John Engler appoints a review team to evaluate Flint's financial condition.
April 22	City reorganization implementation approved.	The city council approves a citywide reorganization that implements many proposals for the 2001–2002 budget year.
April 26	Takeover recommended.	The governor-appointed review team recommends state takeover.
May 21	Rutherford submits petition to run for mayor.	James Rutherford submits a petition to run for mayor and is the only candidate to have enough valid signatures for the August 6 special election.
May 22	Financial emergency declared.	Engler declares financial emergency in Flint.
June 24	City appeals financial emergency.	City appeals state's declaration of financial emergency before state chief deputy treasurer Julie A. Croll.

July 8	Takeover approved.	Engler approves takeover, and Ed Kurtz is named emergency financial manager.
July 11	Judge blocks takeover to hear legal arguments.	Ingham County circuit judge James Giddings grants an injunction, blocking the takeover until legal arguments are heard.
August 6	Rutherford elected mayor.	Rutherford is elected to his second time in this office. He had previously served as mayor from 1975 to 1983; he had also served as Flint's chief of police from 1967 to 1975.
August 12	State appeals court ruling.	State of Michigan appeals Judge Giddings's ruling.
August 20	State Court of Appeals overrules injunction.	State Court of Appeals overrules Giddings's decision, saying Giddings had no authority to grant an injunction.
September 24	Salary and wage study	Kurtz hires an accounting and consulting firm to conduct a salary and wage study of top officials.
September 27	New code enforcement program	Kurtz implements a new code enforcement program that includes plans for annual rental inspections and emergency demolitions.
October 8	Salaries and benefits cut.	Kurtz cuts annual pay of mayor from $107,000 to $24,000, cuts pay of each of the nine council members from $23,000 to $18,000. Health, dental, and vision benefits are also eliminated for the majority of city officials.
October 14	Court battle ends.	City council ends 3-month battle to fight takeover. Court fight costs city more than $245,000.
October 16	Interim financial plan	Kurtz presents interim financial plan, which includes focuses on hiring, overnight travel, and spending.
November 12	Reduction in retiree pensions by 3.7 percent	Kurtz orders city retirement board to end controversial pension benefit, reducing the pensions of about 350 retirees by 3.7 percent and recouping previous overpayments made because of an apparent loophole.
November 12	Elimination of bonus checks for Hurley Medical Employees	A 13th-week bonus paycheck for Hurley Medical Center employees is also targeted.
December	Court rules no authority on retirement system.	State attorney general says Kurtz doesn't have the authority to issue orders to a retirement system.

(continued on next page)

TABLE A3.1 KEY EVENTS FROM FLINT'S MUNICIPAL TAKEOVERS *(continued from previous page)*

Date	Event/order/directive/action	Details
2002 *(cont.)*		
December	City audit indicates $26.6 million deficit.	First city audit completed in 5 years indicates that the city has a $26.6 million deficit.
December	Kurtz makes ultimatum.	Kurtz gives ultimatum of wage and benefit cuts or layoffs to city employees as talks with 6 unions are at a standstill. City audit shows a dent in the deficit.
December	Community centers closed.	Kurtz temporarily closes Flint's recreation centers, laying off 18 workers.
2003		
May	Office of the Ombudsman closed.	Kurtz closes the Office of the Ombudsman.
May	Water bill increased 11 percent.	Kurtz increases water rates by 11 percent.
September	Union agrees to 4 percent pay cut.	Union (AFSCME Local 1600) agrees to 4 percent pay cut.
October	Sewer and road improvement	Kurtz approves more than $1 million for improvements to city roads and sewers.
November 10	Williamson sworn in as mayor.	Don Williamson, a prominent businessman, is sworn into office as mayor of Flint. Williamson butts heads with Kurtz.
December	Budgets reduced.	Financial audits indicate that the city's deficit was reduced to $14 million. Estimates for the 2003–2004 budget reduce the number to $6–8 million.
2004		
February 17	City Retirement Board approves reduction in city contribution.	The city Retirement Board approves four proposals that lower the amount the city has to pay into the system, under Kurtz's threat of massive layoffs and replacement of the board.

March 24	Pay for mayor and city council reinstated.	Kurtz announces that he will reinstate some pay for the mayor and city council members.
May	City layoffs	Kurtz lays off 10 employees as a part of his plan to eliminate 35 jobs for the 2004–2005 budget.
June	End of takeover recommended.	Kurtz recommends that the takeover end. According to the *Flint Journal*, during his time in office he has issued nearly 120 directives. State oversight continues through January 2006.
2005		
June 30		Flint has a $6.1 million general fund surplus (Scorsone and Bateson 2011; Flint 2010, "CAFR"). June 30 is the fiscal year (FY) end.
2006		
January	Ombudsman Jessie Binion resigns post.	Jessie Binion, who had served as Flint Ombudsman with a salary of nearly $200,000 per year, resigns after a prolonged four-year leave of absence due to illness (Snell 2006a).
February 28	City Charter amendments voted down.	A proposal to eliminate the city Office of the Ombudsman, which investigates complaints about city departments, is rejected by a margin of 53–47 (only 8 percent of registered voters voted).
March	Tumultuous process to appoint Ombudsman	Tyrone Croom is appointed city ombudsman on March 9 (Snell 2006a), but he abruptly resigns after corruption allegations surface. Brenda Purifoy, retired Flint police sergeant and active member of Flint NAACP, is appointed on May 9.
June 6	City Council votes to cut funding to Office of Ombudsman.	Despite a budget surplus, the city council votes, 5–4, to "cut the watchdog agency's $460,000 budget in half," with the other half allocated to hiring more police officers (Snell 2006b).
December	Williamson creates Citizen's Service Bureau.	Williamson creates Citizen's Service Bureau within police department, which is met with a lot of controversy.
2007		
July	Williamson announces budget surplus.	Williamson announces budget surplus.

(continued on next page)

TABLE A3.1 KEY EVENTS FROM FLINT'S MUNICIPAL TAKEOVERS (continued from previous page)

Date	Event/order/directive/action	Details
2009		
February 8	Don Williamson resigns as mayor.	Facing a recall election on February 24, Williamson announces he will resign as mayor effective February 14, stating that he is doing so for health reasons.
February 16	Michael Brown is assumes role of interim mayor.	Michael Brown, who was serving as city administrator, succeeds Williamson as interim mayor.
August 5	Dayne Walling elected mayor.	Walling is elected mayor is a special election. He wins 12,266–6876 against Brenda Clack.
2010		
	Discussions on the creation of the Karegnondi Water Authority (KWA)	Representatives from the city of Flint and other city and county officials begin exploring the potential of a new water pipeline, calling it the Karegnondi Water Authority (KWA).
2011		
March 16	PA 4 takes effect.	PA 4 takes effect, expanding the powers of the state-appointed manager, now referred to as EM (rather than EFM).
May 16	Stand Up for Democracy	The Stand Up for Democracy Campaign forms to overturn PA 4.
August 2	Flint mayoral primary election	Incumbent mayor, Dayne Walling, receives the most votes and proceeds to the November run-off election.
August 2	Flint mayor notified of financial review intentions.	Mayor Walling is notified—on the day of the primary—that the State Treasurer's Office is planning to place Flint under financial review.
August 29	Flint financial review announced.	State treasurer, Andy Dillan, announces that Flint is to undergo a financial review under PA 4 to determine probable fiscal distress.
September 30	Financial Review Team appointed.	Governor Rick Snyder appoints an 8-member Financial Review Team to evaluate whether a financial emergency exists in Flint.
November 7	Financial emergency announced.	The State Financial Review Board, led by Bob Henderson, announces a financial emergency in Flint.
November 8	Election day	Mayor Walling is re-elected to his first full term.

November 11	Michael Townsend fired.	Michael Townsend, Flint's finance director, is terminated days after a state review panel declares Flint in a financial emergency.
November 14	City council votes not to appeal.	Flint City Council votes against appealing the findings of the Financial Review Team (7–2 vote, Neeley and Sarginson voted to appeal).
November 15	Walling declines hearing.	Mayor Walling does not request a hearing on the Financial Review Team's recommendation that the state take over the city and appoint an emergency manager.
November 29	Governor Rick Snyder names Michael Brown Flint's emergency manager.	Michael Brown is named emergency manager. Brown had a long history of working in the Flint community: County Commissioner (1981–1984); Flint director of community development and government relations (1987–1991); president of United Way of Genesee and Lapeer Counties (1996–2002); executive vice president of Public Policy for Genesee Regional Chamber of Commerce (2008–2009); interim mayor for city of Flint (2009); and director of Flint Area Reinvestment Office at C. S. Mott Foundation (2009–2011).
December 1	Emergency manager takes office.	Mike Brown takes office as first Flint emergency manager.
December 1	**Executive Order 001:** Termination of Appointments	As noted in the order, "Pursuant to Public Act 4, the Emergency Manager may, at his discretion, remove appointees to any office, board, commission, or other entity which is within or is a component unit of local government." Seven people were are terminated, including Greg Eason (city administrator), Donna Poplar (Human Resources and Labor Relations), Edward Parker (Civil Service Commission), Brenda Purifoy (Office of the Ombudsman), Rhoda Matthews (Citizens Services), Steve Montle (Green City's coordinator), and Kathleen Sheetz (executive secretary).
December 1	**Executive Order 002:** Elimination of Salaries and Benefits for Mayor and City Council	The salary and all compensation for the mayor and members of city council are eliminated. They are later partially restored.
December 8	**Executive Order 003:** Procedures for Purchasing	The contracting or procurement of all goods and services, in any amount, must be authorized by the emergency manager or Purchasing Department; the Purchasing Department may review and approve purchases with accumulated value of $10,000 or less without EM approval.

(continued on next page)

TABLE A3.1 KEY EVENTS FROM FLINT'S MUNICIPAL TAKEOVERS *(continued from previous page)*

Date	Event/order/directive/action	Details
2011 *(cont.)*		
December 8	**Executive Order 004:** Procedure for Submission of Resolutions and Ordinances	Establishes strict guidelines and timelines for submitting resolutions and ordinances.
December 8	**Executive Order 005:** Elimination of Office of the Ombudsman	Established by the 1974 City Charter, the Office of the Ombudsman investigates grievances of city residents regarding city agencies.
December 8	**Executive Order 006:** Elimination of Civil Service Commission	Established by the 1974 City Charter, the Civil Service Commission investigates grievances of city employees. At the time of the office's elimination, it had 15 ongoing cases.
December 13	**Executive Order 007:** Budgetary Oversight and Termination of Line-Item Level	The order notes: "Based on the foregoing, it is hereby ordered that, in light of the City's financial challenges, all City Officials, Department Heads and Division Heads shall adhere to the following budgetary guidelines and responsibilities: 1. Budgetary authority is **not** a mandate to spend. [emphasis in original] 2. Departmental expenses are to be managed within the amounts authorized in the department's budgets. 3. All possible actions are to be taken to keep expenses as low as possible. 4. It is vital that all budgeted revenues are collected. 5. It is extremely important that all are continuously seeking and recommending ways of operating more efficiently and at lesser cost. 6. All budgetary revenues and expenditures must be continually monitored and the Finance Department must be immediately advised of any variances that become apparent, along with recommendations for addressing such variances."
December 16	Flint "Invitation-Only" Community Roundtable on Crime	Governor Snyder, Emergency Manager Brown, and Police Chief Lock hold an "invitation-only" roundtable discussion regarding crime with community members, including "community leaders from local churches, the Genesee Regional Chamber of Commerce, the Charles Steward Mott Foundation, local schools and

December 16	Protest	municipalities." The governor calls for more law enforcement officers, an improved criminal justice system, and more jobs (Longley 2011d).
		Small protest takes place outside the "invitation-only" roundtable, led by Paul Jordan, local activist and former Flint school board member.
December 19	**Executive Order 008:** Advisory Committee	Per the contract for Emergency Manager Services signed with the state, the emergency manager must recommend an advisory committee of 3–5 members: "The membership shall be one representative of the City's elected officials, one representative of the Flint business community, one citizen of Flint and up to two more persons with interest in and knowledge of the Flint community and relevant professional skills to assist the Emergency Manager." Under the order, Brown recommends the following individuals to serve on the advisory committee: Mayor Dayne Walling Councilman Delrico Lloyd, First Ward; international service representative for UAW, region 1-C Kenyetta Dotson, anti-violence activist and founder of Community Action Group/WOW Outreach Latrelle Holmes, VP of Finance at Big Brothers, Big Sisters of Greater Flint Tim Herman, CEO of Flint and Genesee Chamber of Commerce
December 20	**Executive Order 009:** Mayor's Responsibilities and Partial Compensation Restoration	Mayor Walling's pay is partially restored. His role with the city is outlined, including responsibility for community and citizen engagement, intergovernmental affairs and policy, comprehensive master plan, and economic development. The only mention of policy authority is "develop City of Flint policies and procedures to create positive business climate."
December 20	**Executive Order 010:** City Council's Responsibilities and Partial Compensation Restoration	The order reads: "Council shall convene in City Council Chambers one time per month as scheduled by the Emergency Manager for the purpose of listening to public comment, conducting public hearings and addressing other matters submitted by the Emergency Manager. Council members shall address the concerns of their respective constituencies. Individual Council members shall attend ward meetings in their respective wards as directed by the Emergency Manager, and shall be responsible for communicating information about ward meetings to their constituency so as to promote community awareness, including the date, time and location of such meetings. Individual Council members shall serve on committees as directed by the Emergency Manager."

(continued on next page)

TABLE A3.1 KEY EVENTS FROM FLINT'S MUNICIPAL TAKEOVERS *(continued from previous page)*

Date	Event/order/directive/action	Details
2012		
January 11	**Executive Order 011:** Procedure for Submission of Matters Involving Planning Commission Recommendations	Procedures identified for taking action where state or city law requires a recommendation by the City Planning Commission, including zoning ordinances, vacating a street, and street name change. The procedures indicate that the Emergency Manager will "approve or disapprove of the proposal," thus granting final authority to the EM.
January 11	**Executive Order 012:** Monthly Meetings with City Council	EM will hold a monthly meeting with city council to provide a status report and to answer questions of the council members. Meetings will be open to the public and will provide opportunity for public comment. Meetings to be held the second Monday of every month, 5:30–7:30 P.M. Public comment time restricted to 5 minutes, one comment per person. Further restrictions on public comment are outlined as follows: "Any person attending a meeting may be called to order by the Council President or any councilperson for failure to be germane, for vulgarity, for personal attack of persons or institutions, or for speaking in excess of the allotted time. A person called to order shall thereupon take his or her seat until the Council President shall have determined whether he or she is in order. Every question of order shall be decided by the Council President. If a person so engaged in presentation shall be determined by the Council President to be out of order, that person shall not be permitted to continue at the same meeting."
January 15	45-day plan	Brown lays out his 45-day plan, "The Financial and Operating Plan"
January 16	"Occupy for Democracy" Protest in Lansing	A group of Michigan residents, including a busload from Flint, protests outside the governor's home in Lansing.
January 17	Brown submits Financial and Operating Plan to the state.	Identifies the following as the primary goals: "1. Long-term financial stability; 2. An increase in revenue base to provide quality services to its residents; 3. A reduction in government costs through negotiated union contracts, consolidation and shared services, and ongoing professional development of staff;

		4. Continue to maintain and modernize the infrastructure of the city in alignment with the current population counts; 5. To streamline the processes necessary for businesses to locate, and continue operations, in the city; 6. To utilize the Master Plan to stabilize and then increase both the commercial and residential base of the city; 7. To provide public safety services, focusing on reducing violent crime, commensurate with cities of comparable size and resources" (Brown 2012).
February	Ward-based community meetings	"Community engagement" meetings are hosted throughout the city in each of the nine wards: February 2: Ninth Ward February 7: Seventh Ward February 9: Fifth Ward February 16: Second Ward February 20: Fourth Ward February 23: First Ward February 27: Third Ward February 28: Eighth Ward March 1: Sixth Ward
March 7	Governor Snyder delivers public safety address from Flint City Hall.	Governor Snyder calls for re-opening the Flint local jail and increasing the state police presence in the city. In his address he notes budget allocations of $4.5 million to further enhance Flint lockup and $900,000 for prosecutorial support.
March 15	Temporary restraining order against EM Brown actions	Judge grants temporary restraining order against any action by Brown, pending a lawsuit by city employee and head of AFSCME local 1600, Sam Muma, alleging the state violated the Open Meetings Act by appointing Brown without public deliberation.
March 20	Ingham County Circuit Court judge rules in favor of Muma.	Ingham County judge rules in favor of Muma. Brown is removed from office, and authority is restored to mayor and council.
March 26	Michigan Court of Appeals reinstates Brown's authority.	Brown is reinstated by the Michigan Court of Appeals.

(continued on next page)

TABLE A3.1 KEY EVENTS FROM FLINT'S MUNICIPAL TAKEOVERS *(continued from previous page)*

Date	Event/order/directive/action	Details
2012 *(cont.)*		
April 13	**Executive Order 013:** Modification of Settlement Agreement with URGE	Modification of city-approved settlement agreement with United Retired Governmental Employees (URGE) regarding prescription drug coverage, from 2002. Modified to increase required co-pay on non-generic drugs. (Effective May 1, 2012.)
April 20	Barnett Jones appointed public safety administrator	Barnett Jones, former police chief of Ann Arbor, is named public safety administrator to oversee police and fire and develop a public safety plan. His salary is $135,000, paid for by a grant from the C. S. Mott Foundation.
April 24	**Executive Orders 014, 015, 016:** Approval of Collective Bargaining Agreements	Approval of collective bargaining agreements with P.O.L.C-Flint Police Sergeants Union, P.O.L.C.-Flint Police Captains and Lieutenants Union, and I.A.F.F.-Flint Firefighters Union.
April 25	**Executive Order 017:** Approval of 2013 Budget	Approves and adopts FY 2013 budget, which notes that staffing reductions set forth in the FY 2013 budget shall immediately be implemented as an amendment to the current FY 2012 budget, as directed by the emergency manager. The budget includes a new $66 street light assessment and a $143 trash collection fee that replaces the 3-mill waste-collection tax (Executive Orders 028 and 030).
April 25	**Executive Order 018:** Flint Police Officers Association Contract Provision Modification/Termination	The order reads, in part: "As part of our plan to reduce costs, Attorney John Clark and other members of my team have met with the Flint Police Officers Association ('FPOA') in an attempt to meet and confer over our proposed concessions. My team met with the executive committee of FPOA and its attorney on March 15, 2012, March 30, 2012, April 13, 2012, April 17, 2012, and April 19, 2012. The FPOA has refused to agree to any of our proposed concessions." Therefore on April 11, 2012, the EM requested that the state treasurer concur with the modification of certain sections of the Collective Bargaining Agreement. Details of the imposed concessions are specified in the order.

Date	Action	Description
April 25	**Executive Order 019, 020, 021, 022, 023, 024, 025:** Insurance Recipients	Changes/modifications in health insurance coverage for non-union actives and retirees, and modifications to collective bargaining agreements regarding health coverage for P.O.I.C.-Flint Police Sergeants Union Retirees; P.O.I.C.-Flint Police Captains and Lieutenants Union Retirees; Flint Police Officers Association Union Retirees; Flint I.A.F.F.-Flint Firefighters Union Retirees; AFSCME Local 1600 Retirees; and AFSCME Local 1799 Retirees.
April 25	**Executive Order 026:** Contract Provision Modification/Termination with AFSCME Local 1600	The order reads, in part: "As part of our plan to reduce costs, Attorney Kendall Williams and other members of my team have met with the executive committee of AFSCME Local 1600 in an attempt to meet and confer over our proposed concessions. My team met with the executive committee of AFSCME Local 1600 and its attorney on March 7, 2012, April 11, 2012, April 12, 2012, April 13, 2012, April 16, 2012 and April 17, 2012 to confer over our proposed concessions. AFSCME Local 1600 has refused to agree to any of our proposed concessions." Therefore, on April 23, 2012, the EM requested that the state teasurer concur in his modification of certain sections of the Collective Bargaining Agreement. Details of the imposed concessions specified in the order.
April 25	**Executive Order 027:** Approval of Collective Bargaining Agreement with AFSCME Local 1799	Approval of Collective Bargaining Agreement with AFSCME Local 1799.
April 25	**Executive Order 028:** Waste Collection User Fee	Order reads, in part: "The City has collected a special 3 mill property tax levy for waste collection. However, the amount collected from the levy has reduced as property values have fallen, while costs have increased. As a result, the City's General Fund has subsidized waste collection by up to $1.5 million. The City's General Fund can no longer subsidize waste collection. The City has authority to collect a user fee for waste collection, disposal and related activities under the Home Rule City Act, Act 279." The order discontinued the 3-mill levy for waste collection, implementing a user fee in its place.
April 26	Board of Canvassers vote, 2–2, to put referendum on ballot.	The Michigan Board of Canvassers certifies the language for PA 4 referendum.

(continued on next page)

TABLE A3.1 KEY EVENTS FROM FLINT'S MUNICIPAL TAKEOVERS *(continued from previous page)*

Date	Event/order/directive/action	Details
2012 *(cont.)*		
May 30	**Executive Order 029:** Application to State Administrative Board for Approval to Issue Not to Exceed $9,300,00 in Fiscal Stabilization Bonds	The order reads: "Subject to the limitations of Section 4(8) of Act No. 80, the Emergency Manager hereby determines that it is necessary to issue its bonds (the 'Bonds') pursuant to Act No. 80 in the principal amount not to exceed $9,300,000, for the purpose of providing funds to find (i) all or a portion of the accumulated operating deficit for the fiscal year ended June 30, 2011 and a portion of its projected accumulated operating deficit for the fiscal year ended June 30, 2012, (ii) an amount necessary to prepay all or a portion of the principal of and interest on obligations or bonds of the City as in the Bond Authorizing Order, if outstanding when the Bonds are issued and so determined by the City at the time of sale of the Bonds, (iii) a reserve to secure payment of principal of or interest on the Bonds in an amount not exceeding the maximum amount of principal and interest coming due on the Bonds in any fiscal year, if necessary, (iv) a discount of not to exceed 10% of the principal amount of the Bonds, and (v) an amount sufficient to pay all legal, financial, accounting, printing and other expenses related to the issuance of the Bonds. State 'holds off' and requests that the city wait for a better interest rate."
May 30	**Executive Order 030:** Special Assessment for Street Lighting	Imposes a tentative street light assessment of $62 per parcel to cover the FY 2013 budget appropriation of $2,850,000 for street light expenses to operate and maintain 11,292 streetlights citywide. Public Hearing set for May 31 at 11 A.M. to discuss creation of street light assessment district.
May 30	**Executive Order 031:** Water and Sewer Rate Increase	Water and sewer rate is increased.
May 31	Public hearing regarding street light assessment	According to the *Flint Journal*, the public hearing was attended by only 3 people, all of whom objected to the fee. Officials indicated that another public hearing would be set for June.
June 8	Layoff notices of city employees	Nearly 100 city employees received layoff notices as part of the 2013 budget. No police and fire workers were cut because of a $6.9 million federal grant.
June 12	Most violent city	Flint is identified as the most violent city in America for the third straight year.

June 13	Arsons make national news.	For the third consecutive year, Flint is identified as having the most arsons per capita in the nation.
June 14	Hundreds of residents attend June hearing on street light assessment.	More than 200 community members turn out for the June hearing. More than 100 people fill out forms to speak at the hearing.
June 27	**Executive Order 032:** Establishment of Special Assessment for Street Lighting	Street light assessment is set at $66.05 per parcel. Assessment is to be collected July 1, 2012, through a property tax bill for all property owners.
July 11	Brown meets with Flint Police Officers Association (FPOA).	EM Brown and FPOA are unable to come to a "prompt and satisfactory resolution" (as cited in EO 034, August 8).
August 8	**Executive Order 033:** Consolidation of Flint Area Enterprise Community with Economic Development Corporation and Elimination of Citizens District Councils	Consolidates the Flint Area Enterprise Community (FAEC) with the Enterprise Economic Development Corporation (EDC), with the EDC authority and control of the FAEC. The citywide advisory committee, Smith Village Citizen's District Council, I-475 Neighborhood Development Citizens District Council, and Flint Park Lake Citizens District Council are all eliminated.
August 8	**Executive Order 034:** Flint Police Officers Association Union Contract Provision Modification/Termination	Flint Police Officers Association Union retirement plan is transferred to the Municipal Employees' Retirement System of Michigan (MERS) after the EM declares the meeting between parties unsatisfactory.
August 8	Brown signs 30 resolutions on last day as EM.	Resolutions and actions include the following: Resolution to demolish and replace Genesee Towers with "urban plaza" Puts 6-mill public safety tax increase on November ballot to eliminate city's dependence on grants from foundations and federal government Approved development agreement with Genesee Towers to transfer ownership to a new owner for it to be demolished—transfer ownership to Uptown Reinvestment Corp for $1. The agreement is signed by Brown and Uptown president Tim Herman.

(continued on next page)

TABLE A3.1   KEY EVENTS FROM FLINT'S MUNICIPAL TAKEOVERS *(continued from previous page)*

Date	Event/order/directive/action	Details
2012 *(cont.)*		
August 8	State Board of Canvassers places the issue of repealing PA 4 on the ballot.	As directed by the Michigan Supreme Court, the State Board of Canvassers certifies the referendum and places the issue of repealing PA 4 of 2011 on the November 6, 2012, ballot. In so doing, PA 4 is suspended, in accordance with Michigan's Constitution. PA 72 of 1990 is reinstated, in effect.
August 8	Ed Kurtz appointed EFM, under PA 72.	Ed Kurtz is appointed as EFM by the state's Emergency Financial Assistance Loan Board. Brown was is not eligible to serve as EFM under PA 72 because he was an employee, and interim mayor, of the city during the previous 5 years. Brown notes, however, that an EFM is still necessary, indicating that "cash flow is minimal" and that $19 million in past debt is still to be resolved (Longley 2012c).
August 8	Michael Brown appointed city administrator by Kurtz.	Ed Kurtz, incoming EFM, appoints outgoing EM Mike Brown as his city administrator. Kurtz states, "This will keep the current management team in place and offer stability to city government as it continues to rebuild and restructure itself financially" (Longley 2012f).
August 20	Prayer protests and civil rights rally	Concerned Pastors for Social Action and North Flint Reinvestment Corporation organize protest and rally and submit list of "desired outcomes" to EFM.
August 24	**Executive Order EFM001, EFM002, EFM003:** Procedures for Purchasing, Procedures for Submission of Resolutions and Ordinances, Budgetary Oversight	Sets procedures for purchasing, procedures for submission of resolutions and ordinances, and budgetary oversight pursuant to PA 72.
August 24	**Executive Order EFM004:** Advisory Council	Pursuant to PA 72 guidelines and the Contract for Emergency Financial Manager Services signed by the Local Emergency Financial Assistance Loan Board, the EFM recommends the following individuals to serve on the EFM's Advisory Committee:

September 10	City council files lawsuit against Kurt's appointment.	Mayor Dayne Walling Kenyetta Dotson, anti-violence activist and founder of Community Action Group/WOW Outreach Reverend Phillip Thompson, Bethlehem Temple Church Tim Herman, CEO of Flint and Genesee Chamber of Commerce Flint City Council files lawsuit against Kurt's appointment, seeking an injunction.
September 12	Executive Order EFM005: City Treasurer Authorized to Correct Assessments	The order reads: "City Treasurer is authorized to make the necessary correction to an assessment or fee that was placed on the tax roll in the event it is determined that property owner is entitled to a waiver."
September 14	Executive Order EFM006: Overtime	The order notes: "All overtime must be directly approved by the department head in advance, with the exception of emergency overtime that can be clearly documented. In the Police Department, requests for overtime should be directed to Chief Alvern Lock. In the Fire Department, requests for overtime should be directed to Public Safety Administrator Barnett Jones."
October 1	Flint city lock-up opens.	The lockup facility opens for the first time since 2008, housing up to 110 inmates. The estimated operating cost is $2.1 million annually.
October 8	City council adopts Ordinance No. 3826.	On October 8, 2012, Flint City Council adopts Ordinance No. 3826, changing the rental property inspection period from 3 to 5 years.
October 11	Executive Order EFM007: City Council Adoption of Amendment to Rental Inspection Ordinance Null and Void	Ordinance No. 3826 is rendered null and void under the order. As outlined in the order, "The ordinance changes the rental property inspection period from 3 to 5 years" and thus "will result in less revenue for the city." The order notes that the ordinance was adopted without approval of the EFM or approval of the chief legal officer.
October 22	Executive Order EFM008: Poverty Exemption to Street Lighting Assessment	The order states: "The City of Flint recognizes that this special assessment will impose a financial hardship on certain residents. For this reason, the Emergency Manager hereby orders that individuals who qualify for relief from property taxes may also, upon request, be provided relief from the street lighting special assessment."

(continued on next page)

TABLE A3.1 KEY EVENTS FROM FLINT'S MUNICIPAL TAKEOVERS *(continued from previous page)*

Date	Event/order/directive/action	Details
2012 *(cont.)*		
November 6	Michigan voters overturn PA 4.	Michiganders vote 53 percent to 47 percent to strike down a referendum on Public Act (PA) 4.
November 6	Flint voters approve public safety tax increase.	Voters of the city of Flint vote in support of the 6-mill public safety tax increase, with approximately 59 percent of the ballots cast in support of the ballot (25,198 total votes cast).
December 12	**Executive Order EFM009:** Invalidating Council Action	The order is related to City Council Resolution No. 12084.1, which overturned a Freedom of Information Act (FOIA) request by a plaintiff in lawsuit against the city of Flint. The order renders City Council Resolution No. 121084 null and void, "because (1) it was adopted in violation of Flint City Charter, and (2) it violates Public Act 72 by usurping the authority of the Emergency Financial Manager."
December 27	PA 436 approved.	PA 436 is approved by the Michigan State Legislature.
2013		
January 10	Barnett Jones resigns.	Jones, Flint's administrator for public safety, resigns after it is discovered he is also the head of security for the Detroit Water and Sewerage Department.
February 7	Flint Police Officers Association files lawsuit against city over forced concessions.	Forced concessions include a 5 percent wage cut, reduced retirement benefits, and increased hours per shift.
March 15	**Executive Order EFM010:** Grant Applications	Lays out the process for submitting, approving, and accepting grants on behalf of the city. Primary responsibility and authorization for approving rests with the EFM or city administrator (Brown).
March 25	Flint City Council votes to support joining KWA pipeline.	Flint City Council votes to support joining KWA pipeline, though the vote is symbolic.
March 27	**Executive Order EFM011:** Water Services Procedures	New procedures are adopted regarding water services in an effort to address the "substantial financial impact" in the delivery of water services.

March 28	PA 436 goes into effect.	PA 436 goes into effect and effectively repeals PA 72. It is a response to the repeal of PA 4 by a ballot initiative in November 2012. The new law offers some minor changes from PA 4, most notably budget allocations, making it effectively immune from future ballot referenda.
March 28	Ed Kurtz appointed emergency manager.	Kurtz continues his tenure as Flint's second state-appointed manager, but his title switches from EFM to EM under PA 436.
March 28	**Executive Order 001:** Mayor Responsibilities and Partial Restoration of Pay	Identical order to EO 009 under PA 4. But this time it is under the authority of Ed Kurtz, pursuant to his authority under PA 436.
March 28	**Executive Order 002:** City Council's Responsibilities and Partial Restoration of Compensation	In addition to the language found in EO 010 in 2011, this order lays out obligations of the council and requires acknowledgment and agreement to abide in order to be eligible for compensation: "1. Meet once per month (4th Monday) in order to hear concerns from constituents. Council members must be in attendance throughout the meeting. 2. Accept and respond to constituent calls and requests for information. Council members shall submit actionable items to the Emergency Manager in writing 3. Schedule meetings as requested by the Emergency Manager to address issues that have a significant impact on the City, such as the Comprehensive Master Plan, KWA, Charter Revisions, and other issues that may arise. 4. Complete Level One of the Michigan Municipal League (MML) core courses for municipal government and receive the MML Education Award within one year. The City will pay for costs of the actual training, exclusive of travel, lodging and meals. 5. All communication with staff must be in writing and directed through the Emergency Manager's office. 6. Comply with any other request authorized by Public Act 436 from the Emergency Manager on timely basis."
April 16	Kurtz signs agreement with KWA.	EM Kurtz signs agreement with KWA after officials from DWSD make offer to try to keep Flint as a customer. It is reported that it will be at least 2.5 years before the new KWA pipeline will be complete.

(continued on next page)

TABLE A3.1 KEY EVENTS FROM FLINT'S MUNICIPAL TAKEOVERS *(continued from previous page)*

Date	Event/order/directive/action	Details
2013 *(cont.)*		
April 17	Detroit Water and Sewerage Department announces termination of contract.	In response to Flint joining KWA, Detroit Water and Sewerage Department (DWSD) announces termination of water contract, giving the city one year.
May 29	Kurtz submits resignation letter.	Kurtz submits resignation to Governor Snyder, indicating July 3 as his last day.
June 6	**Executive Order 003:** Special Assessment District for Street Lighting	The order effectively increases the street lighting assessment to $67.87 per parcel, an increase of $1.82 per parcel. The order expressly indicates that "all funds will be used exclusively for the purpose intended—for the payment of costs permitted under MCL 117.4d(2)(b), including engineering, financial, legal, administrative services, and operation and maintenance of the lighting system." The order indicates a planned public hearing for June 11, 2013.
June 11	Street light assessment hearing	During the hearing, the city reports that it can no longer provide street lighting without reducing other public services, including fire and police. Brown, currently serving in the role of city administrator to EM Kurtz, reports that he is considering the creation of a special assessment district.
June 13	**Executive Order 004:** Adoption of Fiscal Year 2014 Budget	Kurtz signs his final executive order, adopting the FY 2014 budget.
June 26	Resolution adopted to prepare Flint Water Treatment Plant to treat water.	Kurtz signs a resolution "authorizing approval to enter into a professional engineering services contract for the implementation of placing the Flint Water Plant into operation."
June 26	Brown appointed emergency manager, July 8.	Governor Snyder appoints Michael Brown to serve as emergency manager, effective July 8.
July 3	Ed Kurtz last day as EM	

Date	Event	Description
July 8	Brown takes over as emergency manager.	Mike Brown begins his second term as Flint emergency manager.
July 19	Townsend settlement	Flint settles lawsuit with former finance director, Townsend, for more than $250,000.
September 11	Brown announces resignation.	Michael Brown announces his resignation as EM on September 11. He is replaced by Darnell Earley, former city administrator of Flint (and more recently city administrator of Saginaw).
September 11	New appointments to KWA board	In a series of resolutions, Brown appoints Josh Freeman, Steve Landaal, and Sheldon Neeley to the KWA board.
November 1	**Executive Order 1**: City Council Schedule for Remainder of 2013	Order sets the schedule for council meetings in November and December.
December 11	**Executive Order 2**: Cancellation of City Council Meeting	December council meeting is canceled.
December 11	**Executive Order 3**: Directives to Councilman Eric Mays	Order publicly berates councilman Eric Mays, First Ward, for his behavior and specifies directives for how Mays should communicate with the EM, via e-mail only.
2014		
January 15	**Executive Order 4**: Confirmation of Council Committee Appointments	Order confirms City Council Committee appointments. Notes that all meetings convened on behalf of the committees must be scheduled by the emergency manager or his designee.
January 23	Blue Ribbon Committee	Earley appoints a 23-member Blue Ribbon Committee on Governance.
January 31	**Executive Order 5**: City Council and Council Committee Meeting Schedule	Order approves and posts February meeting schedule.

(continued on next page)

TABLE A3.1 KEY EVENTS FROM FLINT'S MUNICIPAL TAKEOVERS *(continued from previous page)*

Date	Event/order/directive/action	Details
2014 *(cont.)*		
February 25	**Executive Order 6:** Confirmation of City Council Committee Appointments	Order establishes Public Works and Planning and Development Committees and renames Finance as Finance and Administration.
February 25	**Executive Order 7:** Authority for Presentation of Mayor's State of City Address	Order authorizes mayor to give State of the City address on March 3, 2014.
March 5	**Executive Order 8:** Council Meeting Protocol	This orders sets out the policies and procedures for city council meetings to ensure that "the business of the City of Flint conducted at City Council meetings occurs in an orderly, dignifies, and efficient manner." Protocol is as follows: "At meetings of the Flint City Council each Council member shall be afforded five (5) minutes to address matters open before Council; to make referrals; to respond to public comment; or to discuss issues concerning the City of Flint. Council members shall not yield time to fellow members. The period for Council member comment shall appear on the agenda and shall be the last item on the agenda. The City Clerk shall keep time and shall issue a warning when a member has one (1) minute remaining to speak. Otherwise, Council members shall not make comments during Council meetings, other than to respond to roll call or to respond directly to a request of the Council President, or at his recognition. When recognizing a member, the Council President shall limit comments, discussion or debate to a reasonable amount of time."
March 6	**Executive Order 6.1:** Revision to Confirmation of City Council Committee Appointments	Order switches members of Public Works and Planning and Development committees. In addition, the order notes, "This Order No. 6.1 supersedes Order No.6 dated February 25, 2014."
March 21	**Executive Order 9:** Monthly City Council and Committee Schedule	Order provides schedule for April.

April 1	**Executive Order 10:** City Council Agenda	Agenda for meetings is laid out. Limitation on public comment is set at 3 minutes.
April 19	**Executive Order 11 (22):** Street Lighting Assessment FY 2015 and FY 2016	Order notes that the street light assessment set at "$70.94 per parcel in comparison to the current assessment" and for FY 2016 will "tentatively be set at $74.14 per parcel," which is a projected increase of $3.20 per parcel over the FY 2015 assessment.
April 25	Flint switches water supply.	The water supply is switched from pre-treated Lake Huron water from DWSD to Flint River water treated at the Flint Water Treatment Plant. The switch is intended to be a short-term, stop-gap measure as the KWA pipeline is built.
April 30	**Executive Order 12:** Compliance with Public-Funded Health Insurance Contribution Act, Act 152 of 2011	Earley signs order stating that "the city of Flint shall not pay more than eighty (80) percent of the total annual costs of all of the medical benefits it offers or contributes to for its employees and elected officials." The order notes that, effective July 1, 2014, "all active employees and elected officials are obligated to pay twenty (20) percent of the total annual costs of all medical benefit plans."
June 20	**Executive Order 13:** Adoption of Biennial Budget for FY 2015 and FY 2016	The order lays out the process that the EM undertook to engage the mayor, city council, and the public in developing and adopting the biennial budget. Staffing reductions are included in the budget.
June 20	**Executive Order 14:** Adoption of Strategic Plan for City of Flint	Strategic plan, FY 2015–FY 2019, is adopted.
June 20	**Executive Order 15:** Mayor Walling Increased Responsibilities and Compensation	Walling becomes responsible for the day-to-day operations of the Department of Planning and Development and the Department of Public Works. Increased annual compensation rate is $82,500.
June 20	**Executive Order 16:** Flint City Council's Increased Responsibilities	Intent is indicated for the council to move in the direction of transitioning the city back to local control. Compensation is increased to $10,500.

(continued on next page)

TABLE A3.1 KEY EVENTS FROM FLINT'S MUNICIPAL TAKEOVERS *(continued from previous page)*

Date	Event/order/directive/action	Details
2014 *(cont.)*		
June 30	Blue Ribbon Committee	On June 30, 2014, the committee submitted its findings and recommendations to the emergency manager. Six recommendations were made: "shifting to a hybrid form of Council-Manager government with an elected Mayor and an appointed City Manager; reconsideration of the City Council system by a Charter Commission; Ongoing training for all City Council members; City-appointed officials report to and are hired by the City Manager (with the exception of the City Attorney and City Clerk); Elimination of the Civil Service Commission and removal from charter of Ombudsman Office; Adoption of multi-year budgeting, strategic planning, and long-term financial forecasts."
July 1	Walling given control of Departments of Planning and Development, as well as Public Works.	Earley hands control of Departments of Planning and Development and Public Works to Mayor Dayne Walling.
July 15	**Executive Order 18:** Adoption of the Deficit Elimination/Reserve Accumulation Plan	With FY 2013 financial statements indicating a nearly $12.9 million general fund deficit, down from $19.2 million, arising from inter-fund borrowing in the form of cash advances, the order authorizes additional steps to eliminate the deficit and establish reserves.
July 15	**Executive Order 20:** Acceptance and Adoption of Collective Bargaining Agreement with AFSCME Local 1600	Acceptance and adoption of collective bargaining agreement with AFSCME Local 1600
July 15	**Executive Order 21:** Amended Waste Collection User Fee	Waste removal fee is extended to all residential/commercial combination parcels in the city.
July 16	**Executive Order 22:** Acceptance and Adoption of Collective Bargaining Agreement with AFSCME Local 1799	Acceptance and adoption of Collective Bargaining Agreement with AFSCME Local 1799

Date	Event	Description
July 16	**Executive Order 23:** Acceptance and Imposition of Collective Bargaining Agreement with Flint Police Officers Association Union	After unsuccessful negotiations, the order imposes the required changes to the Collective Bargaining Agreement between the city of Flint and the Flint Police Officers Association Union.
August 4–5	Charter amendments placed on ballot.	Earley signs a series of resolutions to place charter amendments on the November ballot.
September 12	**Executive Order 24:** Adoption of Benefit Modifications for Non-Union Employees	The order makes further changes to health benefits of non-union employees.
October 15	**Executive Order 25:** Monthly City Council Meeting Schedule for Remainder of 2014	October meeting is canceled; November and December meeting times and locations are scheduled.
November 4	Flint voters decide on charter amendments.	Proposal 1: Approves Charter Review: approved. Proposal 2: Reduces the number of mayoral staff appointments from no more than 10 to no more than 5: approved. Proposal 3: Adds a charter amendment to require budgetary best practices: approved. Proposal 4: Eliminates the requirement for certain executive departments: defeated. Proposal 5: Eliminates the Civil Service Commission: defeated. Proposal 6: Eliminates the Office of Ombudsman: defeated.

(continued on next page)

TABLE A3.1 KEY EVENTS FROM FLINT'S MUNICIPAL TAKEOVERS *(continued from previous page)*

Date	Event/order/directive/action	Details
2014 *(cont.)*		
November 6	**Executive Order 26:** Acceptance and Adoption of Collective Bargaining Agreement with POLC-Police Sergeants	Acceptance and adoption of Collective Bargaining Agreement with POLC-Police Sergeants.
November 6	**Executive Order 27:** Acceptance and Adoption of Collective Bargaining Agreement with POLC-Police Captains and Lieutenants	Acceptance and adoption of Collective Bargaining Agreement with POLC-Police Captains and Lieutenants.
December 9	**Executive Order 28:** Special Council Meeting	Authorizes council to conduct a special meeting for the sole purpose of approving or disapproving the emergency manager's proposed contract with the International Association of Firefighters.
December 9	Resolution establishing charter review commission	Earley signs a resolution establishing a Charter Review Commission, in accordance with the November 4 passage of proposal 1.
2015		
January	Community meetings on water	City officials host a series of meetings throughout the community to address water-quality concerns among residents.
January 8 (December 12)	**Executive Order 29:** Special Council Meeting	Authorizes council to "conduct a special meeting for the sole purpose *considering an alternative* to Emergency Manager's proposed contract with the International Association of Firefighters."
January 8 (December 29)	**Executive Order 30:** Special Council Meeting	Authorizes council to conduct a special meeting for the sole purpose of appointing two individuals to fill the vacant council positions for the Third and Sixth Wards, noting that "the appointees shall serve until

Date	Event	Description
January 12	Executive Order 31: Acceptance and Imposition of Collective Bargaining Agreement with International Association of Firefighters, Local 352	November of 2015; and the council positions for Ward 3 and Ward 6 shall be subject to an August, 2015, primary election and November, 2015, general election." With negotiations unsuccessful, the order imposes the required changes to the Collective Bargaining Agreement between the city of Flint and the IAF Union.
January 13	Darnell Earley resigns.	Darnell Earley resigns from his post in Flint to take over as the EM of the Detroit Public Schools.
January 13	Gerald Ambrose appointed EM.	Gerald Ambrose is appointed EM.
February 2	Executive Order 1: Bi-monthly City Council and Committee Meetings	Establishes a city council organizational chart, dissolves the council legislative committee, and establishes regular meetings of the council and its committees.
February 2	Executive Order 2: Restructuring Outstanding Water Supply Revenue Bonds	Order restructures Outstanding Water Supply Revenue Bonds series 1999, series 2000, series 2001, and series 2002.
February 14	Water protests	Activists march on Valentine's Day to protest water-quality concerns.
March 18	Executive Order 3: City Administrator	Establishes the role of the city administrator, outlining that the person "shall serve as the City's Chief Administrative Officer at the pleasure of the Mayor, City Council, and Emergency Manager or Receivership Transition Advisory Board (RTAB) in accordance with her contract" (February 23, 2015). Role is outlined in the order.
March 23	Flint City Council votes to reconnect to Detroit water system.	Flint city council votes on resolution from Councilmember Eric Mays (7–1) to do "all things necessary" to end Flint River usage and return to the Detroit water system.

(continued on next page)

TABLE A3.1 KEY EVENTS FROM FLINT'S MUNICIPAL TAKEOVERS *(continued from previous page)*

Date	Event/order/directive/action	Details
2015 *(cont.)*		
April 10	**Executive Order 4:** Mayor/Council Compensation	Reinstates pay for the mayor, outlining his increased responsibilities and his increased training from Michigan Municipal League (MML).
April 28	**Executive Order 7:** Adoption of Biennial Budget for Fiscal Years 2016 and 2017	Ambrose orders that the biennial budget be adopted and shall be "implemented upon direction of the Emergency Manager, or by the City Administrator, if there is no longer an Emergency Manager"
April 28	Ambrose recommends appointment of an RTAB.	Emergency Manager Ambrose recommends the appointment of a Receivership Transition Advisory Board (RTAB). RTAB would serve as an oversight body to monitor the city while the city remains in receivership.
April 30	**Executive Order 5:** Special Street Light Assessment	FY 2017 street light assessment will remain the same as FY 2016.
April 30	**Executive Order 6:** Rescind Certain Emergency Manager Orders Concerning Council	The order rescinds EO 8, 9, and 10 (Earley) related to council protocol, agenda, and schedule. The order also rescinds EO 3 (Earley) regarding the directives for Council Member Eric Mays.
April 30	**Executive Order 8:** Compliance with Public-Funded Health Insurance Contribution Act, Public Act 152	Same as EO 12 (Earley 2013).

Date	Event	Description
April 30	**Executive Order 20:** Measures to Rectify Financial Emergency and Allocation of Responsibilities in the Event of the Appointment of a Receivership Transition Advisory Board	The order outlines the roles and responsibilities of the mayor and city council, as well as the obligations of the city administrator. The executive order explicitly states, "There shall be no funding for the Office of the Ombudsman or the Civil Service Commission."
May 19	City Charter Commission meets.	The first meeting of the City Charter Commission is held.
July 9	Walling drinks water on TV.	Mayor Walling drinks tap water on the local news.
August 20	**Executive Order 7.1:** Amendment of Budget	Amendment to the FY 2015–2016 budget to be in compliance with the State of Michigan Uniform Budgeting and Accounting Act is signed by the state treasurer, Nick Khouri.
September	Report of lead in water.	Virginia Tech team reports findings of their water sampling efforts, followed closely by a report from Dr. Hanna-Attisha. Both report concerns about lead.
November 3	Karen Weaver elected mayor.	Karen Weaver is elected Flint's new mayor. She is the first woman to hold the post.
2016		
January 21	Michael Townsend appointed to RTAB.	Michael Townsend is appointed to the RTAB.
May 26	Provision powers restored to Flint City Council.	Provision powers are restored to Flint City Council.

Sources: Flint Journal, Access World News database (for back issues of *Flint Journal*, 2002–2005), City of Flint, interview transcripts, and Genesee County website. Direct quotes pulled from news articles are cited in the text and listed in the References.

Notes

Prologue

1. McClinton 2014a.
2. Discussed in more detail in Chapter 2, the policy was first referred to as PA 72 and, now, after PA 4 was overturned, the policy is referred to as PA 436.
3. Abowd 2012.
4. Anderson 2016.
5. Oosting 2016.
6. As early as January 2013, officials warned about the feasibility of switching the city's water supply to the Flint River, noting concerns about corrosiveness. See Bridge Staff 2016; Fonger 2015b, 2015d.
7. Hanna-Attisha et al. 2016.
8. See Snyder 2016; White House 2016.
9. Hedden 2014.
10. See Ridley 2014 for information on the protest march; McClinton's speech can be heard on YouTube, McClinton 2014a.
11. Fasenfest and Pride 2016.
12. D. Z. Morris 2016.
13. Conyers 2016; Sapotichne et al. 2015; Scorsone 2014; Pew Charitable Trusts 2013.
14. Ecorse was released from emergency management in April 2013. Hamtramck was later placed under an EM in July, bringing the percentage back up to 49.5, until Pontiac was released in August of that year.
15. Snyder 2012b.

Introduction

1. Nickels 2016.
2. This is particularly true since 2011, after the passage of the statutes PA 4 and PA 436.

3. See Wilde-Anderson 2012 and Scorsone 2014, respectively.

4. This research focuses on municipal takeovers of cities and therefore does not address the takeover literature on school districts or public utilities, unless directly relevant.

5. See, for example, Pew Charitable Trusts 2013 and Spiotto, Acker, and Appleby 2012.

6. Wolman et al. 2007, 1.

7. The concept of policy paradox is borrowed from D. Stone (1997) 2011.

8. Carpenter and Kennedy 2001, 10. See also S. Campbell 2013.

9. D. Stone (1997) 2011.

10. Ibid.

11. Ibid.

12. Ibid., 9.

13. Ibid., 10.

14. See, for example, Berman 1995; Cahill and James 1992; Spiotto, Acker, and Appleby 2012.

15. Spiotto, Acker, and Appleby 2012.

16. Frug 1999, 17.

17. Pew Charitable Trusts 2013; Spiotto, Acker, and Appleby 2012.

18. Cahill and James 1992, 91–92.

19. See, for instance, Cahill and James 1992; Coe 2008; Kloha, Weissert, and Kleine 2005.

20. Kloha, Weissert, and Kleine 2005.

21. Mahler 2011.

22. As cited in Mahler 2011.

23. Kasdan 2014, 1194.

24. Maddow 2011.

25. See Fung 2006 for more discussion of how institutional design shapes participation and decision making.

26. Longley 2012b.

27. CamConnect 2009. The number of voters increased in 2009, as did the number of registered voters. This was, in part, due to the significant voter registration efforts of the Obama campaign in 2008. Yet, in 2009, Camden's voter turnout was half the state average in 2009. See also Nickels 2012.

28. Wilde-Anderson 2012, 587.

29. See also Kossis 2012.

30. See AlHajal 2011 and MRG 2013 for more discussion on public opinion regarding municipal takeover.

31. See, for instance, Berry, Thomson, and Portney 1993; Dahl 1981; Peterson 1981; C. Stone 1989.

32. R. Harris 2016.

33. Loh 2016, 833.

34. Ibid. See also R. Harris 2016; C. Stone 1989.

35. Klein 2007.

36. See Keiser 2014 for a discussion on how shocks, such as scandals, can change governance regimes.

37. North 1990. Douglass North notes that institutions can be understood

as defining the formal and legal rules of the game as well as the informal cultural rules and norms. See also Pierson 1993.

38. Moynihan and Soss 2014, 321.
39. Jacobs and Weaver 2015, 444.
40. See Pierson 1993 for a discussion of how policies create instrumental effects through the allocation of resources and incentives.
41. The premise that policies create politics is well supported by decades of research. See, for example, A. Campbell 2003; Lowi 1964; March and Olsen 1984; Mettler 2005; Pierson 1993; Piven and Cloward 1979; Schattschneider 1935; Schneider and Ingram 1993; Skocpol 1992; Soss and Schram 2007.
42. Hall 2010, 215.
43. Keiser 2014.
44. Goffman 1974; Benford and Snow 2000.
45. D. Stone (1997) 2011, 160.
46. This holds true in other states, as well. For example, in Rhode Island, 87 percent of Central Falls's population is of minority racial and ethnic background, and in East St. Louis, Illinois, 97 percent of the population is Black. Both cities have experienced state intervention.
47. McClinton 2014b.
48. See Eclectablog 2011b; Fasenfest and Pride 2016; Lewis 2013; Nichols 2013.
49. The federal district court judge dismissed, however, numerous other claims made by the plaintiffs: the law did not violate right to due process, to have local government, or to vote in local elections (see ruling, Steeh 2014).
50. As cited in E. White 2016; Associated Press 2016.
51. These included the cities of Allen Park, Benton Harbor, Detroit, Ecorse, Flint, Hamtramck, Highland Park, Lincoln Park, and Pontiac and the Village of Three Oaks.
52. As discussed in more detail below, this book draws on the theoretical propositions of policy feedback theory, relying heavily on the works of policy scholars, political scientists, and sociologists. Some of these scholars include A. Campbell 2003; Mettler 2005; Pierson 1993; Schneider and Ingram 1993; Skocpol 1992; Soss and Schram 2007.
53. Hacker, Mettler, and Soss 2010; Hacker and Pierson 2014.
54. Hacker, Mettler, and Soss 2010, 14.
55. Scorsone and Bateson 2011. See also Sugrue 1996; Gillette 2006.
56. Using the definition of municipal takeover adopted in this book (e.g., the appointment of a single manager/receiver to manage local government), most cities that have experienced this form of state intervention are small cities (i.e., populations of 100,000 or less). In 2010, Flint was on the cusp of 100,000 and has since decreased further according to U.S. Census estimates.
57. U.S. Census Bureau 2010f.
58. The population of Central Falls, Rhode Island, was 19,347 in 2010, when the state's new municipal receivership law went into effect and placed the city under state control.
59. See Seawright and Gerring 2008. This case study uses an iterative approach to data collection and analysis. I applied midrange theory to the case,

using predefined causal mechanisms to both refine current theory and build new microlevel theory. While I argue that context matters, many aspects of my theory for how takeovers reshape democracy are applicable—and testable—in other cities.

60. Hacker and Pierson 2014, 644. See also Fischer 1998; Gerring 2001; Yin 2014.

61. Racial identification was determined by observation or participant disclosure but was not explicitly asked as a part of the interview. The term "Black" is adopted in this book to refer to individuals who identified or presented as Black or African American. The term "Latinx" is adopted as a nongendered referent to individuals that identify as Hispanic, Latino, or Latina.

62. U.S. Census Bureau 2010f.

63. It is also relevant to note that the author is White and not a Flint native. As such, this may have impacted how some residents perceived my presence and thus their willingness to participate in an interview.

64. Throughout the book the names of individuals and their affiliations are disguised to maintain their anonymity. The importance of anonymity to this research project is explained in Appendix 1, where I discuss my methodological approach.

65. D. Stone (1997) 2011. See also the literature on policy feedback (e.g., A. Campbell 2003; Mettler 2005; Pierson 1993; Schneider and Ingram 1993; Skocpol 1992; Soss and Schram 2007).

66. Anne Schneider and Helen Ingram (1993, 1997) examine how policy design "feeds forward," whereas other scholars have adopted the language of "policy feedback," notably Paul Pierson (1993).

67. Gilman 2016, 7.

Chapter 1

1. Gillespie 2016.
2. Jacob and Hendrick 2013, 11.
3. Honadle, Cigler, and Costa 2003; Ladd 1994; Levine, Justice, and Scorsone 2012; Hendrick 2011.
4. Fuchs 1992.
5. Monkkonen 1995, 1.
6. Bradbury 1983.
7. Carl, personal interview, June 2015.
8. Fuchs 1992.
9. Ibid., 6.
10. Ibid., 273, emphasis added.
11. Ibid., 235.
12. Ibid., 237. See also Peterson 1981.
13. Fuchs 1992, 273.
14. See Thelen 2004.
15. McNichol 2012; see also Anzia and Moe 2015; Flavin and Hartney 2015.
16. McNichol 2012.
17. Anzia and Moe 2015.
18. Nollenberger, Groves, and Valente 2003.

19. Hendrick 2004, 81.
20. Tabb 2015.
21. Galster 2015.
22. Ibid. See also Sugrue 1996.
23. Highsmith 2015.
24. Dandaneau 1996.
25. Fonger 2013.
26. City of Flint 2010.
27. Scorsone and Bateson 2011, 9.
28. City of Flint 2002.
29. Note that, throughout the book, the term EM is used when policies implemented under PA 4 or PA 436 are being discussed, but EFM when policies implemented under PA 72 are discussed.
30. City of Flint 2010.
31. As cited in Gantert 2012.
32. Gantert 2012.
33. Scorsone and Bateson 2011, i.
34. Ibid., 14–15.
35. This is the average proportion of Blacks in public-sector, "industry-92-public administration" jobs from 2000 to 2016. These data were extracted from the Quarterly Workforce Indicators tool available from the U.S. Census's Center for Economic Studies.
36. The data used are fourth-quarter employment counts from 2000 to 2016.
37. This analysis does not take a fine-grained look at these data. However, future research should look at the relationship between decreasing local government employees and the decreasing proportion of public-sector employees. My hypothesis is that many of the jobs lost from 2000 to 2016 in the public sector were at the local level, which likely employed more Black people.
38. D. Harris 2011.
39. Scorsone and Bateson 2011.
40. Lederman 2016.

Chapter 2

1. Monkkonen 1995.
2. Weikart 2013.
3. Kossis 2012, 1117.
4. *Meriwether v. Garrett* 1880.
5. Ibid., emphasis added. This is addressed in many states by the adoption of constitutional home rule provisions that protect municipal charters from legislative interference.
6. As cited by Berman 2003, 2.
7. Judd and Swanstrom 2015, 41.
8. Kossis 2012. See also Monkkonen 1995.
9. Kossis 2012, 1113, emphasis added.
10. *Hunter v. Pittsburgh* 1907, emphasis added.
11. Ibid. The federal constitutional opinion in *Hunter v. Pittsburgh* is controversial. For a review of the challenges to this legal opinion, see Kathleen

Morris's article, "The Case for Local Constitutional Enforcement." In addition to highlighting past critiques of the judicial opinion, which has become known as the Hunter Doctrine, she also posits that *Hunter v. Pittsburgh* should be overturned for two reasons: (1) The Hunter Doctrine's position on local government powerlessness "was effectively overruled in 1938 by *Erie v. Tomkins*" (*Erie*, Morris argues, overturns *Hunter* on the grounds that *Hunter* was not decided on constitutional grounds, but rather common law grounds). (2) "The rule of local powerlessness has always stood on shaky analytical ground." Morris continues by acknowledging the normative value of overturning *Hunter* on the grounds that "there are good reasons to support local constitutional enforcement; such enforcement has the potential to promote local power, enhance the democratic legitimacy of constitutional litigation, and shore up local constitutional competency" (2012, 5).

12. Kossis 2012, 1117.
13. Ibid.
14. Weikart 2013.
15. Lehmann 1950.
16. Berman 1995.
17. Kossis 2012.
18. Kloha, Weissert, and Kleine 2005; Scorsone 2014.
19. Cahill and James 1992. See also Pew Charitable Trusts 2013; Scorsone 2014.
20. Scorsone 2014, 11.
21. Pew Charitable Trusts 2013, table 2.
22. Pew Charitable Trusts 2013; Scorsone 2014.
23. Cahill and James 1992, 91.
24. Pew Charitable Trusts 2013.
25. Ibid.
26. See also Nickels 2016.
27. Scorsone 2014.
28. Livengood 2015.
29. See Citizen's Research Council of Michigan (CRC) 1994 for more on Michigan as a strong home rule state.
30. *People v. Hurlbut* 1871. The case was brought to court in response to the legislature's passage of an act that eliminated the city's sewer and water commissions and created a board of public works, which was given "absolute control over the streets, public parks, and grounds of the city, over the construction of the city hall, fire houses, and all other public buildings except school houses, as well as over the water-works and sewer system. The offending feature of the act was that the first members of this powerful board were named in the act itself." This violated that state's constitution, which stated, "Judicial officers of cities and villages shall be elected, and all other officers shall be elected or appointed at such times and in such manner as the legislature shall direct" (McBain 1916, 192). In *People v. Hurlbut*, the court ruled that such intervention was unconstitutional; Cooley wrote, "It would be the boldest mockery to speak of a city possessing municipal liberty where the state not only shaped its government, but at discretion sent its own agents to administer it."
31. Morgan et al. 2015, 17.

32. Ibid.
33. Gross 2011, emphasis added.
34. Nickels 2016.
35. This was unchanged from the version adopted in 1908. In addition to keeping this provision, the 1963 constitution added a preamble that addressed home rule: "The provisions of this constitution and laws concerning counties, townships, cities, and villages shall be liberally construed in their favor."
36. See Fino 1996 for further examination of Michigan's state constitution and home rule provisions.
37. Other states, such as Connecticut, New York, and Massachusetts, allow for and have used special legislation. See Table 2.2.
38. CRC 1994. The report ends with a recommendation that "a constitutional convention might consider self-executing home rule provisions that would clearly establish home rule supremacy on matters of local concern—a constitutionally protected sphere of immunity from state intervention in local affairs."
39. Home Rule City Act, PA 279 of 1909.
40. D. Morris (1971) 1993, 5.
41. Nickels 2016.
42. Article IX, Section 26, establishes an overall limitation on total state spending each fiscal year. The Headlee Amendment also creates two significant limitations on the fiscal relationship between state and local units of government: Article IX, Section 29, prohibits the state from reducing its share of existing state-mandated programs and requires the state to reimburse local governmental units for any new state-mandated programs; Article IX, Section 30, prohibits the state from reducing the proportion of total state spending paid to all units of local government as a group below the proportion in effect in fiscal year 1979.
43. Article IX, Section 30, of the Michigan State Constitution.
44. Kleine 1991.
45. Gross 2011.
46. Wayne County's current population estimate is 1,753,616, making it the nineteenth-most populous in the country (U.S. Census Bureau 2017). In the 1980s, it was the fourth-most populous county (CRC 1987).
47. CRC 1987, 7.
48. Ibid., 11.
49. CRC 1987.
50. Ibid., 8.
51. Kleiman and Sahu 1999, 152.
52. Ibid., 153.
53. Ibid.
54. Kaza 1989.
55. Gross 2011.
56. Scorsone 2010.
57. Ibid.
58. PA 72 of 1990, 4.
59. Ibid.
60. Ibid., 4–5.

61. Scorsone 2010.
62. Ibid., 2–3. See also PA 72 of 1990, 5–6.
63. PA 72 of 1990, 5.
64. Scorsone 2010, 5.
65. Ibid.
66. Ibid.
67. Note that Public Act numbers are assigned based on when they are passed within the year. PA 4 was the fourth bill passed in 2011. PA 101 was replaced by PA 72, which was replaced by PA 4. When PA 4 was repealed, PA 72 went back into effect, until it was replaced by PA 436.
68. The Local Government and School District Fiscal Accountability Act, PA 4 of 2011.
69. Note that, throughout the book, the term EM is used when policies implemented under PA 4 or PA 436 are being discussed, and but EFM under when policies implemented under PA 72 are discussed.
70. PA 4 of 2011, 3.
71. Ibid., 3–4.
72. Ibid., 7.
73. PA 4 of 2011.
74. Ibid., 10–11.
75. Ibid., 11.
76. Ibid.
77. Abowd 2012.
78. Ibid.
79. Luke 2011.
80. Ibid.
81. Quoted in ibid.
82. C. Savage 2012.
83. Scorsone, as cited in Hakala 2016.
84. Sapotichne et al. 2015, 17.
85. Martin, Levey, and Cawley 2012, 18.
86. Ibid., 25.
87. Wilde-Anderson 2012, 28. See also Sapotichne, Scorsone, and Henion 2016.
88. Farnham 2011; Henderson 2010.

Chapter 3

1. Keith, a member of Flint's 2011 EM team, personal interview, July 2015.
2. Snyder 2012a.
3. It was not until Flint experienced a serious public health disaster under the leadership of an EM that the broader public and academic community began to examine the sociopolitical and public health ramifications of such policies. See, for example, Clark and Gorina 2017; Fasenfest 2019; Hammer 2019; and Stanley 2016.
4. Berman 2003, 128.
5. D. Stone (1997) 2011.
6. Ibid.

7. See, for example, Denhardt and Denhardt 2015; Nickels and Rivera 2018.
8. Fasenfest 2019, 36.
9. D. Stone (1997) 2011, 10. See also Denhardt and Denhardt 2015.
10. See, for example, Hunter 1953.
11. See, for example, C. Stone 1989. Urban regime theory was developed by Clarence Stone (1989) and emerged as a dominant paradigm in U.S. urban studies in the 1980s. The urban regime is a conceptual tool for understanding how local governments, business, and community actors cooperate to shape and carry out the local agenda. Urban regime theory contends that local governments must "blend their *capacities* with those of various non-governmental actors," including, but not necessarily exclusively, the business sector, in order to sustain their "influence and impact" in key policy areas (C. Stone 1989, 6; Orr and Stocker 1994).
12. See, for example, Bachrach and Baratz 1962.
13. Anne Schneider and Helen Ingram (1993, 1997) discuss the three faces of power: power to influence behavior; power to control information, including the ability to keep information off the decision-making agenda; and the power to shape or influence values or rationales that underpin decision-making preferences.
14. See Schneider and Ingram 1993. See also Fortner 2016 or Harding 2009 for a summary of the community power debate.
15. Mumby 2004. See also Fortner 2016.
16. Keiser 2015.
17. R. Harris 2016.
18. For a discussion of how Michigan's municipal takeover policy creates opportunities for planning-focused interests, see Loh 2016. For more on the concept of a policy window, see Kingdon 1995.
19. R. Harris 2016. For additional discussions of the role of nonprofit organizations in urban politics, see also Levine 2016 and Marwell 2007.
20. Mahler 2011. See also Executive Order 3 (December 13, 2013), in which Flint councilperson Eric Mays's communication was restricted to e-mail only. https://www.cityofflint.com/wp-content/uploads/CityPDF/OrderNo.3.pdf.
21. See Kasdan 2014, 2016.
22. Keiser 2015, 527.
23. This analysis is rooted in a social constructivist approach but draws on the theoretical contributions of both policy feedback theory rooted in historical institutionalism (e.g., Pierson 1993) and theory of policy design and social construction rooted in social constructivism (e.g., Schneider and Ingram 1993, 1997).
24. See Lowi 1964; March and Olsen 1984; Pierson 1993; Piven and Cloward 1979; Schattschneider 1935; Schneider and Ingram 1993, 1997.
25. See A. Campbell 2003; Mettler 2005; Pierson 1993; Skocpol 1992.
26. Mettler and SoRelle 2014, 152.
27. Moynihan and Soss 2014, 322. See also Schneider and Ingram 2005, 23.
28. Burch 2013, 4.
29. Jacobs and Weaver 2015. See also Mahoney and Thelen 2009.
30. Jacobs and Weaver 2015, 444.
31. Pierson 1993. See also Ingram, Schneider, and DeLeon 2007, 97.

32. A. Campbell 2003; Pierson 1993; Mettler 2005.
33. Jacobs and Weaver 2015.
34. Burch 2013; Soss and Schram 2007; Sharp 2002.
35. Lasswell 1936.
36. There is an important caveat, however. The water crisis changed the political opinions of some policy proponents.
37. Moynihan and Soss 2014, 322.
38. Alexei, personal interview, July 2015.
39. Eclectablog 2011a.
40. Kromer 2010.
41. Lake et al. 2007.
42. See Shragge 2013; Jacobs and Weaver 2015.
43. Schneider and Ingram 1997.
44. See Burch 2013, 1. See also Schneider and Ingram 2005.
45. Ingram, Schneider, and deLeon 2007. See also Schneider and Ingram 2005.
46. Shaun, personal interview, June 2015.
47. Mettler 2002, 352.
48. Ingram, Schneider, and deLeon 2007; Soss 1999.
49. Burch 2013.
50. D. Stone 1989, 300.
51. See also Falleti and Lynch 2009.
52. *Flint Journal* 2002.
53. As cited by Gantert 2011.
54. Keith, personal interview, July 2015.
55. Fuchs 1992.
56. Berman 2003, 128.
57. Sapotichne, Scorsone, and Henion 2016.
58. Kasdan 2016 refers to Michigan's EM law as an "unfortunate necessity" (878).
59. Keith, personal interview, July 2015.
60. Shayne, personal interview, July 2017.

Chapter 4

1. Bruce, former elected official, personal interview, June 2015.
2. The term "redlining" comes from the red lines drawn on residential security maps developed by the Home Owner's Loan Corporation (HOLC) in the 1930s to indicate which neighborhoods were not open to Blacks and other ethnic minorities. The term is used here, however, to reference the discriminatory practices employed by the FHA and bankers of denying services, typically financial services such as home loans, to residents based on race or ethnicity. See Rothstein 2017.
3. Race restrictive housing covenants were a tool for maintaining racial segregation by restricting to whom the property could be sold. See Rothstein 2017.
4. Urban renewal is typically associated with programs carried out in the 1950s and 1960s that demolished Black communities to make way for middle-income White families and/or highway development, which is associated with suburban development. See Rothstein 2017.

5. A. Morris 1984.
6. Francis, personal interview, August 2015.
7. Contentious politics use techniques to disrupt normal activity. Such techniques might include protests, strikes, or civil disobedience. See McAdam, Tarrow, and Tilly 2001 for more on the use of contentious politics.
8. Quoted in McClinton 2014c. Also note that Flint was not the first city to elect a Black mayor. Floyd McCree was one of the first Black mayors in the United States, but he was appointed to the position by the city council, not elected.
9. Rast 2012; Falleti and Lynch 2009.
10. Reuther Library 2010.
11. Dandaneau 1996.
12. Young 2013, 49.
13. As cited in ibid., 48.
14. Highsmith 2015.
15. Ibid., 24.
16. Ibid.
17. Ibid.
18. Ibid., 34–35.
19. Michigan Civil Rights Commission (MCRC) 2017, 2.
20. MCRC 2017.
21. Ibid.
22. U.S. Census Bureau 1950, 1960, 1970, 1980, 1990, 2000, 2010a–i.
23. Fonger 2013.
24. Ainsley, personal interview, August 2015.
25. As cited in Dandaneau 1996, 161.
26. Bradsher 1997.
27. City of Flint 2010; Doidge et al. 2015.
28. U.S. Census Bureau 2014. See also Fonger 2014d.
29. Ibid.
30. See Highsmith 2015.
31. Rosner and Markowitz 2016; see also Hanna-Attisha 2018; Clark 2018.
32. Highsmith 2015.
33. See Bullard and Wright 2012; Mohai and Saha 2007; Starbuck and White 2016.
34. As reported in Carmody 2016.Add citations.
35. Carmody 2016.
36. Leonardi and Gruhn 2001, 70.
37. Bryson 2004, 22.
38. As Baumgartner and Jones (1993) argue, stakeholder support is necessary for creating winning coalitions; and, as John Bryson, Gary Cunningham, and Karen Lokkesmoe (2002) argue, "Key stakeholders must be satisfied, at least minimally, or public policies, organizations, communities, or even countries will fail" (571).
39. Hospitals and universities are often referred to as "anchor institutions." Anchor institutions are nonprofit organizations that typically do not and cannot move locations easily. For more information on anchor institutions, see https://community-wealth.org/strategies/panel/anchors/index.html.

40. See D. Smith 1997; R. Harris 2016; and Leach 2018.
41. R. Harris 2016; Leach 2018.
42. A. Smith 2017; Gilmore 2017.
43. Chetkovich and Kunreuther 2006; see also Ospina and Foldy 2005; Cnaan and Milofsky 2007.
44. Naples 2014; Piven and Cloward 1979.
45. Clark and Nickels 2018.
46. Acosta 2017.
47. City of Flint 2010. See also Scorsone and Bateson 2011.
48. Shelterforce 2014.
49. See the Genesee County Land Bank website: http://www.thelandbank.org/.
50. As of January 30, 2018, the Genesee County Land Bank had 8,990 properties listed on their website.
51. Young 2013, 50.
52. Ibid., 49.
53. Highsmith and Erickson 2016, 568.
54. Ibid.
55. Ibid., 572.
56. Highsmith 2015, 257–258.
57. Ibid. AutoWorld, the "linchpin" of Flint's Great Leap Forward plan, opened in 1984. As Highsmith (2015, 259) notes, the theme park, "like most of the other" economic initiatives in the downtown business district, was funded by public and private dollars: $36 million in public funds, $31 million from the Mott Foundation, $9 million from an East Coast investment firm called Capital Income Properties, and $4 million from private donors.
58. George, personal interview, November 2015.
59. Brenda, personal interview, July 2015.
60. Jennifer, personal interview, July 2017.
61. C. S. Mott Foundation 2016b.
62. Highsmith 2015.
63. Bruce, personal interview, June 2015.
64. Highsmith, cited in McClelland 2015.
65. A. Harris n.d.
66. *Concerned Pastors for Social Action v. Khouri* 2016.
67. Janean, personal interview, November 2015.
68. Zach, personal interview, June 2015.
69. See also Highsmith 2015.
70. Francis, personal interview, August 2015.
71. Zach, personal interview, June 2015.
72. See also Highsmith 2015.
73. Adrian, personal interview, July 2015.
74. Shayne, personal interview, July 2017.
75. Highsmith 2015.
76. As cited in Manns 2013.
77. Duggan 2010; Manns 2013.
78. Bill, personal interview, June 2015.
79. Ibid.

80. Zach, personal interview, June 2015.
81. Adrian, personal interview, July 2015; Peter, personal interview, July 2015.
82. Bill, personal interview, June 2015.
83. Shaun, personal interview, June 2015.
84. Liesel, personal interview, September 2015.
85. Adrian, personal interview, July 2015.
86. Carl, personal interview, June 2015.

Chapter 5

1. Moynihan and Soss 2014, 322.
2. See R. Harris 2016.
3. There are important overlaps between the development regime in Flint and those identified by R. Harris (2016) in Camden; however, Harris uses the term "community development regime."
4. Raymer 2001. There are 366 metropolitan areas in the United States as defined by the U.S. Census Bureau. However, Raymer was not explicit about how her information was derived.
5. LaFaive 2002.
6. Hakim 2002; Ronders 2001.
7. Dresden 2014.
8. Frammolino 2002.
9. As cited in Hakim 2002.
10. *City Council of Flint v. State of Michigan* 2002.
11. As cited in ibid.
12. Mostafavi 2011.
13. LaFaive 2002; LaFaive and Schimmel 2011.
14. As cited in Machniak 2002.
15. Machniak 2002.
16. As cited in ibid.
17. Adams 2013.
18. Scorsone and Bateson 2011.
19. Mostafavi 2011.
20. Whiteside 2007.
21. Ibid.
22. Ibid.
23. Garza 2009.
24. Young 2013, 69.
25. Whiteside 2007.
26. Rutherford was first elected mayor in 1975, running against Floyd McCree, Flint's first Black mayor. Rutherford won with only 169 more votes than his opponent (*Flint Journal* 2002). Finding an ally in the new mayor, a coalition of community leaders, including the Mott Foundation and other civic organizations, put forward a "sweeping revitalization plan for the central business district" (Highsmith 2015, 257–258).
27. Young 2013, 70.
28. Lawlor 2009a.

29. Bruce, personal interview, June 2015. See also Fonger 2009. Ron Fonger also notes that Phil Shaltz, owner of Shaltz Automation and co-founder of Uptown Development Corporation, with close ties to the C. S. Mott Foundation, was very involved in the discussions that led to Brown's appointment.

30. Mickle 2009. Other appointees included Leonard Smorch, former controller for Genesee County, to serve as finance director, Alvern Lock as police chief, Angela Watkins as city attorney, and Tracy Atkinson as constituent services director, as well as Margaret Fredericks and Maxine Murray as aides and Bob Campbell as communications director.

31. Lawlor 2009b.
32. Ibid.
33. Longley 2009.
34. Ibid.
35. Ibid.
36. City of Flint 2013.
37. McClelland 2014.
38. Jennifer, personal interview, July 2017.
39. Scorsone and Bateson 2011, 9.
40. Ibid., 10.
41. Longley 2011a, 2011e; Scorsone and Bateson 2011.
42. Longley 2011c.
43. Michigan Department of Treasury 2011.
44. Ibid.
45. Ibid.
46. Longley 2011b.
47. Ibid.
48. As cited in ibid.
49. Jerry Ambrose was not from Flint, nor had he worked in the area. However, he was tapped by Michael Brown to serve as finance director, and by the time he was appointed EM, he was well known throughout the city. Prior to his tenure in Flint he served as executive assistant to the mayor and served as finance director for the city of Lansing.

50. Patrick, personal interview, July 2015.
51. Brown 2012 [emphasis added].
52. Members of the Emergency Manager Core Team: Mike Brown, emergency manager, former county commissioner, former director of community development and government relations under Collier, former city administrator under Williamson, former president of United Way of Genesee and Lapeer Counties, interim mayor for the city of Flint (February–August 2009), former director of Flint Area Reinvestment Office at the Mott Foundation, president of Prima Civitas; Jerry Ambrose, financial advisor to emergency manager/emergency manager, former finance director of Lansing, Michigan; Elizabeth Murphy, assistant to the emergency manager, former director of public works under Mayor Collier, and current group vice president at Flint and Genesee Chamber of Commerce; Al Lock, police chief; Ward Chapman, civil attorney; Peter Bade, city attorney; Howard Croft, director of public works; Maxine Murray, assistant to the mayor/emergency manager. Advisory Committee chairs (as reported in the forty-five-day plan) included Armando Hernandez, finance

administration chair, member of Governor Snyder's Hispanic/Latino Commission, board chair of the Genesee County Hispanic Latino Collaborative, and assistant vice president for the Security Credit Union; Diana Kelly, public safety chair, program director at Metro Community Development; George Wilkinson, infrastructure development chair, director of operations for Flint and Genesee Chamber of Commerce, pastor at Word of Life Christian Church, member of board of trustees for Community Foundation of Greater Flint, member of board of directors for Genesee Habitat for Humanity (appointed 2014); Sue Peters, grants/DCED chair, programs officer with Michigan LISC, former program officer with Mott Foundation, Pathways out of Poverty; and Ed Kurtz, pension and OPEB underfunding chair, former EFM, former president of Baker College. Members of the Citizens Advisory Committee (two elected officials and three community members): Dayne Walling, mayor; Delrico Loyd, First Ward council member; Kenyetta Dotson, community activist; Latrelle Holmes, pastor at Great Galilee Baptist Church; Tim Herman, CEO of Flint and Genesee Chamber of Commerce, president of Uptown Redevelopment Corporation, former Flint finance director under Collier, member of Governor Snyder's Council for Labor and Economic Growth.

53. Carl, personal interview, June 2015.
54. Longley 2012e, 125.

Chapter 6

1. PA 4 of 2011.
2. Wilde-Anderson 2012.
3. Longley 2011d.
4. As cited in ibid.
5. Longley 2012f.
6. See EO 005 and EO 033. See Appendix 3 for details on executive orders; see also https://www.cityofflint.com/rtab/executive-orders/.
7. Fonger 2014a.
8. Bankert 2016.
9. Longley 2012b. These actions were investigated by the Flint City Council, but no details emerged as to why Brown eliminated the citizens' groups.
10. Ibid.
11. Longley 2012a.
12. Twenty-three members were initially appointed, but one member resigned in March 2014.
13. Adams 2014. Some DDL members argue that the group emerged from this early work (Pauli 2019).
14. Scorsone and Doidge 2014.
15. Bill, personal Interview, June 2015.
16. Adrian, personal interview, July 2015.
17. Attendance at the community meetings was as follows: thirty-four on May 3, 2014; forty-three on May 10; and forty on May 15 (Scorsone and Doidge 2014).
18. Ibid., 24.
19. Ibid., 29.
20. Ibid., 34.

21. Ibid., 35.
22. Elizabeth Jordan August 2014 e-mail, from field notes, July 2015.
23. The November 2014 ballot also included candidates in the governor's race as well as candidates for secretary of state and attorney general.
24. As cited in Fonger 2014b.
25. The inclusion of the Office of the Ombudsman was a significant issue under the charter review process. The new charter, approved by voters in 2017, includes an Office of the Ombudsman.
26. RTAB website, https://www.cityofflint.com/rtab/.
27. Morgan, member of the Emergency Manager team, personal interview, August 2015.
28. Arnstein 1969; Fung 2004.
29. Loh 2016.
30. As cited in A. Savage 2013.
31. A. Savage 2013.
32. Walling, as cited in ibid.
33. Walling, as cited in ibid.
34. Walling, as cited in ibid.
35. Loh 2016, 855.
36. Adrian, personal interview, July 2015.
37. Jennifer, personal interview, July 2017.
38. Morgan, personal interview, August 2015.
39. Longley 2012c.
40. Ibid. The mill rate is also referred to as the millage rate. The mill rate is used to determine property taxes.
41. Longley 2012d.
42. Adrian, personal interview, July 2015.
43. In addition to the sale of the towers, two months later, the Flint Downtown Development Authority (DDA), a quasi-governmental entity, approved the sale of a parking lot next to the Genesee Towers to Uptown Reinvestment Corporation for $95,000 more than its appraised value (Byron 2013). The deal also called for the DDA to give the $200,000 sale price to the Chamber of Commerce for the purchase of another convention center and visitor's bureau. Three members of the DDA serve on the board of the Uptown Reinvestment Corporation. Each of them abstained from voting for the plan.
44. Adrian, personal interview, July 2015.
45. Ibid.
46. Ketchum 2012; Keller 2012.
47. See EO 014, 015, 016, and 027. See Appendix 3 for details on executive orders; see also https://www.cityofflint.com/rtab/executive-orders/.
48. See EO 07, 026. See Appendix 3 for details on executive orders; see also https://www.cityofflint.com/rtab/executive-orders/.
49. See EO 019 to 025. See Appendix 3 for details on executive orders; see also https://www.cityofflint.com/rtab/executive-orders/.
50. *Welch v. Brown* 2013.
51. Ibid.
52. Ibid.
53. For a discussion of Michigan's "neoliberal response to an urban crisis,"

see also Fasenfest 2019. Another mechanism of the neoliberal rationality project is the devolution of service provision to nonprofit organizations, which was also evident in the Flint case.
54. Longley 2012d.
55. Ambrose 2015, 3.
56. Wilson 2016.
57. As cited in Fonger 2014c.
58. Fonger 2014b.
59. See Flint Water Study 2016.
60. Dixon 2016.
61. C. Savage 2012.
62. Shaun, personal interview, June 2015.
63. Wilson, personal interview, November 2015.
64. Jobb 2002.
65. Ibid.
66. McPhail 2002.
67. Morgan, personal interview, August 2015.
68. Patrick, personal interview, July 2015.
69. Keith, personal interview, July 2015, emphasis added.
70. Jeffrey, personal interview, July 2015.
71. Martin, personal interview, July 2015.
72. Carl, personal interview, June 2015.
73. As cited in AlHajal 2011.
74. Shariff 2014.
75. Aaron, personal interview, August 2015.
76. Brenda, personal interview, June 2015.
77. Ibid.
78. Aaron, personal interview, August 2015.
79. Casey, personal interview, August 2015.

Chapter 7

1. Fonger 2015c.
2. D. Stone (1997) 2011.
3. Mettler 2002; Pierson 1993; Schneider and Ingram 2005; Soss 1999; Schneider and Ingram 1993.
4. Shaun, personal interview, June 2015.
5. PICO is a national network of faith-based community organizations. More about the network can be found at their website: http://www.piconetwork.org/about.
6. Shaun, personal interview, June 2015.
7. Entman 1993.
8. Goffman 1974; Benford and Snow 2000.
9. D. Stone (1997) 2011, 160.
10. Snow et al. 1986; Snow and Benford 1992.
11. D. Stone 1989.
12. Ibid.
13. The group that worked in opposition to Stand Up for Democracy and

in support of Michigan's EM law is called Citizens for Fiscal Responsibility and was established by the long-time head of the Michigan Chamber of Commerce's political action group (Smith and Pluta 2012).
14. *MLive* staff 2012.
15. Shariff 2014.
16. McClinton 2014d.
17. Jefferson 2012.
18. Gibbs, as cited in Maynard 2014.
19. McClinton 2014c.
20. Shariff 2014.
21. McClinton 2014b.
22. Lewis 2013; Fasenfest and Pride 2016; Lee et al. 2016.
23. It should be noted, however, that in 2011 Flint's mayor was White and four members of the nine-member city council were also White.
24. McClinton 2014a.
25. See, for example, Goodman 2016.
26. Fonger 2015a.
27. Guzmán 2016.
28. Cleora Magee, presentation to community, July 20, 2017, from author's field notes.

Chapter 8

1. McClinton 2016.
2. Moss 2016.
3. Mott 2015a, emphasis added.
4. Collins 2000, 300.
5. D. Stone 1989.
6. Mays, as cited in Bailey 2016.
7. McClinton 2016; McClinton, as cited as cited in Bailey 2016.
8. Mays, as cited in Dawson 2016.
9. Hooper 2016.
10. Kaufman, as cited in *UM-Flint News* 2016b.
11. C. S. Mott Foundation 2015b.
12. Wilkinson, as cited in Flint and Genesee Chamber of Commerce 2016a.
13. Borrego 2016.
14. Shariff 2016.
15. McClinton, as cited in Bailey 2016.
16. Mays, as cited in Dawson 2016.
17. Palladino 2017. Camp Promise was a demonstration site affiliated with the Water Is Life movement, which aimed to call attention to the Flint water crisis and demand clean water for Flint residents. Local activists joined activists from across the country in setting up a protest camp in Flint's Kearsley Park.
18. McClinton 2016.
19. Lee et al. 2016; Fasenfest and Pride 2016.
20. MCRC 2017, 2.

21. *UM-Flint News* 2016a.
22. FlintNow 2016.
23. Highsmith 2015.
24. Highsmith and Erikson 2015, 571.
25. Ibid.
26. White, as cited in C. S. Mott Foundation 2015b. White did release a statement in May 2016 that was much more critical of the government's role in the water crisis.
27. Jones 2016.
28. Herman 2016.
29. Gaskin 2016.
30. C. S. Mott Foundation 2016a.
31. Flint and Genesee Chamber of Commerce 2016c.
32. R. White 2016.
33. Flint and Genesee Chamber of Commerce 2016c.
34. Flint and Genesee Chamber of Commerce 2016b.
35. Palladino, as cited in May 2016.
36. Mays 2016.
37. Jefferson 2016.
38. Walters 2016
39. Mays 2017.
40. Shariff 2017.
41. McClinton, as cited in Bailey 2016.
42. Jefferson 2017.

Conclusion

1. D. Stone (1997) 2011.
2. Lasswell 1936.
3. David Easton's (1965, 50) definition of politics is also useful here. He defines politics as the "authoritative allocation of values," which is influenced by the distribution and use of power. In this way, both Lasswell and Easton posit that politics is shaped by top-down decision-making processes. Deborah Stone, on the other hand, defines politics as a "dispute over interpretation," wherein a "society decides whether needs are real or legitimate" ([1997] 2011). It is from this definition that we can best understand the political nature of the grassroots responses.
4. Hohman 2011.
5. Highsmith 2015; Young 2013.
6. Dreier, Mollenkopf, and Swanstrom 2001, 154.
7. Balfour, Adams, and Nickels 2019.
8. See Ungar 2011; Conaway 2013.
9. Scorsone, as cited in Fehr and Murphy 2016.
10. Berman 2003.
11. Ibid. See also Niquette 2013; Sapotichne, Scorsone, and Henion 2016.
12. Fung 2004.
13. Gilman 2016, 7.

Appendix 1

1. Hacker, Mettler, and Soss 2010; Hacker and Pierson 2014.
2. Hacker, Mettler, and Soss 2010, 14.
3. Scorsone and Bateson 2011. See also Sugrue 1996; Gillette 2006.
4. See Yanow 2007, 412.
5. Seawright and Gerring 2008, 299.
6. See Hacker, Mettler, and Soss 2010; D. Stone (1997) 2011.
7. Hacker, Mettler, and Soss 2010, 14; Hacker and Pierson 2014.
8. Schneider and Ingram 1993, 1997; Gerring 2001.
9. D. Stone (1997) 2011; Schneider and Ingram 1993.
10. See, for example, Silverman and Patterson 2015; Schram and Caterino 2006.
11. Carpenter 2010, 20.
12. See Ungar 2011; Marcus and Livio 2016.
13. George and Bennett 2005.
14. I followed Facebook pages, such as Flint Strong, Black Lives Matter-Flint, Communities First (Flint), City of Flint, and Flint Neighborhoods United; and blogs, such as Flint Expatriates.
15. City reports, documents, and other materials (including past video recordings and transcripts of city council meetings) are readily available on the city's website (www.cityofflint.com).
16. Nonelectronic data from 2000 to 2008 was photographed at the Genesee County Clerk's Office. This was combined with readily available electronic documentation available on the county website (www.gc4me.com).
17. I walked through downtown and parts of the Carriage Town neighborhood, north of the Flint River. However, due to limited familiarity with the city and the lack of public transportation, I spent most of my time driving through the city.
18. Ostrander 2013; Silverman and Patterson 2015. See also Kapiszewski, MacLean, and Read 2015.
19. City council meetings are recorded and posted on YouTube (https://www.youtube.com/playlist?list=PLom4-mJ5N8tY10N8aYUc8j-LtaslW-4vR). I was able to attend only two of the meetings in person, but I observed others via video recording.
20. Silverman and Patterson 2015.
21. Racial identification was determined by observation or self-identified at the time of the interview. This was not explicitly asked as a part of the interview.
22. Yanow 2013, 133.
23. City of Flint 2013.
24. Dandaneau 1996; Highsmith 2015; Young 2013.
25. Mahoney 2010.
26. Gerring 2007, 45; George and McKeown 1985, 35–36.
27. Creswell 2013, 76.
28. Schneider and Ingram 1997.
29. Ibid., 73.
30. Creswell 2013, 82.
31. D. Stone (1997) 2011.

References

Abowd, Paul. 2012. "Michigan's Hostile Takeover." *Mother Jones*, February 15. http://www.motherjones.com/politics/2012/02/michigan-emergency-manager-pontiac-detroit.
Acosta, Roberto. 2017. "Flint Charter Update Coasts to Approval on Election Day." *Flint Journal*, August 9. http://www.mlive.com/news/flint/index.ssf/2017/08/flint_charter_update_coasts_to.html.
Adams, Dominic. 2013. "A Timeline of State Control over Flint." *Flint Journal*, September 11. http://www.mlive.com/news/flint/index.ssf/2013/09/a_look_at_michael_browns_tenur.html.
———. 2014. "A List of Who Is on the Flint Blue Ribbon Committee on Governance." *Flint Journal*, January 9. http://www.mlive.com/news/flint/index.ssf/2014/01/flints_blue_ribbon_committee_m.html.
AlHajal, Khalil. 2011. "Flint Residents Argue for and against Fighting Emergency Financial Manager Appointment." *Flint Journal*, November 14. http://www.mlive.com/news/flint/index.ssf/2011/11/flint_residents_argue_for_and.html.
Ambrose, Gerald. 2015. "Exit Letter to Governor Snyder." City of Flint. https://www.cityofflint.com/wp-content/uploads/Emergency-Manager-Exit-Letter.pdf.
Anderson, Elisha. 2016. "Legionnaires'-Associated Deaths Grow to 12 in Flint Area." *Detroit Free Press*, April 11. https://www.freep.com/story/news/local/michigan/flint-water-crisis/2016/04/11/legionnaires-deaths-flint-water/82897722/.
Anzia, Sarah F., and Terry M. Moe. 2015. "Public Sector Unions and the Costs of Government." *Journal of Politics* 77 (1): 114–127.
Arnstein, Sherry R. 1969. "A Ladder of Citizen Participation." *Journal of the American Planning Association* 35 (4): 216–224.

Associated Press. 2016. "Court Rejects Challenge to Michigan's Emergency Manager Law." *MLive.* September 12. http://www.mlive.com/news/index.ssf/2016/09/court_rejects_challenge_to_mic.html.

Bachrach, Peter, and Morton S. Baratz. 1962. "Two Faces of Power." *American Political Science Review* 56 (4): 947–952.

Bailey, Kristian Davis. 2016. "The Untold Story of Flint: The Assault on Democracy for Poor and Black People." *Black Bottom Archives.* http://www.blackbottomarchives.com/blackpapersocialjustice/the-untold-story-of-flint-the-assault-on-democracy-for-poor-black-people.

Balfour, Danny, Guy Adams, and Ashley E. Nickels. 2019. *Unmasking Administrative Evil.* 5th ed. New York: Routledge.

Bankert, Terry. 2016. "Flint Ombudsman's Office Needs Filled." *Flint Water Scandal* (blog), January 17. http://flintwaterscandal.com/flint-ombudsmans-office.

Baumgartner, Frank R., and Bryan D. Jones. 1993. *Agendas and Instability in American Politics.* Chicago: University of Chicago Press.

Benford, Robert D., and David A. Snow. 2000. "Framing Processes and Social Movements: An Overview and Assessment." *Annual Review of Sociology* 26 (1): 611–639.

Berman, David R. 1995. "Takeovers of Local Governments: An Overview and Evaluation of State Policies." *Publius* 25 (3): 55–70.

———. 2003. *Local Government and the States: Autonomy, Politics, and Policy.* New York: M. E. Sharpe.

Berry, Jeffrey M., Ken Thomson, and Kent E. Portney. 1993. *The Rebirth of Urban Democracy.* Washington, DC: Brookings Institution Press.

Borrego, Susan E. 2016. "2016 State of the University Address." University of Michigan-Flint. https://www.umflint.edu/chancellor/chancellors-desk#accordion-state-of-the-university-address.

Bradbury, K. L. 1983. "Structural Fiscal Distress in Cities: Causes and Consequences." *New England Review* (January/February): 33–44.

Bradsher, Keith. 1997. "G.M. to Close Car Factory, Delivering Big Blow to Flint." *New York Times,* November 22. https://www.nytimes.com/1997/11/22/business/gm-to-close-car-factory-delivering-big-blow-to-flint.html.

Bridge Staff. 2016. "Disaster Day by Day: A Detailed Flint Crisis Timeline." https://www.bridgemi.com/truth-squad-companion/disaster-day-day-detailed-flint-crisis-timeline.

Brown, Michael. 2012. "Financial and Operating Plan." City of Flint, Office of the Emergency Manager. https://www.cityofflint.com/finance/finanical-reports/.

Bryson, John M. 2004. "What to Do When Stakeholders Matter: Stakeholder Identification and Analysis Techniques." *Public Management Review* 6 (1): 21–53.

Bryson, John M., Gary L. Cunningham, and Karen J. Lokkesmoe. 2002. "What to Do When Stakeholders Matter: The Case of Problem Formation for the African American Men Project of Hennepin County, Minnesota." *Public Administration Review* 62 (5): 568–584.

Bullard, R. D., and B. H. Wright. 2012. *The Wrong Complexion for Protection:*

How the Government Response to Disaster Endangers African American Communities. New York: New York University Press.
Burch, Tracy. 2013. *Trading Democracy for Justice: Criminal Convictions and the Decline of Neighborhood Political Participation.* Chicago: University of Chicago Press.
Byron, Shaun. 2013. "Flint Farmer's Market Moves to Downtown Location in 2014." *MLive,* March 8. http://www.mlive.com/business/mid-michigan/index.ssf/2013/03/flint_farmers_market_comes_bac.html.
Cahill, Anthony G., and Anthony J. James. 1992. "Responding to Municipal Fiscal Distress: An Emerging Issue for State Governments in the 1990s." *Public Administration Review* 52 (1): 88–94.
CamConnect. 2009. "Voter Participation Report." http://camconnect.org/fact/VoterParticipationReport.htm.
Campbell, Andrea Louise. 2003. *How Policies Make Citizens: Senior Political Activism and the American Welfare State.* Princeton, NJ: Princeton University Press.
Campbell, Scott D. 2013. "Sustainable Development and Social Justice: Conflicting Urgencies and the Search for Common Ground in Urban and Regional Planning." *Michigan Journal of Sustainability* 1:75–91. https://quod.lib.umich.edu/m/mjs/12333712.0001.007?view=text;rgn=main.
Carmody, Tim. 2016. "Factories and People Have Been Dumping Sewage, Chemicals, and Road Salt in the Flint River for More Than a Century." *The Verge,* February 26. http://www.theverge.com/2016/2/26/11117022/flint-michigan-water-crisis-leadpollution-history.
Carpenter, Daniel. 2010. *Reputation and Power: Organizational Image and Pharmaceutical Regulation at the FDA.* Princeton, NJ: Princeton University Press.
Carpenter, Susan L., and W.J.D. Kennedy. 2001. *Managing Public Disputes: A Practical Guide for Professionals in Government, Business and Citizen's Groups.* New York: John Wiley and Sons.
Chetkovich, Carol A., and Frances Kunreuther. 2006. *From the Ground Up: Grassroots Organizations Making Social Change.* Ithaca, NY: Cornell University Press.
Citizen's Research Council of Michigan (CRC). 1987. *A Review of the Effects of Home Rule on Wayne County Government.* Citizen's Research Council of Michigan. Report No. 286, September.
———. 1994. *Michigan Constitutional Issues.* Citizen's Research Council of Michigan. Report No. 301-09, October.
City Council of Flint v. State of Michigan. 2002. 253 Mich. App. 378.
City of Flint. 2002. "Comprehensive Annual Financial Report." June 30.
———. 2010. "Comprehensive Annual Financial Report." June 30. https://www.cityofflint.com/wp-content/Cafr/2010/City%20of%20Flint%20CAFR%2006-30-10.pdf.
———. 2013. "Imagine Flint: Master Plan for a Sustainable Flint." http://www.imagineflint.com/Documents.aspx.
Clark, Amanda D., and Ashley E. Nickels. 2018. "Calling for Community Control: Local Organizing and Implications for Community Development

Policy." In *Community Development and Public Administration Theory: Empowerment through the Enhancement of Democratic Principles,* edited by Ashley E. Nickels and Jason D. Rivera, 46–65. New York: Routledge.

Clark, Anna. 2018. *The Poisoned City: Flint's Water and the American Urban Tragedy.* New York: Metropolitan Books.

Clark, Anna Fountain, and Evgenia Gorina. 2017. "Emergency Financial Management in Small Michigan Cities: Short-Term Fix of Long-Term Sustainability." *Public Administration Quarterly* 41 (3): 532–568.

Cnaan, Ram A., and Carl Milofsky, eds. 2007. *Handbook of Community Movements and Local Organizations.* New York: Springer.

Coe, Charles C. 2008. "Preventing Local Government Fiscal Crises: Emergency Best Practices." *Public Administration* 68 (1): 759–767.

Collins, Patricia Hill. 2000. *Black Feminist Thought: Knowledge, Consciousness, and the Politics of Empowerment.* Rev. ed. New York: Routledge.

Conaway, Laura. 2013. "In #Michigan, 'Financial Martial Law' in Action. Report Says#Wisconsin's Next." *The MaddowBlog* (blog), April 18. http://www.msnbc.com/rachel-maddow-show/michigan-financial-martial-law.

Concerned Pastors for Social Action v. Khouri. 2016. 194 F.Supp. 3d 589. (U.S. District Court, E.D. Michigan, Southern Division).

Conyers, John. 2016. "Flint Is the Predicted Outcome of Michigan's Long, Dangerous History with 'Emergency Managers.'" *The Nation,* February 17. https://www.thenation.com/article/flint-is-the-predicted-outcome-of-michigans-long-dangerous-history-with-emergency-managers/.

Creswell, John W. 2013. *Qualitative Inquiry and Research Design: Choosing among Five Approaches.* 3rd ed. Thousand Oaks, CA: Sage.

C. S. Mott Foundation. 2015a. "The Flint: A Good River with a Bad Reputation." *C. S. Mott Foundation* (blog), December 2. https://www.mott.org/news/articles/flint-good-river-bad-reputation/.

———. 2015b. "Gov. Rick Snyder: Move Back to Detroit Water Provides Best Protection for Public Health: State, City, Mott Foundation Join to Fund Switch until KWA Is Ready." *C. S. Mott Foundation,* October 8. https://www.mott.org/news/releases/gov-rick-snyder-move-back-to-detroit-water-provides-best-protection-for-public-health-in-flint/.

———. 2016a. "Expanded Double Up Food Bucks Program Will Help More Flint Residents Use the Power of Healthy Food to Combat Effects of Lead." C. S. Mott Foundation, April 26. https://www.mott.org/news/articles/expanded-double-food-bucks-program-help-flint-residents-combat-effects-lead/.

———. 2016b. "90 Years Young: 2016 Annual Report." https://www.mott.org/wp-content/uploads/2017/11/AR2016.pdf.

Dahl, Robert. 1981. *Who Governs? Democracy and Power in an American City.* New Haven, CT: Yale University Press.

Dandaneau, Steven P. 1996. *A Town Abandoned: Flint Michigan Confronts Deindustrialization.* Albany: State University of New York Press.

Dawson, Mackenzie. 2016. "Flint Mom Shares the Heartbreak of Giving Her Kids Poisoned Water." *The Stir,* January 28, 2016. https://thestir.cafemom.com/politics_views/195368/flint_mom_shares_the_heartbreak.

Denhardt, Janet V., and Robert B. Denhardt. 2015. "The New Public Service." *Public Administration Review* 75 (5): 664–672.

Dixon, Jennifer. 2016. "How Flint's Water Crisis Unfolded." *Detroit Free Press*, n.d. http://www.freep.com/pages/interactives/flint-water-crisis-timeline/.

Doidge, Mary, Eric Scorsone, Traci Taylor, Josh Sapotichne, Erika Rosebrook, and Danielle Kaminski. 2015. "The Flint Fiscal Playbook: An Assessment of the Emergency Manager Years (2011–2015)." Michigan State University Extension White Paper, July 31. https://www.canr.msu.edu/uploads/resources/pdfs/Flint-Fiscal-Playbook.pdf.

Dreier, Peter, John Mollenkopf, and Todd Swanstrom. 2001. *Place Matters: Metropolitics for the 21st Century*. Lawrence: University of Kansas Press.

Dresden, Eric. 2014. "A Timeline of Perani Arena's History in Flint and Teams that Have Called It Home." *Flint Journal*, December 9. http://www.mlive.com/news/flint/index.ssf/2014/12/a_timeline_of_perani_arenas_hi.html.

Duggan, Daniel. 2010. "Flint's 'Uptown Six' Developers Share Tips to Reinventing a Factory Town." *Crain's Detroit*, November 10. http://www.crainsdetroit.com/article/20101110/C03/101119988/flints-uptown-six-developers-share-tips-to-reinventing-a.

Easton, David. 1965. *A Systems Analysis of Political Life*. New York: John Wiley.

Eclectablog. 2011a. "Benton Harbor Emergency Financial Manager Gets Right to Work." *Eclectablog*, April 18. http://www.eclectablog.com/2011/04/benton-harbor-emergency-financial-mgr.html.

———. 2011b. "Half of Michigan African Americans Will Soon Be under the Rule of an Emergency Manager." *Eclectablog*, December 1. http://www.eclectablog.com/2011/12/half-of-michigan-african-americans-will.html.

Entman, Robert M. 1993. "Framing: Toward Clarification of a Fractured Paradigm." *Journal of Communication* 43 (4): 51–58.

Falleti, Tulia G., and Julia F. Lynch. 2009. "Context and Causal Mechanisms in Political Analysis." *Comparative Political Studies* 42 (9): 1143–1166.

Farnham, Alan. 2011. "Bankrupt Cities Using Financial Managers to Recover." *ABC News*, May 2. http://abcnews.go.com/Business/bankrupt-cities-benton-harbor-mi-emergency-financial-managers/story?id=13472258.

Fasenfest, David. 2019. "A Neoliberal Response to an Urban Crisis: Emergency Management in Flint, MI." *Critical Sociology* 45 (1): 33–547.

Fasenfest, David, and Theodore Pride. 2016. "Emergency Management in Michigan: Race, Class, and the Limits of Liberal Democracy." *Critical Sociology* 42 (3): 331–334.

Fehr, Stephen, and Mary Murphy. 2016. "Flint Water Crisis Could Spur Changes to Michigan's Emergency Manager Law." Pew Charitable Trusts. March 23. https://www.pewtrusts.org/en/research-and-analysis/articles/2016/03/23/flint-water-crisis-could-spur-changes-to-michigans-emergency-manager-law.

Fino, Susan A. 1996. *Michigan State Constitution: A Reference Guide*. Westport, CT: Greenwood Publishing.

Fischer, Frank. 1998. "Beyond Empiricism: Policy Inquiry in Postpositivist Perspective." *Policy Studies Journal* 26 (1): 129–146.

Flavin, Patrick, and Michael T. Hartney. 2015. "When Government Subsidizes Its Own: Collective Bargaining Laws as Agents of Political Mobilization." *American Journal of Political Science* 59 (4): 896–911.

Flint and Genesee Chamber of Commerce. 2016a. "FGCC Hosts Orientation for Flint Small Business Grant Program." Flint and Genesee Chamber of Commerce, March 30. https://www.flintandgenesee.org/fgcc-hosts-orientations-flint-small-business-grant-program/.

———. 2016b. "Moving Flint Forward Initiative." Flint and Genesee Chamber of Commerce, April 5. https://www.flintandgenesee.org/moving-flint-forward-initiative/.

———. 2016c. "Moving Flint Forward Leadership Summit Planned for June 14." Flint and Genesee Chamber of Commerce, April 26. https://www.flintandgenesee.org/moving-flint-forward-leadership-summit-planned-june-14/.

Flint Journal. 2002. "Desperate Flint Needs Kurtz, Not Council Suit." *Flint Journal*, July 9. Access World News Database.

FlintNow. 2016. "Ten Philanthropies Will Help Flint Recover and Rise from the Water Crisis." *FlintNow*, May 11. http://flintnow.org/press-releases/ten-philanthropies-will-help-flint-recover-and-rise-from-water-crisis/.

Flint Water Study. 2016. *Flintwaterstudy.org Guide*. http://flintwaterstudy.org/guide-to-flintwaterstudy-org/.

Fonger, Ron. 2009. "Businessman Phil Shaltz Brokered Michael Brown's Appointment as Flint City Administrator." *Flint Journal*, February 11. http://www.mlive.com/news/flint/index.ssf/2009/02/businessman_phil_shaltz_broker.html.

———. 2013. "GM Weld Tool Center Closing: General Motors History in Flint Area Has Been Full of Highs and Lows." *Flint Journal*, January 13. http://www.mlive.com/news/flint/index.ssf/2013/01/highlights.html.

———. 2014a. "Flint Charter Proposal 6: Amendment Would Eliminate Flint Ombudsman's Office." *Flint Journal*, October 19. http://www.mlive.com/news/flint/index.ssf/2014/10/proposal_6_charter_amendment_f.html.

———. 2014b. "Flint Emergency Manager Says 'No Plans' to Reopen Ombudsman's Office." *Flint Journal*, December 5. http://www.mlive.com/news/flint/index.ssf/2014/12/flint_emergency_manager_says_n_1.html.

———. 2014c. "Flint Gets Final Permit Approvals from State to Use Flint River." *Flint Journal*, April 10. http://www.mlive.com/news/flint/index.ssf/2014/04/flint_gets_final_permit_approv.html.

———. 2014d. "Flint's Population Falls below 100,000 for First Time since 1920s." *Flint Journal*, May 22. http://www.mlive.com/news/flint/index.ssf/2014/05/flints_population_falls_below.html.

———. 2015a. "Emergency Manager Calls City Council's Flint River Vote 'Incomprehensible.'" *Flint Journal*, March 24. https://www.mlive.com/news/flint/2015/03/flint_emergency_manager_calls.html.

———. 2015b. "Flint Democracy Defense League Plans Four Meetings on City's Water Problems." *Flint Journal*, January 29. http://www.mlive.com/news/flint/index.ssf/2015/01/flint_democracy_defense_league_1.html.

———. 2015c. "Lead Leaches into 'Very Corrosive' Flint Drinking Water, Researchers Say." *Flint Journal*, September 2. http://www.mlive.com/news/flint/index.ssf/2015/09/new_testing_shows_flint_water.html.

Fortner, Michael J. 2016. "Straight No Chaser: Theory, History and the Muting of the Urban State." *Urban Affairs Review* 52 (4): 591–621.

Frammolino, Ralph. 2002. "Mayor Is Ousted in a Town Divided: Voters in the Debt-Ridden City Recall a Three-Term Incumbent. Race Is a Subtext Writ Large." *Los Angeles Times*, March 7. http://articles.latimes.com/2002/mar/07/news/mn-31628.

Frug, Gerald E. 1999. *City Making: Building Cities without Building Walls*. Princeton, NJ: Princeton University Press.

Fuchs, Ester. 1992. *Mayors and Money: Fiscal Policy in New York and Chicago*. Chicago: University of Chicago Press.

Fung, Archon. 2004. *Empowered Participation: Reinventing Urban Democracy*. Princeton, NJ: Princeton University Press.

———. 2006. "Varieties of Participation in Complex Governance." *Public Administration Review* 66 (s1): 66–75.

Galster, George. 2015. "A Structural Diagnosis and Prescription for Detroit's Fiscal Crisis: Response to William Tabb's 'If Detroit Is Dead, Some Things Need to Be Said at the Funeral.'" *Journal of Urban Affairs* 37 (1): 17–20.

Gantert, Tom. 2011. "Are Michigan Emergency Managers Overpaid?" *CAPCon: Michigan Capital Confidential*, December 31.

———. 2012. "Union Contracts a Major Reason for City's Financial Problems." *CAPCon: Michigan Capital Confidential*, July 26. https://www.michigancapitolconfidential.com/17223.

Garza, Ryan. 2009. "Don Williamson Out as Mayor of Flint; Many Won't Miss His Brash Style." *Flint Journal*, February 9. http://www.mlive.com/news/flint/index.ssf/2009/02/williamson_profile.html.

Gaskin, Jamie. 2016. "Interview with United Way of Genesee County CEO, Jamie Gaskin." *Flint News Talk 1470 WFNT* [transcript], February 15.

George, Alexander L., and Andrew Bennett. 2005. *Case Studies and Theory Development in the Social Sciences*. Cambridge, MA: MIT Press.

George, Alexander L., and Timothy J. McKeown. 1985. "Case Studies and Theories of Organization Decision Making." *Advances in Information Processing in Organizations* 2:21–58.

Gerring, John. 2001. *Social Science Methodology: A Critical Framework*. New York: Cambridge University Press.

———. 2007. *Case Study Research: Principles and Practices*. New York: Cambridge University Press.

Gillespie, Patrick. 2016. "Flint, Michigan: A Hollow Frame of a Once Affluent City." *CNN Money*. March 7. http://money.cnn.com/2016/03/06/news/economy/flint-economy-democratic-debate/index.html.

Gillette, Howard. 2006. *Camden after the Fall: Decline and Renewal in a Postindustrial City*. Philadelphia: University of Pennsylvania Press.

Gilman, Hollie Russon. 2016. *Democracy Reinvented: Participatory Budgeting and Civic Innovation in America*. Washington, DC: Brookings Institution Press.

Gilmore, Ruth Wilson. 2017. "In the Shadow of the Shadow State." In *The Revo-

lution Will Not Be Funded: Beyond the Non-profit Industrial Complex, rev. ed., edited by INCITE!, 41–52. Durham, NC: Duke University Press.

Goffman, Erving. 1974. *Frame Analysis: An Essay on the Organization of Experience*. Cambridge, MA: Harvard University Press.

Goodman, Amy. 2016. "'Thirsty for Democracy: The Poisoning of an American City': Special Report on Flint's Water Crisis." *Democracy Now*, February 17. https://www.democracynow.org/2016/2/17/thirsty_for_democracy_the_poisoning_of.

Gross, Evan. 2011. "Michigan: A State of Home Rule, Local Autonomy, and Emergency Managers." *Michigan Policy Network*, December 3. http://michiganpolicy.com/index.php/urban-affairs-the-news/current-issues-9/1155-michigan-a-state-of-home-rule-local-autonomy-and-emergency-managers.

Guzmán, Martina. 2016. "Water Warriors: How Four Activists Let the World Know about Water Crises in Flint and Detroit." *Sojourners*, May 25. https://sojo.net/articles/water-warriors.

Hacker, Jacob S., Suzanne Mettler, and Joe Soss. 2010. "The New Politics of Inequality: A Policy-Centered Perspective." In *Remaking America: Democracy and Public Policy in an Age of Inequality*, edited by Joe Soss, Jacob Hacker, and Suzanne Mettler, 3–23. New York: Russell Sage Foundation.

Hacker, Jacob S., and Paul Pierson. 2014. "After the 'Master Theory': Downs, Schattschneider, and the Rebirth of Policy-Focused Analysis." *Perspectives on Politics* 12 (3): 643–662.

Hakala, Josh. 2016. "How Did We Get Here? A Look Back at Michigan's Emergency Manager Law." *Michigan Radio*, February 3. http://michiganradio.org/post/how-did-we-get-here-look-back-michigans-emergency-manager-law#stream/0.

Hakim, Danny. 2002. "For Flint, Mich., Takeover Adds to the List of Woes." *New York Times*, July 10. http://www.nytimes.com/2002/07/10/us/for-flint-mich takeover-adds-to-the-list-of-woes.html.

Hall, Peter A. 2010. "Historical Institutionalism in Rationalist and Sociological Perspective." In *Explaining Institutional Change: Ambiguity, Agency, and Power*, edited by James Mahoney and Kathleen Ann Thelen, 204–233. New York: Cambridge University Press.

Hammer, Peter J. 2019. "The Flint Water Crisis, the Karegnondi Water Authority, and Strategic-Structural Racism." *Critical Sociology* 45 (1): 103–119.

Hanna-Attisha, Mona. 2018. *What the Eyes Don't See: A Story of Crisis, Resistance, and Hope in an American City*. New York: Random House.

Hanna-Attisha, Mona, Jenny LaChance, Richard Casey Sadler, and Allison Champney Schnepp. 2016. "Elevated Blood Levels in Children Associated with the Flint Drinking Water Crisis: A Special Analysis of Risk and Public Health Response." *AJPH Research* 106 (2): 283–290.

Harding, Alan. 2009. "The History of Community Power." In *Theories of Urban Politics*, 2nd ed., edited by Jonathan S. Davies and David L. Imbroscio, 27–39. London: Sage.

Harris, Alfred L. n.d. "History of the Concerned Pastors for Social Action." http://www.concernpastors.org/?page_id=785.

Harris, David. 2011. "Flint's East Side Bears Worst Arson Scars: 'They Burned the Whole Block.'" *Flint Journal,* January 8. http://www.mlive.com/news/flint/index.ssf/2011/01/flints_east_side_bears_worst_a.html.

Harris, Richard A. 2016. "Farewell to the Urban Growth Machine: Community Development Regimes in Smaller, Distressed Cities." In *Urban Citizenship and American Democracy,* edited by Amy Bridges and Michael Javen Fortner, 125–158. Albany: State University of New York Press.

Hedden, Adrian. 2014. "Councilman Leads Protest at Flint City Hall, Addresses Police Chases, Water Rates." *Flint Journal,* July 14. https://www.mlive.com/news/flint/2014/07/councilman_leads_protest_at_fl.html.

Henderson, Tom. 2010. "Dillon Scouts Talent for Turnaround Team." *Crain's Detroit Business,* December 13–19. http://www.crainsdetroit.com/assets/PDF/CD719441212.PDF.

Hendrick, Rebecca. 2004. "Assessing and Measuring the Fiscal Health of Local Governments: Focus on Chicago Suburban Municipalities." *Urban Affairs Review* 40 (1): 78–114.

———. 2011. *Managing the Fiscal Metropolis: The Financial Policies, Practices, and Health of Suburban Municipalities.* Washington, DC: Georgetown University Press.

Herman, Tim. 2016. "Let's Keep Lines of Communication Open." Flint and Genesee Chamber of Commerce, February 24. https://www.flintandgenesee.org/lets-keep-lines-communication-open/.

Highsmith, Andrew R. 2015. *Demolition Means Progress: Flint, Michigan and the Fate of the American Metropolis.* Chicago: University of Chicago Press.

Highsmith, Andrew R., and Ansley T. Erickson. 2015. "Segregation as Splitting, Segregation as Joining: Schools, Housing, and the Many Modes of Jim Crow." *American Journal of Education* 121 (4): 563–595.

Hohman, James M. 2011. "Mackinac Center Recommendations Found in New Financial Emergency Legislation." *Mackinac Center for Public Policy* (blog), March 17. http://www.mackinac.org/14756.

Honadle, Beth, Beverly Cigler, and James Costa. 2003. *Fiscal Health for Local Governments.* Amsterdam: Academic Press.

Hooper, Amanda. 2016. "The Flint Water Crisis Is a Feminist Issue." National Women's Law Center. https://nwlc.org/blog/the-flint-water-crisis-is-a-feminist-issue/.

Hunter, Floyd. 1953. *Community Power Structure: A Study of Decision Makers.* Chapel Hill: University of North Carolina Press.

Hunter v. Pittsburgh. 1907. 207 U.S. 161 (U.S. Supreme Court).

Ingram, Helen, Anne L. Schneider, and Peter deLeon. 2007. "Social Construction and Policy Design." In *Theories of the Policy Process,* edited by Paul A. Sabatier, 93–126. Cambridge, MA: Westview Press.

Jacob, Benoy, and Rebecca Hendrick. 2013. "Assessing the Financial Conditions of Local Governments: What Is Financial Condition and How Is It Measured?" In *Handbook of Local Government Fiscal Health,* edited by Helisse Levine, Jonathan B. Justice, and Eric A. Scorsone, 11–42. Burlington, MA: Jones and Bartlett Learning.

Jacobs, Alan M., and R. Kent Weaver. 2015. "When Policies Undo Themselves:

Self-Undermining Feedback as a Source of Policy Change." *Governance* 28 (4): 441–457.
Jefferson, Bernadel. 2012. "Bishop Jefferson Talks Democracy, Voting Rights at Michigan United against the War on Women Rally." Peace Education Center (transcript), April 29. https://www.youtube.com/watch?v=z4tiifHRN6w.
———. 2016. "Flint Water Crisis: Bernadel Jefferson." AFL-CIO (transcript), March 17. https://www.youtube.com/watch?v=3iW3A0fy-mk.
———. 2017. "Poison Water Is Not the Only Crisis Flint Is Facing." Transcript, January 13. https://www.youtube.com/watch?v=TO7RwFYUus0.
Jobb, Bela. 2002. "Can't Trust Kurtz." Letter to the editor. *Flint Journal*, December 31. Access World News Database.
Jones, Miyako. 2016. "Honors Students Create Flint Water App." University of Michigan–Flint Honors Program, July 25. https://blogs.umflint.edu/honors/2016/07/25/honors-students-create-flint-water-app/.
Judd, Dennis R., and Todd Swanstrom. 2015. *City Politics*. 9th ed. New York: Routledge.
Kapiszewski, Diana, Lauren M. MacLean, and Benjamin L. Read. 2015. *Field Research in Political Science: Practices and Principles*. Cambridge: Cambridge University Press.
Kasdan, David Oliver. 2014. "A Tale of Two Hatchet Men: Emergency Financial Management in Michigan." *Administration and Society* 46 (9): 1092–1108.
———. 2016. "Emergency Manager 2.0: This Time, It's Financial." *Urban Affairs Review* 52 (5): 862–882.
Kaza, Greg. 1989. "Ecorse's Grand Experiment." Mackinac Center for Public Policy, August 21. https://www.mackinac.org/V1989-07.
Keiser, Richard. 2015. "Urban Regime Change: A Silver Lining for Scandals." *Urban Affairs Review* 51 (4): 504–532.
Keller, A. 2012. "Pastors Petition Flint's EFM with List of 'Desired Outcomes.'" *WNEM*, August 22. http://www.cbs46.com/story/19344557/pastors-petition-flints-efm-with-list-of-desired-outcomes#ixzz46Icx7tmh.
Ketchum, William E., III. 2012. "Crim Protest by Flint Pastor Reginald Flynn Draws Nearly 100." *Flint Journal*, August 25. https://www.mlive.com/news/flint/2012/08/crim_protest_by_flint_pastor_r.html.
King, Kate. 2016. "Christie Links Atlantic City Takeover and Northern New Jersey Casino Expansion." *Wall Street Journal*, March 31. https://www.wsj.com/articles/christie-links-atlantic-city-takeover-and-northern-new-jersey-casino-expansion-1459471361.
Kingdon, John W. 1995. *Agendas, Alternatives, and Public Policies*. 2nd ed. Boston: Addison-Wesley Educational Publishers.
Kleiman, Robert T., and Anandi P. Sahu. 1999. "Privatization as a Viable Alternative for Local Governments: The Case Study of a Failed Michigan Town." In *Contracting Out Government Services*, edited by P. Seidenstat, 151–165. Westport, CT: Praeger.
Klein, Naomi. 2007. *The Shock Doctrine: The Rise of Disaster Capitalism*. New York: Picador.
Kleine, Robert. 1991. "The Headlee Amendment—Aid to Local Government."

Public Sector Consultants, June 20. http://www.publicsectorconsultants.com/wp-content/uploads/2017/01/062091_ppa.pdf.

Kloha, Philip, Carol S. Weissert, and Robert Kleine. 2005. "Someone to Watch Over Me: State Monitoring of Local Fiscal Conditions." *American Review of Public Administration* 35 (3): 236–255.

Kossis, Lyle D. 2012. "Examining the Conflict between Municipal Receivership and Local Autonomy." *Virginia Law Review* 98 (5): 1109–1148.

Kromer, John. 2010. *Fixing Broken Cities: The Implementation of Urban Development Strategies.* New York: Routledge.

Ladd, H. 1994. "Big-City Finances." In *Big City Politics, Governments, and Fiscal Constraints*, edited by G. E. Peterson, 201–269. Washington, DC: Urban Institute.

LaFaive, Michael D. 2002. "Mayoral Recall May Foreshadow Flint Bankruptcy." *Mackinac Center for Public Policy* (blog), March 7. https://www.mackinac.org/article.aspx?ID=4106.

LaFaive, Michael D., and Louis H. Schimmel. 2011. "State Should Reform Public Act 72 of 1990." *Mackinac Center for Public Policy* (blog), January 10. http://www.mackinac.org/14290.

Lake, Robert W., Kathe Newman, Philip Ashton, Richard Nisa, and Bradley Wilson. 2007. *Civic Engagement in Camden, New Jersey: A Baseline Portrait.* New York: MDRC and the Ford Foundation.

Lasswell, Howard D. 1936. *Politics: Who Gets What, When, How.* New York: Whittlesey House. http://www.policysciences.org/classics/politics.pdf.

Lawlor, Joe. 2009a. "Flint Mayor Don Williamson Appoints Longtime Community Leader Mike Brown as New City Administrator to Replace Darryl Buchanan." *Flint Journal*, February 4. http://www.mlive.com/news/flint/index.ssf/2009/02/flint_mayor_don_wiliamson_shak.html.

———. 2009b. "Temporary Mayor Michael Brown's Proposed Budget Cuts Police, Fire Hardest." *Flint Journal*, April 7. http://www.mlive.com/news/flint/index.ssf/2009/04/temporary_mayor_michael_browns.html.

Leach, Kirk A. 2018. "Cross-Sector Community Partnerships and the Growing Importance of Nonprofits in Urban Governance: A Case Study of Camden, NJ." In *Community Development and Public Administration Theory: Empowerment through the Enhancement of Democratic Principles*, edited by Ashley E. Nickels and Jason D. Rivera, 211–228. New York: Routledge.

Lederman, Jacob. 2016. "Flint's Water Crisis Is No Accident. It's the Result of Years of Devastating Free-Market Reforms." *In These Times*, January 22. http://inthesetimes.com/article/18794/flint-water-crisis-neoliberalism-free-market-reforms-rick-snyder.

Lee, Shawna J., Amy Krings, Sara Rose, Krista Dover, Jessica Ayoub, and Fatima Salman. 2016. "Racial Inequality and the Implementation of Emergency Management Laws in Economically Distressed Urban Areas." *Children and Youth Services Review* 70 (Supplement C): 1–7.

Lehmann, Henry W. 1950. "The Federal Municipal Bankruptcy Act." *Journal of Finance* 5 (3): 241–256.

Leonardi, Joseph M., and William J. Gruhn. 2001. "Flint River Assessment." State of Michigan Department of Natural Resources, Report Number 27. https:// www.canr.msu.edu/michiganlakes/uploads/files/Leonardi%20and%20 Gruhn%202001.pdf.

Levine, Helisse C., Jonathon B. Justice, and Eric A. Scorsone, eds. 2013. *Handbook of Local Government Fiscal Health*. Burlington, MA: Jones and Bartlett Learning.

Levine, Jeremy R. 2016. "The Privatization of Political Representation: Community-Based Organizations as Nonelected Neighborhood Representatives." *American Sociological Review* 81 (6): 1251–1275.

Lewis, Chris. 2013. "Does Michigan's Emergency-Manager Law Disenfranchise Black Citizens?" *The Atlantic*, May 9. http://www.theatlantic.com/politics/archive/2013/05/does-michigans-emergency-manager-law-disenfranchise-black-citizens/275639/.

Livengood, Chad. 2015. "Orr Named Advisor to Atlantic City's New EM." *Detroit News*, January 22. https://www.detroitnews.com/story/news/local/wayne-county/2015/01/21/ex-em-orr-taking-gamble-atlantic-city/22144539/.

Loh, Carolyn G. 2016. "The Everyday Emergency: Planning and Democracy under Austerity Regimes." *Urban Affairs Review* 52 (5): 832–863.

Longley, Kristin. 2009. "Walling Plans to 'Go to Work' for Flint after Definitive Mayoral Victory over Clack." *MLive* (blog), August 5. http://blog.mlive.com/flint-city-beat/2009/08/walling_plans_to_go_to_work_fo.html.

———. 2011a. "City of Flint Hopes to Avoid State Takeover of Finances by Borrowing $20M." *Flint Journal*, January 10. http://www.mlive.com/news/flint/index.ssf/2011/01/city_of_flint_hopes_to_avoid_s.html.

———. 2011b. "Emergency Financial Manager Recommended for Flint Same Day Mayor Dayne Walling Re-elected." *Flint Journal*, November 10. http://www.mlive.com/news/flint/index.ssf/2011/11/emergency_financial_manager_re.html.

———. 2011c. "Former Finance Director Suing City under Whistleblower Act." *Flint Journal*, December 22. http://www.mlive.com/news/flint/index.ssf/2011/12/former_finance_director_suing.html.

———. 2011d. "Gov. Rick Snyder Talks Crime, Police Patrols in Flint at Public Safety Discussion." *Flint Journal*, December 16. http://www.mlive.com/news/flint/index.ssf/2011/12/gov_rick_snyder_talks_crime_po.html.

———. 2011e. "Special Flint City Council Meeting to Consider $8 Million Bond." *Flint Journal*, March 23. http://www.mlive.com/news/flint/index.ssf/2011/03/special_flint_city_council_mee.html.

———. 2012a. "Call to Action: Flint Council Takes Steps to Investigate Emergency Manager Actions, Overturn New Appointment." *Flint Journal*, August 13. http://www.mlive.com/news/flint/index.ssf/2012/08/call_to_action_council_takes_s.html.

———. 2012b. "Council Questions Emergency Manager Eliminating Citizens' Groups, Shuffling Political Appointees before Leaving Office." *Flint Journal*, August 13. http://www.mlive.com/news/flint/index.ssf/2012/08/city_council_questioning_emerg.html.

———. 2012c. "Genesee Towers: A Storied History in Downtown Flint." *Flint

Journal, September 27. http://www.mlive.com/news/flint/index.ssf/2012/09/genesee_towers_timeline_histor.html.
——. 2012d. "Genesee Towers to Be Demolished; Flint Seeks Safety Tax for Police, Firefighters." *Flint Journal*, August 9. http://www.mlive.com/news/flint/index.ssf/2012/08/genesee_towers_to_be_demolishe.html.
——. 2012e. "Michael Brown Appointed City Administrator under New Emergency Financial Manager Ed Kurtz." *Flint Journal*, August 8. http://www.mlive.com/news/flint/index.ssf/2012/08/michael_brown_appointed_city_a.html.
——. 2012f. "Residents Invited to Open Forum with Flint Emergency Manager Michael Brown." *Flint Journal*, February 9. http://www.mlive.com/news/flint/index.ssf/2012/02/residents_invited_to_open_foru.html.
Lowi, Theodore J. 1964. "American Business, Public Policy, Case Studies, and Political Theory." *World Politics* 16 (4): 676–715.
Luke, Peter. 2011. "Gov. Rick Snyder Says Fighting over Labor Issues Is a Budget Distraction." *MLive*, February 22. http://www.mlive.com/politics/index.ssf/2011/02/snyder_says_fighting_over_labo.html.
Machniak, Christofer. 2002. "The Story of Flint's Takeover—Recall Pushes Senator to Act." *Flint Journal*, July 14. Access World News Database.
Maddow, Rachel. 2011. "Tyrants Replacing Local Government." *The Rachel Maddow Show*, December 8. http://www.nbcnews.com/video/rachel-maddow/45607138.
Magee, Cleora. 2017. Presentation to community, July 20.
Mahler, Jonathan. 2011. "Now that the Factories Are Closed, It's Tee Time in Benton Harbor, Mich." *New York Times*, December 15. http://www.nytimes.com/2011/12/18/magazine/benton-harbor.html.
Mahoney, James. 2010. "After KKV: The New Methodology of Qualitative Research." *World Politics* 62 (1): 120–147.
Mahoney, James, and Kathleen Thelen. 2009. *Explaining Institutional Change: Ambiguity, Agency, and Power*. New York: Cambridge University Press.
Manns, Myron. 2013. "Uptown Drives Downtown Flint." *MyCity Magazine*, July 1. http://www.mycitymag.com/uptown-drives-downtown-flint/.
March, James G., and Johan P. Olsen. 1984. "The New Institutionalism: Organizational Factors in Political Life." *American Political Science Review* 78 (3): 734–749.
Marcus, Samantha, and Susan K. Livio. 2016. "Christie Announces State Takeover of Atlantic City Finances." *New Jersey Politics*, January 26. http://www.nj.com/politics/index.ssf/2016/01/christie_atlantic_city_1.html.
Martin, Lawrence L., Richard Levey, and Jenna Cawley. 2012. "The 'New Normal' for Local Government." *State and Local Government Review* 44 (1 supplemental): 17–28.
Marwell, Nicole P. 2007. *Bargaining for Brooklyn: Community Organizations in the Entrepreneurial City*. Chicago: University of Chicago Press.
May, Jake. 2016. "Flint Water Crisis Protest at Two-Year Mark Urges Change." *Flint Journal*, April 26. http://www.mlive.com/news/flint/index.ssf/2016/04/residents_urge_change_blame_sn.html.
Maynard, Mark. 2014. "Everything You Ever Wanted to Know about the Emergency Manager Takeover of Michigan, and How We Allowed It to

Happen." *MarkMaynard.com*, July 29. http://markmaynard.com/2014/07/everything-you-ever-wanted-to-know-about-the-emergency-manager-takeover-of-michigan-and-how-we-allowed-it-to-happen/.
Mays, Melissa. 2016. "Melissa Mays of Water You Fighting For? Flint, MI." Interview by April Watters. Independent Media [Interview Transcript]. March 19. https://www.youtube.com/watch?v=bdVSOILP800.
———. 2017. "Judge Approves Settlement to Replace Flint's Lead-Tainted Water Lines." Interview by Ari Shapiro. *All Things Considered,* NPR, March 28.
McAdam, Doug, Sidney Tarrow, and Charles Tilly. 2001. *Dynamics of Contention*. New York: Cambridge University Press.
McBain, Howard Lee. 1916. "The Doctrine of an Inherent Right of Local Self-Government: The Extent of Its Application by American Courts." *Columbia Law Review* 16 (3): 190–216.
McClelland, Edward. 2014. "Inside Flint's First Master Plan Since 1960." *Next City,* February 6. https://nextcity.org/daily/entry/inside-flints-first-master-plan-since-1960.
———. 2015. "Demolition Means Progress? An Interview with Author Andrew Highsmith." *Belt Magazine,* September 22. http://beltmag.com/demolition-means-progress-an-interview-with-author-andrew-highsmith/.
McClinton, Claire. 2014a. "Claire McClinton Speaking after Water March." Posted August 10. YouTube video. https://www.youtube.com/watch?v=lL3l0CNWoSI.
———. 2014b. "Democracy: Are Flint Citizens Ready to Live without It?" *People's Tribune,* March. http://peoplestribune.org/pt-news/2014/03/democracy-flint-citizens-ready-live-without/.
———. 2014c. "Flint Protest Exposes Emergency Manager Order to Silence Public." *People's Tribune,* June. http://peoplestribune.org/pt-news/2014/06/flint-protest-exposes-emergency-manager-order-silence-public/.
———. 2014d. "What's the Matter with Michigan?" *People's Tribune,* August. http://peoplestribune.org/pt-news/2014/08/%EF%BB%BFwhats-matter-michigan/.
———. 2016. "Dictatorship in Michigan: Flint Water Warriors Expose the Truth." *People's Tribune,* March. http://peoplestribune.org/pt-news/2016/02/dictatorship-in-michigan-flint-water-warriors/.
McNichol, Elizabeth. 2012. "Some Basic Facts on State and Local Government Workers." Center for Budget and Policy Priorities. https://www.cbpp.org/research/some-basic-facts-on-state-and-local-government-workers.
McPhail. D. L. 2002. "Listen to Line Workers—Flint Journal Letter to the Editor." *Flint Journal,* December 27. Access World News database.
Meriwether v. Garrett. 1880. 102 U.S. 472 (U.S. Supreme Court).
Mettler, Suzanne. 2002. "Bringing the State Back in to Civic Engagement: Policy Feedback Effects of the G.I. Bill for World War II Veterans." *American Political Science Review* 96 (2): 351–365.
———. 2005. *Soldiers to Citizens: The G.I. Bill and the Making of the Greatest Generation*. New York: Oxford University Press.
Mettler, Suzanne, and Mallory SoRelle. 2014. "Policy Feedback Theory." In *Theories of the Policy Process,* edited by Paul A. Sabatier and Christopher Weible, 151–181. 3rd ed. Boulder, CO: Westview Press.
Michigan Civil Rights Commission (MCRC). 2017. "The Flint Water Crisis: Sys-

tematic Racism through the Lens of Flint." February 17. https://www.michigan.gov/documents/mdcr/VFlintCrisisRep-F-Edited3-13-17_554317_7.pdf.
Michigan Department of Treasury. 2011. "Report of the Flint Financial Review Team." State of Michigan Department of Treasury, Lansing, MI. https://www.michigan.gov/documents/treasury/Flint-ReviewTeamReport-11-7-11_417437_7.pdf.
Mickle, Bryn. 2009. "New Flint Administration Makes Big Changes at City Hall." *Flint Journal*, February 18. http://www.mlive.com/news/flint/index.ssf/2009/02/new_flint_administration_makes.html.
MLive staff. 2012. "Michigan Election Results: Proposals 1–6." *MLive*, November 6. http://www.mlive.com/politics/index.ssf/2012/11/2012_michigan_election_results.html.
Mohai, Paul, and Robin Saha. 2007. "Racial Inequality in the Distribution of Hazardous Waste: A National-Level Reassessment." *Social Problems* 54 (3): 343–370.
Monkkonen, Eric H. 1995. *The Local State: Public Money and American Cities*. Stanford, CA: Stanford University Press.
Morgan, Dennis F., Kent S. Robinson, Dennis Strachota, and James A. Hough. 2015. *Budgeting for Local Governments and Communities*. New York: Routledge.
Morris, A. D. 1984. *The Origins of the Civil Rights Movement: Black Communities Organizing for Change*. New York: Free Press.
Morris, David. (1971) 1993. "The Nature and Purpose of a Home Rule Charter, Report No. 311." Citizens Research Council of Michigan, Detroit. Reprint, July 1993. https://crcmich.org/PUBLICAT/1990s/1993/rpt31003.pdf.
Morris, David Z. 2016. "Did Michigan's Emergency Manager Law Cause the Flint Water Crisis?" *Fortune*, February 18. http://fortune.com/2016/02/18/michigan-public-act-436-flint/.
Morris, Kathleen S. 2012. "The Case for Local Constitutional Enforcement." *Harvard Civil Rights–Civil Liberties Law Review* 47:1–45.
Moss, Kary. 2016. "Legislature Should Repeal Emergency Manager Law." *Detroit Free Press*, January 18.
Mostafavi, Beata. 2011. "What Happened Last Time? A Look Back at Flint's 2002 State Takeover." *Flint Journal*, November 10. http://www.mlive.com/news/flint/index.ssf/2011/11/what_happened_last_time_a_look.html.
Moynihan, Donald P., and Joe Soss. 2014. "Policy Feedback and the Politics of Administration." *Public Administration Review* 74 (3): 320–332.
MRG. 2013. "Statewide Poll: Overwhelming Support for Emergency Financial Manager for Detroit." *Marketing Resource Group*, March 26. http://mrgmi.com/2013/03/statewide-poll-overwhelming-support-for-emergency-financial-manager-for-detroit/.
Mumby, Dennis M. 2004. "Discourse, Power and Ideology: Unpacking the Critical Approach." In *The Sage Handbook of Organizational Discourse*, edited by D. Grant, C. Hardy, C. Oswick, and L. Putnam, 237–258. Thousand Oaks, CA: Sage.
Naples, Nancy A. 2014. *Grassroots Warriors: Activist Mothering, Community Work, and the War on Poverty*. New York: Routledge.

Nichols, John. 2013. "Bankrupting Democracy in Detroit: The Citizens of One of Our Largest Cities Are Being Shut Out of the Decisions that Will Affect Their Future." *The Nation*, July 31. http://www.thenation.com/article/bankrupting-democracy-detroit/.

Nickels, Ashley E. 2012. "Threats to Urban Democracy? Municipal State Takeover and Implications for Civic [and Political] Engagement." Paper presented at the American Public Policy Analysis and Management Fall Research Conference, November.

———. 2016. "Approaches to Municipal Takeover: Home Rule Erosion and State Intervention in Michigan and New Jersey." *State and Local Government Review* 48 (3): 194–207.

Nickels, Ashley E., and Jason D. Rivera, eds. 2018. *Community Development and Public Administration Theory: Promoting Democratic Principles to Improve Communities*. New York: Routledge.

Niquette, Mark. 2013. "Flint Balances Books at Cost of Services Citizens Need." *Bloomberg*, March 26. http://www.bloomberg.com/news/articles/2013-03-27/flint-balances-books-at-cost-of-services-citizens-need.

Nollenberger, Karl, Sanford Groves, and Maureen G. Valente. 2003. *Evaluating Financial Condition: A Handbook for Local Government*. 4th ed. Washington, DC: International City/County Management Association.

North, Douglass. 1990. *Institutions, Institutional Change and Economic Performance*. Cambridge: Cambridge University Press.

Oosting, Jonathon. 2016. "Sued Firm Says Flint, State Rejected Corrosion Controls." *Detroit News*, June 24. https://www.detroitnews.com/story/news/michigan/flint-water-crisis/2016/06/24/sued-firm-says-flint-state-rejected-corrosion-controls/86362528/.

Orr, M. E., and Gerry Stoker. 1994. "Urban Regimes and Leadership in Detroit." *Urban Affairs Review* 30 (1): 48–73.

Ospina, Sonia, and Erica Foldy. 2005. "Toward a Framework of Social Change Leadership." Paper presented at the Annual Meeting of the Public Management Research Association, Los Angeles.

Ostrander, Susan. 2013. *Citizenship and Governance in a Changing Society: Somerville, MA*. Philadelphia: Temple University Press.

Palladino, Tony. 2017. "Flint Town Hall." *TYT* [transcript], April 2. https://www.youtube.com/watch?v=BcWh2X8WKgc.

Pauli, Benjamin. 2019. *Flint Fights Back: Environmental Justice and Democracy in the Flint Water Crisis*. Cambridge, MA: MIT Press.

People's Tribune. 2016. "Dictatorship in Michigan: Flint Water Warriors Expose the Truth." *People's Tribune*, March. http://peoplestribune.org/pt-news/2016/02/dictatorship-in-michigan-flint-water-warriors/.

People v. Hurlbut. 1871. 24 Mich. 44.

Peterson, Paul E. 1981. *City Limits*. Chicago: University of Chicago Press.

Pew Charitable Trusts. 2013. "The State Role in Local Government Financial Distress." Pew Charitable Trusts, July, Washington, DC.

Pierson, Paul. 1993. "When Effect Becomes Cause: Policy Feedback and Political Change." *World Politics* 45 (4): 595–628.

Piven, Frances F., and Richard A. Cloward. 1979. *Poor People's Movements: Why They Succeed and How They Fail*. New York: Random House.

Rast, Joel. 2012. "Why History (Still) Matters: Time and Temporality in Urban Political Analysis." *Urban Affairs Review* 48 (1): 3–36.
Raymer, Marjory. 2001. "Population Growth in Suburbs, Decline in Flint." *Flint Journal*, December 31. NewsBank (database).
Receivership Transition Advisory Board (RTAB). n.d. City of Flint, Michigan. https://www.cityofflint.com/rtab/.
Reuther Library. 2010. "Subject Focus: Remembering the Flint Sit-Down." *Teller's Blog*, December 17. http://reuther.wayne.edu/node/7092.
Ridley, Gary. 2014. "Protesters March on Bricks in Downtown Flint over High Water Rates." *Flint Journal*, August 8. http://www.mlive.com/news/flint/index.ssf/2014/08/protesters_march_on_bricks_in.html.
Ronders, E. L. 2001. "Flint Fire Department Budget Woes." *Flint Journal*, December 31. Access World News Database.
Rosner, David, and Gerald Markowitz. 2016. "Building the World that Kills Us: The Politics of Lead, Science, and Polluted Homes, 1970–2000." *Journal of Urban History* 42 (2): 323–345.
Rothstein, Richard. 2017. *The Color of Law: A Forgotten History of How Government Segregated America*. New York: Liveright Publishing.
Sapotichne, Joshua, Erika Rosebrook, Eric Scorsone, Danielle Kaminski, Mary Doidge, and Traci Taylor. 2015. "Beyond State Takeovers: Reconsidering the Role of State Government in Local Financial Distress, with Important Lessons for Michigan and Its Embattled Cities." Michigan State University Extension White Paper, August 31. http://msue.anr.msu.edu/uploads/resources/pdfs/beyond_state_takeovers.pdf.
Sapotichne, Joshua, Eric Scorsone, and Andy Henion. 2016. "Flint Crisis Reveals Deeper Problem in Michigan's Fiscal Policy." *MSUToday,* January 26. http://msutoday.msu.edu/news/2016/flint-crisis-reveals-deeper-problem-in-michigans-fiscal-policies/.
Savage, Anne. 2013. "Interview: Flint Mayor Dayne Walling, Part 1—The Community-Driven Reinvention of Flint." *Eclectablog*, November 5. https://www.eclectablog.com/2013/11/interview-flint-mayor-dayne-walling-part-1-the-community-driven-reinvention-of-flint.html.
Savage, Chris. 2012. "The Scandal of Michigan's Emergency Managers." *The Nation,* February 15. http://www.thenation.com/article/scandal-michigans-emergency-managers/.
Schattschneider, Elmer Eric. 1935. *Politics, Pressure, and the Tariff.* Ann Arbor: University of Michigan Press.
Schneider, Anne L., and Helen Ingram. 1993. "Social Construction of Target Populations: Implications for Politics and Policy." *American Political Science Review* 87 (2): 334–347.
———. 1997. *Policy Design for Democracy.* Lawrence: University of Kansas Press.
———. 2005. *Deserving and Entitled: Social Constructions and Public Policy.* Albany: State University of New York Press.
Schram, Sanford F., and Brian Caterino. 2006. *Making Political Science Matter: Debating Knowledge, Research, and Method.* New York: New York University Press.
Scorsone, Eric A. 2010. "An Analysis of Emergency Financial Conditions in Local Units of Government." *State Notes*, Fall. http://www.senate.michigan.gov/sfa/publications%5Cnotes%5C2010notes%5Cnotesfal10es.pdf.

---. 2014. "Municipal Fiscal Emergency Laws: Background and Guide to State-Based Approaches." Mercatus Center, Report No. 14-21. http://mercatus.org/sites/default/files/Scorsone-Municipal-Fiscal-Emergency.pdf.

Scorsone, Eric A., and Nicolette Bateson. 2011. "Long-Term Crisis and System Failure: Taking the Fiscal Stress of America's Older Cities Seriously." Case Study: City of Flint, Michigan. Michigan State University Extension. https://www.cityofflint.com/wp-content/uploads/Reports/MSUE_Flint Study2011.pdf.

Scorsone, Eric A., and Mary Doidge. 2014. "2014 Flint Blue Ribbon Committee Final Report." City of Flint, Office of the Emergency Manager. https://www.cityofflint.com/wp-content/uploads/BRC-Final-Report-071714.pdf.

Seawright, Jason, and John Gerring. 2008. "Case Selection Techniques in Case Study Research: A Menu of Qualitative and Quantitative Options." *Political Science Quarterly* 61 (2): 294–308.

Shariff, Nayyirah. 2014. "Flint Activists Put Emergency Manager on Notice." *People's Tribune,* April. http://peoplestribune.org/pt-news/2014/04/flint-activists-put-emergency-manager-notice/.

---. 2016. "'Gov. Snyder Should Be Arrested': Flint Residents Demand Justice over Water Poisoning." *Democracy Now* (interview), January 8. https://www.democracynow.org/2016/1/8/gov_snyder_should_be_arrested_flint.

---. 2017. "Flint Water Crisis, Day 1007 (Part 4)." Root Branch Review Activist Conference, Dallas, TX, February 7. https://www.youtube.com/watch?v=AHoRPRxiPbM.

Sharp, Elaine. 2002. *Does Local Government Matter? How Urban Policies Shape Civic Engagement.* Minneapolis: University of Minnesota Press.

Shelterforce. 2014. "Q: Is a Land Bank the Same Thing as a Land Trust?" *Shelterforce,* October 2. https://shelterforce.org/2014/10/02/answer_land_banks_land_trusts/.

Shragge, Eric. 2013. *Activism and Social Change: Lessons for Community Organizing.* 2nd ed. Ontario, Canada: University of Toronto Press.

Silverman, Robert Mark, and Kelly L. Patterson. 2015. *Qualitative Research Methods for Community Development.* New York: Routledge.

Skocpol, Theda. 1992. *Protecting Soldiers and Mothers: The Political Origins of Social Policy in the United States.* Cambridge, MA: Harvard University Press.

Smith, Andrea. 2017. "Introduction: The Revolution Will Not Be Funded." In *The Revolution Will Not Be Funded: Beyond the Non-profit Industrial Complex,* rev. ed., edited by INCITE!, 1–18. Durham, NC: Duke University Press.

Smith, David H. 1997. "Grassroots Associations Are Important: Some Theory and a Review of the Impact Literature." *Nonprofit and Voluntary Sector Quarterly* 26 (3): 269–306.

Smith, Lindsey, and Rick Pluta. 2012. "Who's behind the Group Citizens for Fiscal Responsibility?" *Michigan Radio,* April 10. http://michiganradio.org/post/whos-behind-group-citizens-fiscal-responsibility#stream/0.

Snell, Robert. 2006a. "City Post Filled in Marathon Session—Council Takes 7 Hours to Name Ombudsman." *Flint Journal,* March 6, A01. NewsBank Database.

---. 2006b. "Money Earmarked for Ombudsman Goes to Cops Instead." *Flint Journal,* June 6, A03. NewsBank Database.

Snow, David A., and Robert D. Benford. 1992. "Master Frames and Cycles of Protest." In *Frontiers in Social Movement Theory*, edited by A. D. Morris and C. McClurg Mueller, 133–155. New Haven, CT: Yale University Press.

Snow, David A., E. B. Rochford Jr., S. K. Worden, and Robert D. Benford. 1986. "Frame Alignment Processes, Micromobilization, and Movement Participation." *American Sociological Review* 51 (4): 464–481.

Snyder, Rick. 2012a. "Michigan Decides 2012: Gov. Rick Snyder Urges Yes Vote on Emergency Manager Ballot Proposal (Guest Column)." *MLive.com*, September 27. http://www.mlive.com/opinion/index.ssf/2012/09/emergency_manager_ballot_gov_r.html.

———. 2012b. "Why Michigan Needs Its Emergency Manager Law." *Office of Governor Snyder, Reinvention Blog*, August 2. http://www.michigan.gov/snyder/0,4668,7-277-57577_60279-283632—,00.html.

———. 2016. "Declaration of Emergency." State of Michigan. January 5. http://www.michigan.gov/documents/snyder/2016-01-05_Flint_Water_Governors_Declaration_Final_509966_7.pdf?20160105162343.

Soss, Joe. 1999. "Lessons of Welfare: Policy Design, Political Learning, and Political Action." *American Political Science Review* 93 (2): 363–380.

Soss, Joe, and Sanford Schram. 2007. "A Public Transformed? Welfare Reform as Policy Feedback." *American Political Science Review* 101 (1): 111–127.

Spiotto, James E., A. E. Acker, and L. E. Appleby. 2012. *Municipalities in Distress? How States and Investors Deal with Local Government Financial Emergencies*. Washington, DC: Chapman and Cutler.

Stanley, Jason. 2016. "The Emergency Manager: Strategic Racism, Technocracy, and the Poisoning of Flint's Children." *Good Society* 25 (1): 1–45.

Starbuck, Amanda, and Ronald White. 2016. "Living in the Shadow of Danger: Poverty, Race, and Unequal Chemical Facility Hazards." Center for Effective Government Report, January. https://www.foreffectivegov.org/shadow-of-danger.

Steeh, G. C. 2014. "Order Granting in Part and Denying in Part Defendants' Motion to Dismiss (Doc #41) and Denying Defendant's Motion to Stay Proceedings (Doc. #47)." November 19. http://www.eclectablog.com/wp-content/uploads/2014/11/PAlawsuit.pdf.

Stone, Clarence. 1989. *Regime Politics: Governing Atlanta 1946–1988*. Lawrence: University of Kansas Press.

Stone, Deborah A. 1989. "Causal Stories and the Formation of Policy Agendas." *Political Science Quarterly* 104 (2): 281–300.

———. (1997) 2011. *Policy Paradox: The Art of Political Decision Making*. 3rd ed. New York: W. W. Norton.

Sugrue, T. 1996. *The Origins of the Urban Crisis: Race and Inequality in Postwar Detroit*. Princeton, NJ: Princeton University Press.

Tabb, William. 2015. "If Detroit Is Dead, Some Things Need to Be Said at the Funeral." *Journal of Urban Affairs* 37 (1): 1–12.

Thelen, Kathleen. 2004. *How Institutions Evolve: The Political Economy of Skills in Germany, Britain, the United States and Japan*. New York: Cambridge University Press.

UM-Flint News. 2016a. "New UM-Flint Research Shows Location of Lead Pipes in Flint." *UM-Flint News*, February 22. https://news.umflint.edu/2016/02/22/new-um-flint-research-shows-location-of-lead-pipes-in-flint/.

———. 2016b. "UM-Flint Response to Flint Water Crisis Featured in Big Ten Network PSA." *UM-Flint News,* March 8. https://news.umflint.edu/2016/03/08/um-flint-response-to-flint-water-crisis-featured-in-big-ten-network-psa/.

Ungar, R. 2011. "Gov. Scott Walker Reportedly Planning Financial Martial Law in Wisconsin." *Forbes,* April 16. http://www.forbes.com/sites/rickungar/2011/04/16/gov-scott-walker-reportedly-planning-financial-martial-law-in-wisconsin/2/. Accessed April 23, 2012.

U.S. Census Bureau. 1950. "Flint, Michigan Census Tracts." Census of the Population. https://www2.census.gov/library/publications/decennial/1950/population-volume-3/41557421v3p2ch03.pdf.

———. 1960. "Part 24: Michigan, Chapter 3." Characteristics of the Population, General Population Characteristics. https://www2.census.gov/library/publications/decennial/1960/population-volume-1/37722966v1p24ch3.pdf.

———. 1970. "Part 24: Michigan." Characteristics of the Population, General Population Characteristics. https://www2.census.gov/prod2/decennial/documents/1970a_mi-01.pdf.

———. 1980. "Part 24: Michigan." Characteristics of the Population, General Population Characteristics. https://www2.census.gov/library/publications/decennial/1980/volume-1/michigan/1980censusofpopu80124uns_bw.pdf.

———. 1990. "Part 24: Michigan." Characteristics of the Population, General Population Characteristics. https://www2.census.gov/library/publications/decennial/1990/cp-2/cp-2-24-1.pdf.

———. 2000. Community Facts. "Allen Park City, Michigan," "Benton Harbor City, Michigan," "Detroit City, Michigan," "Ecorse City, Michigan," "Flint City, Michigan," "Hamtramck City, Michigan," "Highland Park City, Michigan," "Pontiac City, Michigan," and "Three Oaks, Michigan." Profile of General Demographics, Census 2000 Summary File.

———. 2010a. "Community Facts: Three Oaks, Michigan." Profile of General Demographics: Census 2000 Summary File.

———. 2010b. "QuickFacts: United States; Allen Park City, Michigan." https://www.census.gov/quickfacts/fact/table/allenparkcitymichigan,US/PST045218.

———. 2010c. "QuickFacts: United States; Benton Harbor City, Michigan." https://www.census.gov/quickfacts/fact/table/bentonharborcitymichigan,US/PST045218.

———. 2010d. "QuickFacts: United States; Detroit City, Michigan." https://www.census.gov/quickfacts/fact/table/detroitcitymichigan,US/PST045218.

———. 2010e. "QuickFacts: United States; Ecorse City, Michigan." https://www.census.gov/quickfacts/fact/table/ecorsecitymichigan,US/POP010210.

———. 2010f. "QuickFacts: United States; Flint City, Michigan." http://www.census.gov/quickfacts/table/PST045215/00,2629000.

———. 2010g. "QuickFacts: United States; Hamtramck City, Michigan." https://www.census.gov/quickfacts/fact/table/hamtramckcitymichigan,US/PST045218.

———. 2010h. "QuickFacts: United States; Highland Park City, Michigan." https://www.census.gov/quickfacts/fact/table/highlandparkcitymichigan,US/PST045218.

———. 2010i. "QuickFacts: United States; Pontiac City, Michigan." https://www.census.gov/quickfacts/fact/table/pontiaccitymichigan,US/PST045218.

———. 2014. "Community Facts: United States, Flint City, Michigan." American Community Survey, 5-Year Estimates.
———. 2017. "QuickFacts: United States; Wayne County, Michigan." https://www.census.gov/quickfacts/waynecountymichigan.
Walters, LeeAnne. 2016. "LeeAnne Walters: Statement to Congress." Transcript, February 3. https://www.youtube.com/watch?v=t6687jtuyv8.
Weikart, L. A. 2013. "Monitoring the Fiscal Health of America's Cities." In *Handbook of Local Government Fiscal Health*, edited by H. Levine, J. B. Justice, and E. A. Scorsone, 387–404. Burlington, MA: Jones and Bartlett Learning.
Welch v. Brown. 2013. 935 F.Supp. 2d 875 (E.D. Mich.).
White, Ed. 2016. "Appeals Court Upholds Michigan's Emergency Manager Law." *Detroit Free Press,* September 12. https://www.freep.com/story/news/local/michigan/2016/09/12/appeals-court-upholds-michigans-emergency-manager-law/90274784/.
White, Ridgway. 2016. "Flint Crisis Raises Questions—and Cautions—about the Role of Philanthropy." *Philanthropy News Digest,* April 8. https://philanthropynewsdigest.org/commentary-and-opinion/flint-s-crisis-raises-questions-and-cautions-about-the-role-of-philanthropy.
White House. 2016. "President Obama Signs Michigan Emergency Declaration." White House, January 16. https://obamawhitehouse.archives.gov/the-press-office/2016/01/16/president-obama-signs-michigan-emergency-declaration.
Whiteside, M.A.C. 2007. "Don Williamson." *Flint Journal,* May 15. http://blog.mlive.com/flintjournal/decision2007/2007/05/bio_don_williamson.html.
Wilde-Anderson, Michelle. 2012. "Democratic Dissolution: Radical Experimentation in State Takeovers of Local Governments." *Fordham Urban Law Journal* 39 (3): 577–623.
Wilson, S. 2016. "The River Plan." *MLive.* http://www.mlive.com/news/flint/index.ssf/2015/10/how_the_flint_water_crisis_eme.html#4.
Wolman, Harold, Robert McMammon, Michael Bell, and David Brunori. 2007. "Comparing Local Government Autonomy across the States." GWIPP (George Washington Institute of Public Policy) Working Paper. https://gwipp.gwu.edu/sites/g/files/zaxdzs2181/f/downloads/Working_Paper_035_GovernmentAutonomy.pdf.
Yanow, Dvora. 2007. "Qualitative-Interpretive Methods in Policy Research." In *Handbook of Public Policy Analysis,* edited by F. Fischer, G. J. Miller, and M. S. Sidney, 405–416. Baton Rouge, FL: CRC Press.
———. 2013. "Interpretive Analysis and Comparative Research." In *Comparative Policy Studies: Conceptual and Methodological Challenges,* edited by I. Engeli and C. Rothmayr Allison, 131–159. London: Palgrave Macmillan.
Yin, Robert. 2014. *Case Studies Research Design and Methods.* 5th ed. Thousand Oaks, CA: Sage.
Young, Gordon. 2013. *Teardown: Memoir of a Vanishing City.* Berkeley: University of California Press.

Index

Page numbers followed by the letter *t* refer to tables. Page numbers followed by the letter *f* refer to figures.

Agenda setting, 53–55, 62, 64, 90, 133, 146, 152, 161
Ambrose, Gerald (emergency manager), 100, 102, 118, 150, 205t–206t
Anchor institutions, 13, 78, 171, 219n39
Anzia, Sarah, 25

Bankert, Terry, 106
Bateson, Nicolette, 28
Baumgartner, Frank, 219n38
Berman, David, 33
Blue Ribbon Committee on Governance, 108–110, 127, 135, 139, 199t, 202t
Brown, Michael (emergency manager), 1, 28, 58, 95, 96, 99, 104, 106, 125, 131, 161
Bryson, John, 219n38
Burch, Tracey, 56

Cahill, Anthony, 10, 34
Carpenter, Daniel, 169
Carpenter, Susan, 8–9
Causal stories, 62, 132, 147, 150, 153, 154, 156

Cawley, Jenna, 49
CDCs (community development corporations), 13, 14, 107
Charles Stewart (C. S.) Mott Foundation, 20, 76, 77t, 81–83, 86–88, 93, 96, 97, 101, 102, 104, 106, 113, 114, 130, 143, 144, 152, 161, 171, 172, 185t, 190t, 222n29
Charter review, 21, 99, 110, 130, 137
Chew Charitable Trusts, 33
Citizens Research Council (CRC) of Michigan, 38–39, 40
City Council of Flint v. State of Michigan, 91–92
Coalition building, 137, 146
Collective bargaining, 5, 25, 46, 47, 51, 57, 102, 103, 117, 119, 133, 142, 160, 161, 190t–204t
Collins, Patricia Hill, 145–146
Community development, 13, 14, 55, 80, 94t, 101, 104, 107, 185t
Community Development Block Grants, 12
Community development corporations (CDCs), 13, 14, 107

Concerned Pastors for Social Action (CPSA), 77t, 84, 85, 105, 117, 130, 137, 194t
Contagion, 8, 9, 159. *See also* Spillover effect
Contentious politics, 21, 27, 66, 77t, 130
Cooley, Thomas, 37, 214n30; Cooley Doctrine, 37
Council-manager, 38, 109, 202t
CPSA (Concerned Pastors for Social Action), 77t, 84, 85, 105, 117, 130, 137, 194t
CRC (Citizens Research Council) of Michigan, 38–39, 40
C. S. Mott Foundation. *See* Charles Stewart (C. S.) Mott Foundation
Cunningham, Gary, 219n38

DDL (Flint Democracy Defense League), 3, 59, 78, 129–133, 136, 137, 143
Deindustrialization, 26
Democracy Defense League (DDL), 3–4, 5f, 15, 21, 59, 77t, 78, 126, 129–133, 136–138, 142, 143, 150
Department of Environmental Quality, 3, 151
Detroit Water and Sewerage Department (DWSD), 2, 41, 196t, 198t
Development agenda, 21, 81–87, 89–104, 107, 119, 127. *See also* Development regime; Economic development
Development regime, 20, 88, 90, 93, 103–128, 143–146, 152, 158, 160, 161. *See also* Development agenda; Economic development
Dillon, John, 31–32, 101; Dillon's Rule, 32, 37
Doidge, Mary, 108
Downtown economic development, 81, 82, 85, 86
Dreier, Peter, 162
DWSD (Detroit Water and Sewerage Department), 2, 41, 196t, 198t

Earley, Darnell (emergency manager), 46, 91, 98, 100, 108, 110, 119, 137
Easton, David, 227n3

Economic development, 80, 82, 85, 86, 96, 101, 104, 119, 137, 161. *See also* Development agenda; Development regime
Economic development groups, 55, 78, 80, 82
EFM (emergency financial manager), 27, 28, 42, 43, 44
EM. *See* Emergency manager
Emergency financial manager (EFM), 27, 28, 42, 43, 44
Emergency manager (EM): authority of, 12, 34, 36t, 45–47, 57, 58, 64, 105, 112; definition, 34, 45–47, 127; in Flint, 102t, 111–115, 126–128, 133, 134, 143, 151; limitations on authority of, 48, 52, 118, 121; relationships with community, 85, 101, 105, 120, 125
Emergency manager law (EM law), 1, 4, 8, 15, 48, 59, 105–108, 108f, 126, 128, 132, 135, 143, 150, 151, 152, 218n58, 225–226n13
Emergency Municipal Loan Act (PA 243), 40, 41
EM law. *See* Emergency manager law
Environmental pollution, 75
Environmental Protection Agency (EPA), 3, 147
Erickson, Ansley, 81
Executive orders, 20, 58, 60, 80, 102, 160, 186t–207t

FACT (Flint Area Congregations Together), 85, 130, 131, 137
Fasenfest, David, 53
Fiscal emergency laws, 8, 33, 34
Fiscal health, 23
Flint and Genesee Chamber of Commerce, 20, 86, 87, 93, 94t, 95, 104, 143, 149, 153, 161, 187t, 199t
Flint Area Congregations Together (FACT), 85, 130, 131, 137
Flint Democracy Defense League (DDL), 3, 5f, 59, 78, 129–133, 136, 137, 143
Flint Journal. 62–63, 90–91, 92–93, 96–97, 107, 120, 122, 123, 183t, 192t
Flint River, pollution of, 75, 145. *See also* Water crisis, Flint; Water pollution

Fonger, Ron, 222n29
Fuchs, Ester, 24, 25

Galster, George, 26
Gaskin, Jamie, 154
General Motors (GM), 20, 27, 69–73, 87, 91
Genesee Chamber of Commerce, 85, 86, 88, 102, 104, 106, 108, 143, 161
Genesee County Land Bank, 80, 113
Gerring, John, 168
Gillespie, Patrick, 23
GM (General Motors), 20, 27, 69–73, 87, 91
Goodman, Amy, 137
Governance, 109; urban, 54

Hacker, Jacob, 17, 167
Hanna-Attisha, Mona, 3, 119
Harris, Alfred, 105
Harris, Joseph, 10, 55
Harris, Richard, 54–55, 221n3
HCNP (High-capacity non-profits), 76, 88, 101, 102, 130, 143, 146, 148, 149, 150, 152, 154, 156, 158
Henderson, Natasha, 105, 110–111
Hendrick, Rebecca, 23, 26
Herman, Tim, 87, 94t, 105, 108, 153, 161, 187t, 193t, 195t
High-capacity non-profits (HCNP), 76, 88, 101, 102, 130, 143, 146, 148, 149, 150, 152, 154, 156, 158
Highsmith, Andrew, 70, 81, 82, 84, 220n57
Home rule, 9, 10, 37–40, 139
Home Rule City Act, 38, 123, 124, 139, 191t
Hunter v. Pittsburgh, 32, 213–214n11

Imagine Flint, 97, 112
Ingram, Helen, 59, 175, 212n66, 217n13
Issue framing, 15, 16, 131–133, 137, 145, 147, 150, 158

Jacob, Benoy, 23
Jacobs, Alan, 56
James, Anthony, 10, 34
Jefferson, Bernadel, 147, 156, 157–158
Jobb, Bela, 122–123

Jones, Barnett, 190t, 195t, 196t
Jones, Bryan, 219n38

Kasdan, David, 10
Kaufman, Martin, 149
Kennedy, W.J.D., 8–9
Kleiman, Robert, 41
Klein, Naomi, 13–14
Kossis, Lyle, 32
Kurtz, Ed (emergency manager), 28, 92, 93, 100, 102t, 106, 108, 118, 122, 123, 181t–183t, 194t, 197t–198t

LaFaive, Michael, 63
Lake, Robert, 59
Lasswell, Howard, 160, 227n3
Lederman, Jacob, 29
Leonardi, Joseph, 144–145
Levey, Richard, 49
Local Government Fiscal Responsibility Act (PA 72), 42–46, 91–92, 100, 101, 102t, 177t, 179t, 194t, 196t, 197t
Local Government Fiscal Responsibility Act (PA 101), 4, 42, 179t
Loh, Carolyn, 114
Lokkesmoe, Karen, 219n38
Longley, Kristen, 99

Maddow, Rachel, 11, 137
Magee, Cleora, 139, 140
Martin, Lawrence, 49
Mayor-council, 79
Mays, Melissa, 85, 147, 148, 151, 155, 156
McClinton, Claire, 4, 5f, 15, 134, 135, 136, 142–143, 147, 151, 157
MCRC (Michigan Civil Rights Commission), 70–71
McCree, Floyd (mayor), 82, 84, 94t, 219n8, 221n26
McPhail, D. L., 123
Meriwether v. Garrett, 31, 32
Mettler, Suzanne, 17, 167
Michigan Civil Rights Commission (MCRC), 70–71
Michigan Department of Treasury, 45, 98, 105, 172
Michigan Home Rule City Act. *See* Home Rule City Act

Mobilization: grassroots, 130–138; of opposition, 57, 59, 135
Moe, Terry, 25
Mollenkopf, John, 162
Monkkonen, Eric, 23–24, 31
Morris, David, 38–39
Morris, Kathleen, 214n11
Moss, Kary, 143
Moynihan, Donald, 89
Municipal autonomy. *See* Home rule
Municipal Bankruptcy Acts, 32
Municipal Fiscal Emergency Laws, 8. *See also* Municipal takeover
Municipal takeover: definition, 1, 7, 11, 159; in Flint, 89–102, 112, 119, 133, 160; history of, 30, 37; implications, 12–14, 30, 52, 53, 56, 111, 129, 162–164; and race, 15, 135, 150, 162; water, 143

North, Douglass, 210–211n37

Office of the Ombudsman, Flint, 58, 60, 92, 100, 106, 109, 110, 111t, 139, 140, 183t, 203t
Oppression, 62, 135–137, 142, 145, 148, 158
Organizational restructuring, 57–59
Orr, Kevin, 37

PA 4 (Public Act 4), 1, 44–47, 98, 100, 101, 124, 128, 131, 132, 161
PA 72 (Public Act 72), 42–46, 91–92, 100, 101, 102t, 177t, 179t, 194t, 196t, 197t
PA 101 (Public Act 101), 4, 42, 179t
PA 436 (Public Act 436), 4, 48, 100, 112, 128, 132, 141, 161
Palladino, Tony, 151, 155
Participatory access, 21, 103–112, 160
People's Tribune, 126–127
People v. Hurlbut, 214n30
Pierson, Paul, 57
Policy feedback, 56, 57, 137, 160; instrumental feedback effects, 21, 57, 58, 160; symbolic feedback effects, 6, 21, 53, 56, 57, 59–64, 103, 120
Policy paradox, 8, 9, 17, 20, 51–66, 93, 129, 159, 160

Political stakeholders, 76, 81, 83
Public Act 4 (PA 4), 1, 44–47, 98, 100, 101, 124, 128, 131, 132, 161
Public Act 72 (PA 72), 42–46, 91–92, 100, 101, 102t, 177t, 179t, 194t, 196t, 197t
Public Act 101 (PA 101), 4, 38, 42, 179t
Public Act 436 (PA 436), 4, 48, 100, 112, 128, 132, 141, 161

Racial segregation in Flint, 70, 71, 75, 76, 83, 90, 91, 152, 153, 157
Rational-fiscal perspective, 10, 129
Rationality project, 9, 10, 15, 53, 57, 89, 119, 120, 159, 160, 166
Receivership, 31–33, 161
Receivership Transition Advisory Board (RTAB), 110–112, 141, 171, 205t, 206t, 207t
Rutherford, James (mayor), 72, 82, 95, 180t–181t

Sahu, Anandi, 41
Sapotichne, Joshua, 49
Schimmel, Louis, 41
Schneider, Anne, 59, 175, 212n66, 217n13
Scorsone, Eric, 27, 28, 33, 36t, 44, 108, 162
Seawright, Jason, 168
Shariff, Nayyirah, 126–127, 134–135, 147, 150–151, 157
Sharp, James, Jr. (mayor), 84, 94t
Shrinking city, 27, 72
Snyder, Rick (governor), 44, 47, 52, 98, 128, 134, 135, 150, 184t–198t
Soss, Joe, 17, 89, 167
Spillover effect, 9, 29, 159. *See also* Contagion
Stand Up for Democracy, 48, 132, 137, 184t
Stanley, Woodrow (mayor), 84, 90, 91, 94t, 100, 126, 179t, 180t
State government, role of, 9–11, 49, 50, 55
State intervention, 8–12, 30–40, 49, 51–53, 64, 124, 138, 159, 177t–178t, 179t
Stone, Clarence, 217n11
Stone, Deborah, 9, 20, 53, 62, 119–120, 131, 132, 166, 175, 227n3

Suspension of (local) democracy, 12, 13, 53, 55, 65, 105, 112, 120, 123, 138 142, 143
Swanstrom, Todd, 162

Technocratic rationality, 53, 55, 64, 164

UAW (United Automobile Workers), 69, 76, 77t, 87, 88, 131, 180t, 187t
Unions, 20, 28, 48, 51, 87, 88, 90, 117, 122; contracts, 44, 47, 53, 100, 102, 103, 122, 188t, 193t
United Automobile Workers (UAW), 69, 76, 77t, 87, 88, 131, 180t, 187t
Uptown Developments, LLC, 77t, 86, 87, 95, 96, 115, 134, 161
Uptown Reinvestment Corporation, 86, 87, 115, 116, 134, 161, 193t
U.S. Census Bureau, 27, 74

Walling, Dayne (mayor), 3, 93, 96, 97, 98, 99, 106, 107, 108
Walters, LeeAnne, 3, 147, 156

Water: quality of, 75, 119, 137, 145, 150, 154, 156; rates for, 5, 92, 103, 118, 119, 129, 134, 140, 156, 182t
Water crisis, Flint, 2, 119, 132, 137, 142–146, 148, 151, 154–158, 162. *See also* Flint River, pollution of; Water pollution
Water pollution, 75, 119. *See also* Flint River, pollution of; Water crisis, Flint
Water Rate Protest, 4, 5f, 129, 136f
Weaver, Karen (mayor), 84, 86, 93, 94t, 207t
Weaver, R. Kent, 56
Welch v. Brown, 118
White, Ridgway, 153
Wilde-Anderson, Michelle, 8, 12, 49–50
Wilkinson, George, 149
Williamson, Don (mayor), 93, 94t, 95, 96, 182t–184t
Wolman, Harold, 8

Yanow, Dvora, 173
Young, Gordon, 95

ASHLEY E. NICKELS is an Assistant Professor of Political Science at Kent State University. She is the co-editor of *Community Development and Public Administration Theory: Promoting Democratic Principles to Improve Communities.*

www.ingramcontent.com/pod-product-compliance
Lightning Source LLC
Chambersburg PA
CBHW040902250426
43672CB00034B/2983